MOTICHUR

MOTICHUR

Sultana's Dream and Other Writings of Rokeya Sakhawat Hossain

Translated from Bengali by
Ratri Ray and Prantosh Bandyopadhyay

Oxford University Press is a department of the University of Oxford. It furthers the University's objective of excellence in research, scholarship, and education by publishing worldwide. Oxford is a registered trademark of Oxford University Press in the UK and in certain other countries

Published in India by
Oxford University Press
22 Workspace, 2nd Floor, 1/22 Asaf Ali Road, New Delhi 110 002, India

First Edition published in 2015

ISBN-13: 978-0-19-945037-4
ISBN-10: 0-19-945037-4

Typeset in Adobe Garamond Pro 10.5/16
by Sai Graphic Design, New Delhi 110 055
Printed and bound in India at Repro India Ltd., Mumbai

Contents

Translators' Note vii
Dedication Page of Motichur, *Vol. I (1st Edition)* ix
Dedication Page of the 2nd Edition ix
An Explanation xi
Advertisement xiii
Foreword by Farah Ghuznavi xv

PART I

Thirst 3
The Degradation of Women 14
The Inoffensive Bengali 38
The Better Half 43
The Good Housewife 55
The Burkha 69
Home, Sweet Home 77

PART II

Dedication 93
Foreword 95
Advertisement 97

The Light of Islam 99
The Solar System 125
Sultana's Dream 154
The Murder of Delicia 168
The Fruit of Knowledge 194
The Creation of Woman 204
Nurse Nellie 209
Childcare 227
The Fruit of Freedom 236
Creation 262

About the Author and the Translators 269

Translators' Note

In translating the works of this 'lass unparallel'd' we have tried to be faithful to her tone, language, and sentence-structure, in that order. The language and tone, for example, of *Thirst* is high-pitched and poetic though not accurate. We have tried to convey this.

When translating verse we have been careful to observe the line-division and rhyme-scheme of the original passage. Couplets have been translated as couplets, quatrains as quatrains, etc.

At times, in order to get her tone, we have taken recourse to Latin phrases. They are very well-known, commonplace phrases. For example, at the end of the *Dedication* to the second edition, we have given 'Requiescat in pace'. We plead guilty to having added two words to Hazrat Hussain's speech at the end of Section I of *Thirst*. The phrase we have added conveys pathos and solemnity because they were the words uttered by Christ before he gave up the Ghost: 'Quietus est'.

Finally and most important, we have obtained the meaning and English transliteration of certain Urdu, Arabic, and Persian words from Suleiman Ahmed of Delhi, a fine scholar, who has given unstinted help and encouragement whenever we needed them.

Dedication Page of *Motichur*, Vol. I (1st Edition)

I have never crossed the threshold of either a girls' school or a college. I got a little education through the limitless love and care of my elder brother. The other relatives, far from encouraging me in the pursuit of knowledge, indulged in satire and mockery. Even then, by the grace of God, I myself never hung back, nor was my brother discouraged from teaching me English by the sarcasm of anyone. I am dedicating this book, as a mark of my love, to this elder brother whose extraordinary generosity enabled me to acquire the little knowledge I have and taught me to think for myself.

Dedication Page of the 2nd Edition

To whom shall I dedicate this second edition of *Motichur*? Where is he to whom the first edition had been dedicated? I have looked all over this wide world for him, and yet not found him anywhere. These eyes will not behold him again and I have been deprived, forever, of his love. I dedicate this edition to my brother. Requiescat in pace.

An Explanation

Some of the readers of *Motichur* have expressed in their criticism, the thought that according to them the language and the subject of the book has been taken from the writings of other well-known writers. Such thoughts are not unnatural when they find similarities between this book and some others.

Since I do not have either the daring or the expertise to misappropriate the subject and the style of others, such an effort is impossible for me. I have never set my eyes on Kaliprasanna Babu's book *Bhranti-Binod*, nor have I had the opportunity of reading all the works of Bankim Babu. If there is any similarity between *Motichur* and any other works, it is just a coincidence.

I too have been surprised to see some articles in Urdu periodicals, parts of which seem to be translations of passages in *Motichur*. But I believe the ladies writing them were ignorant of Bengali.

I had not read Marie Corelli's novel *The Murder of Delicia* before writing *Motichur*, yet parts of this book resemble the sentiments expressed in *Motichur*.

One might ask: Why does this happen? How is it that the same subject and sentiments swell up from places as diverse as Bengal, Punjab, Deccan (now Hyderabad), Bombay (now Mumbai), and England? The answer perhaps lies in the spiritual unity among the women of the British Empire.

A few sympathetic readers have pointed out that many English words used in *Motichur* have not been translated into Bengali. In this edition the meanings of English words have been given as far as possible. I am grateful to those readers who have pointed out this defect.

All the other flaws in the book are the result of the writer's lack of knowledge and intelligence and experience. The kind reader, it is hoped, will forgive them.

The Authoress

Advertisement

The essays in this collection had been published in the monthly periodicals *Naba-Prabha*, *Mahila*, and *Naba-Nūr*.

In the present edition the essays have been partially changed and corrected.

Foreword

The opportunity to write the foreword for this latest volume of Rokeya Sakhawat Hossain's *Motichur* came about most serendipitously. Not that this was my first encounter with her, of course. Far from it. Begum Rokeya, as she is commonly known in Bangladesh, is revered as an icon among progressives and an inspiration for the feminist movement, and every schoolgirl—and most boys—grow up knowing exactly who she is.

While some of her work is very well known, other pieces are less familiar to many. So I was delighted to hear about a forthcoming translation to be published by Oxford University Press (OUP). After my panel session at the Jaipur Literary Festival 2014, I had an interesting meeting with the OUP representative who was attending the festival. And one of the things that emerged from that discussion was his suggestion that I should write the Foreword for this book, a collection of essays and fiction by a truly remarkable woman.

Yet although I was very familiar with Rokeya Sakhawat Hossain's story while growing up, I did not actually make one rather important connection until quite recently. In 2005, University Press Limited (UPL) brought out an anthology of English-language writing from Bangladesh titled *From the Delta*. The collection spanned a century. Beginning with *Sultana's Dream*, one of Rokeya's most famous pieces, written in 1905, it ended with my first short story *A Small Sacrifice*, written in 2005.

My father's inordinate pleasure at this coincidence finally made sense when I realized that my great-great-grandmother, Karimunnessa Khanam, had in fact been the beloved older sister of Rokeya. I was vaguely aware of some kind of family connection, but had not (I now confess to my embarrassment) explored it in any detail prior to that.

The role that Karimunnessa played in Rokeya's learning and development is well known to those who are familiar with the latter's life. Indeed, in the second part of *Motichur*, it is to her sister that Rokeya dedicates the book, saying that Karimunnessa was the only one who had encouraged her to learn Bengali at a time when girls from respectable families were at best taught Urdu or Persian—that too, in a decidedly mechanistic fashion. Herself a poet, Karimunnessa was passionate in her support of her younger sister's literary aspirations.

Her faith was justified. In these two volumes of *Motichur*, Rokeya brings to bear her considerable talents as an essayist, satirist, and fiction writer, drawing upon a range of stylistic innovations. These include the reframing of myth, the creative use of fantasy and fable, and her inimitable voice as a passionate social campaigner. From the fate suffered by Kangalini—mother of 14 sons, who paid dearly for neglecting her daughters—in 'Freedom Fruit', to the far happier domestic situation of Gauhar Ali and his nine daughters in 'Solar System', Rokeya's writings display her political colours proudly on her sleeve. Her seminal work 'Sultana's Dream' is only the most famous example of that.

There is much to savour in these pages, but in order to do her work any justice, I have chosen to focus—for the purposes of this Foreword—on the issue perhaps closest to her heart, equality between the sexes. To that end, my observations here will mostly relate to her essays, including 'The Degradation of Women'.

In her writings, no aspect of society or culture is safe from Rokeya's critical eye. And she is brutally honest in her assessments. She does not hesitate to examine the practices of a number of world religions, including Christianity and Hinduism, to show the underlying misogyny of some of the gatekeepers. Though she takes care to point out that the discriminatory practices are often the result of patriarchal interpretation rather than the fundamental tenets of any of the religions.

In assessing the state of women and societal development (or lack thereof) in her own surroundings, Rokeya draws upon examples of progress as far away as Turkey, France, and South Africa. She also discusses the pervasiveness of gender-based discrimination elsewhere in the world, including examples embedded in the cultural traditions of Japan, thereby making it clear that India is not alone in her harmful conservatism. It is evident that she was not only a voracious reader, but that she searched far and wide for information to support her arguments in favour of women's emancipation.

The range of her interests and the breadth of her knowledge are all the more impressive when one takes into consideration the obstacles that she faced in pursuing an education. Rokeya feels those are barriers to learning keenly—not only on her own behalf, but also on behalf of all other women. She acknowledges that the state of many women in her own society is pitiable. But her analysis of the reasons behind women's dependence on men provides not only an explanation for the status quo, but also a set of solutions aimed at bringing about change.

The strongest of these measures is the campaign for female education. Women's arms can only be strengthened and their brains sharpened through use, she argues: 'The sun does not enter our bedrooms and likewise our minds are not visited by the light of knowledge, for there are hardly any schools or colleges for us.' As a result of such factors—from the absurd and humiliating feminine fear of insects, to the endemic lack of intellectual stimulation and physical exercise—Rokeya draws a picture of how the minds and bodies of women suffer equally due to this unnaturally constrained lifestyle. In turn, this state of affairs attracts further mockery from men, who see such weaknesses as the natural state of women.

Long-held views about the roles of husbands versus wives—as, respectively, providers and dependents—perpetuate and worsen the existing backwardness among women. The expectations of the two are thus, correspondingly, very different: 'While the husband is measuring the distance between the Earth and the sun and the stars, the wife is measuring a pillow in order to sew a case for it!' And she holds women just as responsible as men for sustaining the grossly unequal status quo. As women became increasingly incapable of differentiating between independence and slavery, Rokeya states, men gradually became the lords of the land, the house, and 'finally our own lords (*swami*) and we came to be included among their domestic animals or valuable possessions'.

In her essay titled 'The Degradation of Women', Rokeya does not pull any punches, lamenting how in the 'civilized twentieth century', women continue to remain slaves. 'Having lost our self-respect, we no longer feel ashamed to accept the charity meted out to us. We too have become the slaves of idleness, or rather, of males. Even our minds have become enslaved.' Reading this passage, I was reminded of the assertion by the Nobel prize-winning economist Amartya Sen, nearly a century later, to the effect that an oppressor's greatest success lies in coercing members of a marginalized group into collaborating in their own oppression, thereby making them part of perpetuating that very system of oppression.

As she proceeds with her passionate denunciation of patriarchy, Rokeya does not stop at describing the servitude of women as slavery. She also decries the ornaments that women treasure so much, terming them mere symbols of their servitude: 'Dogs wear collars and we imitate them in our jewelled chokers … Opium tastes bitter, but the addict treasures it.' Such utterances were probably considered as scandalous as her outrage that widows were singled out in their misery by being forbidden to wear bangles. After all, she lived in a time where each person was expected to know his or her place, and the place of Hindu widows, in particular, was firmly at the bottom of the heap. But then, what set Rokeya apart from the herd was her singular refusal to accept her place, by virtue of her sex, as a second-class member of society.

She also has an answer for the men who blame women for their own enslavement. To those who ask why women have allowed themselves to be enslaved, Rokeya responds, 'O men! Why have you allowed foreigners to sit on the throne of India?' The essence of her approach seems to be that while things may go wrong, often due to one's own errors of judgement, there is no excuse not to attempt to set them right.

Not that she is unaware of the dangers of being a pioneer. She mentions Galileo, who was imprisoned for saying that the Earth revolves around the sun, pointing out that groundbreaking theories by great men were never received with ease. And therefore, Rokeya advises pioneers: 'Do not bother with what society says. This world does not appreciate good deeds or good messages,' adding 'Was Columbus not called mad when he decided on his voyage of discovery? So what is the fact that woman wants to claim her rights and establish equality with men but an equally insane project?'

To her sisters, whether or not they agree with her, Rokeya also provides some bracing advice to the effect that God helps those who help themselves. After all, as she points out, unless women worry about themselves, 'no one else is going to worry for us, and even if they do, we are not going to benefit from it to the fullest extent'. There is no substitute for direct action and personal responsibility in *her* world.

Her battle, she clarifies, is not with the purdah as such, but with 'mental enslavement'. The example of the Parsi women, who were brought out of purdah by their men, possibly in an attempt to follow 'civilized' Western mores, is cited as only a partial solution. On the one hand, the sky did not fall on their heads as a result of this measure, contrary to the warnings of the doomsayers; on the other hand, the 'mental enslavement' that Rokeya is so concerned about has not been fully addressed by a measure that is, in her view, largely cosmetic. Of such Parsi women, she says, 'At present their Purdah-slavery is gone, but has their mental enslavement also vanished? No, certainly not ... Their men have brought them out only as a step in their imitation of the West ... They [the women] remain the same living luggages that they had been earlier.'

It is full equality with men that she seeks, and her determination and ambition are limitless: 'If we get freedom by ... earning our own living, then we will do that ... We will become, if and when needed, lady clerks, lady magistrates, lady barristers, lady judges—anything and everything. Fifty years later, we will become Lady Viceroy (or, if you prefer it, Vicereine) ... Why will we not earn our living? ... What do we lack? Can we not spend the same labour over our own business concerns as we do over the domestic chores of our "masters"?' To that end, she comes back once again to her treasured dream of families educating their daughters and letting them go out into the world to earn a living for themselves. I can only imagine how alarmingly radical these ideas must have seemed to her compatriots at the time. They would still be considered so, in some parts of the world today.

In an observation that was to be fiercely campaigned over in subsequent decades by the successive waves of feminists who came after her, Rokeya observes that the unfair treatment of women is manifestly evident in the limited number of cases where women have entered the workforce, since men earn more money and sometimes even get paid double for the same work done by their female counterparts. Not to mention that even in cases where 'impoverished women have to bring up their families by charring and working as seamstresses, the useless man is still the lord and master'.

Her pinpointing of the gender gap in wages, as well as her indignation over how women usually received lower wages for similar work and had so little control over their income, precede and carry within it the echo of slogans such as 'equal pay for equal work' and 'equal pay for work of equal value'. Perhaps most challenging to the status quo, however, was her head-on confrontation with the issue of inheritance rights. To this day, that remains one of the clearest instances of discrimination against women in South Asian society. It takes many forms, and has many apologists; and it is still true that in the division of parental property, for a daughter to get an equal share (and in many cases, *any* significant share) remains the exception rather than the rule.

But if some of the things that she said appeared outrageous or extreme to those around her, Rokeya was strategic enough to frame some of her arguments in terms that would appeal to the interests—or, at least, remain within the understanding—of those whom she was addressing. Among the reasons she put forward to support her view that all women needed an education, was that even if a woman's ultimate aspiration was to be a housewife, she would need certain skills to be a *good* housewife, such as having sufficient knowledge of accounting to manage and maintain the household budget, nutrition to nurture the family, medicine in order to nurse the sick, and above all, progressive ideas in order to raise children who could realize their fullest potential. Furthermore, she adds that she has nothing against cookery and needlework, since food and clothing are among the necessities of life; it is just that life should not be lived within the four walls of the kitchen. The latter is a telling observation—and one that is hard to disagree with!

Perhaps Rokeya's most traditional attitudes emerge when it comes to childcare. Here, she seems to take the view that the hand that rocks the cradle has much to contribute to the world. She defends traditional practices related to the seclusion of the new mother, and the importance of breastfeeding for at least the first year of a child's life. But she also touches on the effects of the mother's health and food intake, as well as the role of child marriage, in contributing to higher infant mortality rates. In her words, '… when a girl has to become a mother at thirteen, a grandmother at twenty-six, and a great-grandmother at forty, when will she ever have the chance to learn the things that she needs to?'

In some ways, of course, Rokeya was a woman of her time. Her view of beggars as lazy is perhaps not so surprising—least of all, given her own prodigious levels of energy. And to be fair, she has little respect for the idle rich! But a gentler challenge to class hierarchies is evident in her desire to help the poor women of the neighbourhood, among other things, by buying the garments and needlework they produce, and in her insistence that children should be trained to be kind to servants. Also, the utter scorn with which she refers to the way that some people 'flatter white-skinned masters to gain titles like Rajah or Nawab' makes it clear that racial hierarchies are no more exempt from her critiques, than are gender hierarchies.

In her clarion call for equality between the sexes, Rokeya emphasizes concepts of social interdependence between women and men, reflecting how the different elements in nature are complementary and interdependent. She is passionate in arguing that physical strength cannot be the only factor in deciding the status of women relative to men, especially when women constitute half the body politic. As she points out, 'It is not that the interests of men are different from those of women—they are the same. We have the same aim in life as they ... Instead of being burdens on them we should help them by becoming fit companions in life, in work, in religion.' With those arguments in mind, she concludes, 'I hope from now on, instead of husbands or masters, the phrase "the other half" will be used'. It is eminently clear that she does not think of male spouses as 'the better half' of any couple.

Finally, if Rokeya was overly optimistic in her hope that patriarchy could be dismantled in three decades, she is perceptive in her assessment, when she says, 'And I say to men—brothers, you will not be free till we too are. Know this for sure: you will remain slaves for as long as we do. You tyrannize over us, and see another race is terrorizing over you. For God is just ... You are being paid in your own coin.' Given the persistence of gender inequality in various parts of the globe in the twenty-first century, I think there are many today who would agree with Rokeya that as long as some in our midst remain bound by outdated social conventions, none of us can truly consider ourselves free.

Farah Ghuznavi

Part I

Thirst

(Muharram)

'Thou wert ready to send me away yesterday
But thou thyself art gone away today.
… …
Sorrow without end—thou hast left
Me burning with thirst, of you bereft.
Wherever I look at field or brook
"Thirst" burns at me incandescent
"Thirst" resounds in grave accent.'[1]

My heart burns in the fire of a terrible thirst. There is no end to this burning, and no intermission—it is eternal. At whichever direction this parched heart looks it sees its own reflection. I am blind to everything else. The spectacle of the joyous, fertile earth passes me by. I cannot see the wonderful beauty of the world. What is it that

I see then? If it were possible to take a photograph of the heart, if it were possible to paint the portrait of one's heart with the brush of an artist, then, indeed, could I have shown you my heart. But, alas, that is not possible.

There go the flags and the Tazia[2] of Muharram. The drums beat, people run about—is this itself Muharram? But this is just a pastime, an entertainment for the eyes. Who calls this Muharram? But then, what is Muharram? I do not know, I cannot answer the question. I cannot even think of it—I do not know what happens to me the minute I think of it. Darkness spreads before my eyes, I grow dizzy. So I cannot tell you what Muharram is.

All right then, let it be. Let the game continue with flags and the Tazia. But does not the entire spectacle bring to the mind an old sorrow? The long pennants sway in the breeze—cannot you see 'Thirst, oh thirst' clearly imprinted on them? Does not the memory of a heart-searing grief awakein one's heart? Man is born to die, but how many can die thus?[3]

I dreamt once that I had gone to Karbala. A terrible desert it was—hot sand everywhere, the wind moaning everywhere, as though searching for someone. I just heard 'Thirst, oh, thirst'. Each grain of sand had 'thirst' imprinted on it. I looked around myself—only emptiness, but dreaded Thirst had taken on a body and came before mine eyes.

Oh it was terrible—I left the place and went farther off. But what I saw there was more awful still—more searing to the heart. I saw the sands of the desert red with blood.[4] But the blood had not flowed, for the desert sands had sucked in every drop as it fell. The marks of the blood screamed out—'Thirst, oh, thirst'.

The youth Ali Akbar (Hussain's son), returning from the battle-field, cried out to his father '*Al-atsh, al-atsh*' ('Thirst, oh, thirst').

Hussain told his son to suck his tongue in the hope that it will give him some relief. But what relief can be there—the tongue was dry. The cry resounded from the horizons—'Thirst, oh, thirst'.

Hussain (P.B.H.) is praying for water from the heavens for his child Asgar, but who listens to him? He looks imploringly at the sky-but the sky is clear, too clear. He is enduring his own thirst. He has consoled his people. Sakina and the other girls do not ask for water, they know they cannot get it. But Asgar is too young to understand all this. His mother's breasts are dry because of starvation. The child is thirsty.

Shahr Bano has endured much, but today Asgar's sufferings are too much for her. She gives Asgar to Hussain and tells him, 'No one else is asking for water, but please get a little for his child. Let the enemy hold the drinking cup himself, let him not let you touch it.'

Hussain (P.B.H.), seeing the pitiful condition of his wife and son, is forced to ask for water. He says, 'I'm a stranger, your guest. Torture me as much as you like, I'm ready to bear it. But this child has not harmed you. He is dying of thirst, give him a drop. This will not harm your generosity in any manner.' The enemy said, 'Now this man is getting too much for us. Give him something and get rid of him.'

Instead of giving him water they shot arrows at the child:

I asked the cloud to quench my thirst
Instead, from it the thunder burst.

What hospitality indeed! Hussain (P.B.H.) returned the injured Asgar to his mother and said, 'His thirst is quenched forever. He will not make others cry by crying for water. He will not say any more—"thirst, oh, thirst". This is the end. *Quietus est.*'

What does Shahr Bano see? Thirst and wounded, Asgar is in her lap and in front of her the blood-bespattered body of martyred Akbar! Mother Earth had been proud to have such a treasure in her lap—and this Akbar did not get a drop of water when wounded and dying. 'Thirst, oh, thirst' is written in tears of blood. The martyr's closed eyes still say, 'Thirst, oh, thirst'. A heartrending scene, and it is a mother who is looking at it. Woe is me, alas, alas.

The bud to blossom at dawn is torn in the night.
No dew is there, it is washed in blood from the fight.

I saw further that glorious Hussain (P.B.H.) is defeated in the battle. The field is strewn with thirsty martyrs. Their parched throats were hoarsely whispering, 'Thirst, oh, thirst'. Hussain's sister Zainab, with her long loose hair flying, half-demented with grief, is bidding farewell to her brother. She calls on him loudly, 'Oh, dear brother, I am leaving you in the desert. I had come here with you, but I am leaving without you. I had come decked with many jewels, but I am leaving with an empty heart. Let us bid farewell for the last time. Say but one word and I will go. Open your eyes but once and look at our wretchedness and I will go.' The very winds sighed, 'Alas, alas' with Zainab, and 'Alas, alas' echoed back the far horizon.

The dream is gone and I am awake. The wolves and foxes are baying, 'Thirst, oh, thirst?' What is happening, am I going mad? Why do I see 'Thirst' imprinted everywhere, hear 'Thirst' echo at me everywhere?

I went to the grave of my treasure, my loved one.[5] Passing through the forest, I heard the trees murmuring, 'Thirst, oh, thirst'. The leaves rustled, 'Thirst, oh, thirst'. My treasure's grave whispered 'Thirst, oh, thirst'. Oh it was not to be borne. My treasure, my jewel did not get a drop of water when breathing his last, the doctor had forbidden it. It was a thirsty death for him.

Oh, who had created such a medical system? Forbidding water for a particular disease—who had been so stony-hearted as to order it? When you cannot save the patient let him at least quench his thirst. Do not obey the doctor at such a time, or you will burn with thirst for the rest of your life like me.

A certain patient had said the day before he died, 'Dad, give me water from your pitcher'. He knew that the water from his father's pitcher will definitely be cool. The father, knowing that his son's time was drawing near, had brought him the pitcher with his own hands. The other friends, more foes than friends, had not allowed him to have his fill of water. Does not his soul still wander about like the martyrs of Karbala, crying, 'Thirst, oh, thirst'? But no, there is no thirst in heaven. It is only the living who burn with thirst! One who is sleeping the eternal sleep of peace is not troubled with thirst. It is the one who is burning with the memory of what is past who is thirsty.

But I think of something, and say something different. The one who was the joy of my life had asked his mother to give him water the day before his death. No one gave him water as the doctor had forbidden it. His mother, frightened, had given him a little water. He had suffered from thirst when he passed away. Oh, who knew what a terrible thirst it was!

My soul's joy knew that I would not give him water. I was a slave of the doctor. Obeying his command, I would not give him water. So he did not ask for it while I was there. Oh, what great endurance was there! He asked for tea, asked for hot tea when he was thirsting for cool water. Tea came at once. The man who had brought the tea could not hold the cup, so hot it was. The thirsty patient took the cup in both hands as though it were a treasure and drank the tea. Oh, what a thirst it was! A thirst made up of fire, or was it a thirst made of poison!

Perhaps at that time his senses had become dull otherwise how could he hold a cup so hot in his hands? He was a child of only eight years, holding a hot cup in his soft hands. And the hot tea—had he been in good health it would surely have burnt his throat and his little hands would have melted in the heat. That tea was the last thing he took—he did not eat anything else.

I die every moment—why didn't I give him water? I had hopes he would get well. But he did not, then why didn't I give? This is the reason why, night and day, I hear, 'Thirst, oh, thirst'. I burn in hell. That hot cup hangs before mine eyes, burns at my heart, burns my very soul. If I close my eyes I see the words burning in the darkness, 'Thirst, oh, thirst'.

I went up to the roof at night. The sky was clear. The moon was shining along with a myriad stars. My accursed eyes saw the stars spelling out, diamond bright and diamond hard, 'Thirst, oh, thirst'. Here am I, burning with thirst myself, and on top of that the universe is flinging its thirst at me; echoing the word at me. Perhaps what I see is only the reflection of my own thirst or perhaps the universe is itself suffering from thirst!

What do I see in the garden full of flowers? The flowers sway and murmur, 'Thirst, oh, thirst'. The leaves have 'Thirst' printed on them. I cannot see the smile of the flower. I see the waterlily thirsting for the moon.

What do I hear in the song of birds? What but 'Thirst'? That one word reverberates in different tunes at different times—in the *bhairabī* of the morning, in the *behāg* at night—but it is the same word. The *cātaka* bird thirstily cries '*phatic jal*' and the cuckoo gives its mournful '*cu-ckoo*', raining down on me the pain of the thirst of a thousand souls. Oh, what has happened, why does everything make me hear the language of heart-searing thirst? Oh, where is the place, where I will not hear 'Thirst, oh, thirst'?

Come, my heart, let us go to the river. Maybe there is no thirst there. But listen, the Ganges is singing in soft accents. The liquid sound of the flowing waters sings 'Thirst'. But why—you are yourself water, how can you be thirsty? I heard the answer, 'I thirst for the sea'. Yes, yes, everyone in the world is thirsty. Then maybe the sea itself, at whose feet thou, Mother Ganges, pourest thyself, is not thirsty. Let us see.

Sitting on the wet sands by the seashore I was counting the waves. The waves were continually breaking on the sands, impelled by some unknown pain. What were they pining for? I asked the sea in great puzzlement:

'Thy restless waves spell out, "Oh thirst"
Water's what all thirst quencheth
Thou thyself earth's water holdeth
Tell me, sea, what is thy thirst?'

Still the sea rumbled in deep bass, 'Thirst, oh, thirst!' Ah, this thirst is driving me out of my own country, and yet here too I hear the same cruel word. I closed my eyes—I did not want to see 'thirst' printed on the crest of every wave. But the sea's deep thunder rolled all about me. I understood its language clearly saying, 'Thirst, oh thirst'.

'Thirst, oh, thirst'—oh ignorant Man, do you not know what thirst this is? Who told you that the sea itself is not thirsty? How can I show the insatiable thirst of my heart? The deeper the heart is the keener the thirst. Who is not thirsty in this world? Thirst, yearning, longing—don't you understand it? The rich thirst for wealth, the famous thirst for fame, the worldly thirst for the world. The lotus yearns for the sun, the *cakora* bird yearns for the moon; even fire itself has longings. Don't you understand this basic fact? With what aim would the galaxy revolve if it had no longings? My heart yearns for love—so long as I exist, this yearning also exists. The lover yearns for love, nature yearns for God. Don't you understand this?

Now, now I know why my heart laments all the time, why it is aching all the time. This heart does not yearn for mere water. It yearns for everlasting love. God is the goal of all yearnings and everyone yearns for Him, thirsts for the love of the Great Beloved.

No, I am not mad. The thirst that I see everywhere is not just an imaginary one, it is real. The thirst I hear is not imaginary—it is real. God is love and the universe thirsts for love.

(First pub. in Roy, Gyanendralal and Roy, Harendralal ed., *Nabaprabhā*, Caitra 1308 and Baiśākh, 1309. Rpt in Kazi Nazrul Islam ed., *Dhūmketu*, Bhādra 1329—the Muharram edn.)

Notes

1. Whenever translating poetry, we have tried to keep the line-division and rhyme-scheme the same as in the original (added by the translators).

2. A tazia is a structure, small and light enough to be carried by one person, made of sticks and coloured paper. It represents the tomb at Mecca and is carried in the procession of Muharram.

3. Once Jainul Abedin (the son of Hussain) asked a butcher, 'You have brought this goat for sacrifice, but have you fed it?' The butcher said, 'Yes, I've just now made it drink a lot of water'. Then he said, 'You have quenched the goat's thirst before sacrificing it, but Shamar burnt my father with thirst for three whole days before sacrificing him.'

Jainul was ailing at the time of the battle of Karbala and was thus not subjected to martyrdom.

4. After the demise of the Prophet, one after the other, Abu Bakr Siddiq, Umar Kattab, and Usman Ghani became the Caliph. When time came for the fourth Caliph, there was difference of opinion about appointing Ali or Muawiyah. One group was in favour of Muawiyah while the other group said, 'Ali is the Prophet's son-in-law, so he is the proper successor to the throne'. That was how dissension began.

After this Muawiyah's son Yazid determined to destroy Ali's sons Hassan and Hussain. Yazid killed great Hassan (Peace be upon Him [P.B.H.]) with poison. A year after this he invited the saintly Hussain (P.B.H.), taking him to Karbala and killed him in combat.

But not just in combat in the field of battle Yazid's army cordoned off the banks of the Euphrates. They did not allow anyone belonging to Hussain's (P.B.H.) party to take water. So the latter were halfdead with thirst as it was. The battle was one only in name and Hussain (P.B.H.) and all his friends and relatives were killed on the same day. There is difference of opinion about this. Some say the battle went on for three days, some say just one. Yazid had shown unparalleled cruelty in depriving them of the water of the river.

Kasim, the 18-year-old son of Hassan (P.B.H.), married Sakina the daughter of Hussain (P.B.H.) the night before his death. Karbala saw Sakina as a bride and then, but a few hours later, as a widow. Widowed on the very day of marriage! Woe to thee, Karbala! Why did you not become blind rather than to have seen this? The men went away to fight and what were the women doing? Even while they were mourning for one, they got the news of the death of another. Even while weeping for Kasim, they got the dead body of Ali Akbar. Their mourning turned towards Akbar. And while weeping for Akbar, they got the corpse of the child Asgar. But the one and the same mother had to put down Akbar from her lap and take up Asgar—but how far can endurance go? Even while she was still dazed with grief for her son, the enemy sent the head of her treasure, Hussain (P.B.H.). While she was looking at it, Hussain's young daughter Fatima was crying inconsolably on seeing the head of her father. Even while Shahr Bano was trying to console her, she died. For how long can she, who is but a child, endure hunger and thirst? Death came to her all on a sudden. What will Shahr

Bano do now—wipe away the tears of Sakina or take the dead Fatima on her lap?

Ah, but who on earth can endure so much? My grief-stricken sisters, sorrowing for your sons, do but cast a glance at the limitless sorrow of Shahr Bano and Zainab. You are overwhelmed with grief for just one person and the world has become dark for you. What about this piling up of sorrows, one upon the other? You can weep your fill for one person, but this is denied to them. What can Zainab do—cry for her son, or look after her nephew, or wash the forehead of her dear brother Hussain with her tears. There is no other water to wash it with!

Oh my heroes! Just think of the heroism and endurance of Hussain (P.B.H.). There he is—standing in the river. No other soldier is there; all are dead. He is alone in the battlefield. He has somehow managed to reach the river. See, he is taking up water with joined palms, perhaps he is going to drink? Oh no, he is not going to drink. Asgar has died for this water, Akbar has sucked his tongue for this water—and is he going to drink it? He takes the water; he can drink if he wants. But no, he drops it back into the river. There is heroism for you!

The Sunnis do not join the Shias in observing Muharram—those who say this are grievously mistaken. Ali (P.B.H.) and his descendants are revered by both the sects. What Sunni would indulge in merriment at the time of observing their death? Children might enjoy it, but no devout Sunni would call Muharram a festival.

The Sunnis do not approve of the pomp and ceremony of the Shias. They do not believe that beating the breast or wearing mourning expresses grief. Difference of opinion also occurs in that the Shias disparage Hazrat Ayesha (the stepmother of Fatima) for having given the throne for Muawiyah and not to Ali. But we do not find any fault in her except for the fact that she was the stepmother-in-law of Ali. The Prophet (P.B.H.) had not uttered the name of the fourth Caliph—had pointed with his finger. Both Muawiyah and Ali were standing at the same place and so dissension arose. Some said that Ali was the fourth Caliph and some said it was Muawiyah.

It is not that Ayesha was prompted by jealousy in naming Muawiyah. She too had only inferred it. The Sunnis cannot bear any disparagement of reverend Ayesha. There is this difference of opinion between the Shias and the Sunnis and so there is dissension between them.

5. The person she is writing about is an eight-year-old boy (added by the translators).

The Degradation of Women

My sisters, have you ever reflected on the wretchedness of your life? What are we in this civilized twentieth century? Why, we are slaves! Yes, I have heard that slavery has been abolished, but has it been abolished for us? No. But why are we slaves? There are many reasons for this.[1]

Nobody knows what happened in primitive times, but it seems as if at that time when there was no civilization, no social bondages, our condition had not been like this. For some unknown reason, one part of humanity (man) went on developing in many directions, but the other part (woman) could not progress in a likewise manner. So instead of being a companion, she became a slave.

Can anyone indicate the reasons for this worldwide degradation? Perhaps the main reason is the lack of opportunity. Woman has withdrawn from worldly affairs because of the lack opportunity. Men, seeing that women were weak, started helping them, and the more help they got the weaker and the less efficient they became. We can easily be compared with the beggars of our country. The more the wealthy spend on charity, the greater the number of beggars. Now begging has become a job for the idle. They no longer feel ashamed to beg.

In the same way, having lost our self-respect, we no longer feel ashamed to accept the charity meted out to us. We too have become the slaves of idleness, or rather, of males. Even our minds have become enslaved,[2] and we have become habituated to slavery through long use. The higher tendencies of the mind, like independence, courage, etc., have been repeatedly nipped in the bud and so perhaps they do not come forth these days. It has become easy for men to say: 'The five worst maladies that affect the female mind are: indocility, discontent, slander, jealousy and silliness ... such is the stupidity of her character, that it is incumbent on her, in every particular, to distrust herself and to obey her husband.' (Japan, the Land of the Rising Sun)[3]

Some say, 'Exaggeration and lies are adornments for a woman's tongue.' Some say we are unreasonable. They started to despise us because they found these faults in us. That is but natural. Let us take an example. Sons-in-law are much respected in our country—even a witch adores her son-in-law. But a resident son-in-law (*ghar-jāmāi*) is not respected much. So, when we ourselves became incapable of differentiating between independence and slavery, between progress and regress, men gradually became lord of the land, lord of the house, and finally our own lords (swami)[4] and we came to be included among their domestic animals or valuable possessions.

Then with the coming of civilization and the rise of social customs the rules of society were created in accordance with the whims of the Elders of society. This too is quite natural: 'might is right'. Now I ask—who is responsible for our degradation and downfall?

And our treasured ornaments, these are but symbols of our servitude. They are used at present in the hope of enhancing the beauty of the wearer, but many esteemed persons say that these were originally badges of slavery.[5] Prisoners wear iron rings on their legs and we wear treasured rings (*mal*) made of silver or gold. They wear handcuffs of iron and we wear handcuffs or bangles, of gold or silver. It goes without saying that iron bangles are also worn on the arms.

Dogs wear collars and we imitate them in our jewelled chokers. Elephants and horses are chained with iron chains, and we deck ourselves with gold chains and think, 'I'm wearing a necklace'. The owner of a cow passes a rope through her nose, and our owners too have given us nose rings which are the sign of marriage, or rather, the sign that the husband is living. So you see, sisters mine, your treasured ornaments are nothing but symbols of slavery. Moreover, how ironical it is that the more symbols of slavery a woman wears, the more respect does she gain in society!

How women do pine for ornaments! It is as though their happiness and prosperity depend on them! So the impoverished woman who cannot get bangles of gold or silver wears glass ones, thereby glorifying her existence as a slave! The widow, not allowed to wear bangles, is wretched beyond compare. How very important habit is! We have become habituated to slavery and so we admire the symbols of slavery. Opium tastes bitter but the addict treasures it. However destructive a drug might be, the addict cannot do without it. We are proud to bear on our bodies the symbols of our own slavery!

Some of my sisters might think me to be the devil's advocate or a spy from the camp of males. That is, they might think that I want to turn women against ornaments in order to save men's money from the clutches of goldsmiths. It is definitely not that—I just want to say certain things to you. If ornaments are meant to make men spend money, then there are many other ways of doing that. Let me mention a few of them.

Take that jewelled collar of yours and put it round the neck of your pet dog. When you go out to take the air in your carriage, put your costly necklace around the neck of the horse pulling the carriage. Use your bangles as curtain rings in your drawing room. That will take care of the money of your owner ('swami'). Actually, ornaments are meant to display your wealth, isn't it? So you can display your wealth in this way too. Why bear the symbols of slavery on your own body? When you start using your ornaments in this way, people, at first, will say you are mad, but there is no need to pay them any attention.[6] What good work has ever been done in this wretched world without any trouble? Galileo had to go to prison because he said that the earth goes around the sun. What great man is there who has been able to explain his theories easily? So what I say is, do not bother with what society says. This world does not appreciate good deeds or good messages these days.

Actually ornaments are nothing but symbols of slavery. Is it any less reprehensible to regard them as means to enhance one's beauty rather than a symbol of slavery? Is not the desire to enhance one's beauty a sign of mental weakness? Men think ornaments to be the signs of defeat. When they argue about anything they say, 'If I cannot prove what I say, I will wear bangles'. The poet Sa'adi, wanting to encourage men, told them, 'O heroes! try to be conquerors, do not pact on the garments of women'. They feel insulted to put on our garments! Let us see what these garments are—after all the clothes are very similar to each other. Is there much difference between a sari and a dhoti? In many countries males as well as females wear trousers. One hears of ladies' jackets as well as of gents' jackets. Then perhaps Sa'adi's phrase '*jamae-janan*' (women's clothes) merely meant feminine weaknesses.

Men tell us they have treasured us in their bosoms and threaten us by saying that we will not find such love and caress anywhere else. So we are melting with their caresses. Actually it is their charity that has been the ruin of us. They have imprisoned us in their heart and deprived us of fresh air and the light of knowledge and that is what has gradually killed us. They say, 'They are delicate, we will carry things for them—why should they exert themselves when we are there? We thank such people for their generous words but, dear brother, the world is not just a poet's beautiful dream—it is a painful, iron-hard truth. It is real, not a poem:

It is my life—not a novel or poem.
Nor a theatre-stage—It is my home

And that is where the difficulty lies. Otherwise your bounty would have been enough for us. Your imagination paints the Bengali woman as a delicate darling from which, gradually getting more and more etherealized, she would have got an aerial body[7] and vanished into thin air. But in actual fact conditions are not all that pleasant. Let me humbly say: Do this favour to us—don't shower favours on us. Too much care often spoils many things. The garment folded away with great love often becomes moth-eaten. The poet says:

'Why did the lamp go out?
I guarded it with the greatest care
Wakeful all the bridal night
So my treasured lamp went out.'

One can see that the extreme care men lavish on us serve to ruin us.

Over-protected from the harshness of life, we have lost our courage and strength. We have become helplessly dependent on our husbands because we have lost self-dependence. The least bit of danger, and we retire into a corner and our lamentations reach the skies. Our brothers mock us, talk of our 'affected tears' and we silently bear it. I die of shame when I think of how wretchedly cowardly we have become.[8]

We are alarmed at the sight of cockroaches, leeches, and such insects—what to talk of lions and tigers! Some ladies even faint at the sight! A nine- or ten-year-old boy will take a cockroach or a leech and put it inside a bottle and enjoy himself frightening all the women of the household. The women scream and run and the boy runs laughing after them with the bottle. Have you not seen such a scene? I have, and, thinking of it, I am ready to die to shame. To tell you the truth, I too had enjoyed myself at that time, but now—to think of it makes my blood boil. Oh, at whose feet have we sacrificed our physical strength and mental courage? And on top of everything, we do not have the ability even to reflect on this wretched condition.

I have shown a picture of cowardice, now I will show one of physical weakness. We have become such 'living luggages' that we are nothing but drawing-room ornaments. Dear reader, have you ever seen the living luggage called the daughter-in-law of a wealthy Muslim family of Bihar? I will show you the portrait of such a begum. She should have been kept in a museum to show fitting respect to women. There is this dark room with two doors, one of which is kept closed and the other open. So, (because of the ruling of purdah) fresh air and sunlight cannot enter the room. There is a bedstead covered with red velvet beside a four-poster. On that smaller bed sits the '*dulhin-begum*' (the daughter-in-law of the mistress of the house), decked out with ornaments, lips reddened with betel juice, with a pleased and smiling face. She carries the burden of ornaments worth Rs 10,240.[9] I think it is necessary to give a list of how much gold she is wearing in the different parts of her body:

1. 1/2 *seer* (40 *tolas*) on the head;[10]
2. A bit more than a *pau* (25 tolas) on her ears;
3. 1 1/2 seer (120 tolas) around the neck;
4. Almost 2 seer (150 tolas) on her delicate arms;
5. Almost 3 paus (65 tolas) around the waist;
6. Exactly 3 seers (240 tolas) on her two feet.

The nose ring has a diameter of 4 inches.[11] Her clothes are stiff with gold-thread embroidery and sequins. The poor begum could hardly stir a finger!

It is almost impossible to move about with a load of eight seers of gold, so what could the dulhin-begum do but become a living luggage! She is constantly suffering from headaches. There are three reasons for this: tightly bound braid of hair, loads of ornaments on braid and head, and, half of the head is covered with silver dust and sequins. The eyebrows are covered with sequins. The forehead is decorated with sequins and many-coloured moons and stars made of metal foils. The body has become motionless and more so the mind.

Life becomes a burden for such a motionless object. The health is ruined for lack of exercise. Her feet ache when she goes from one room to another. Her arms are useless. Lack of appetite and indigestion become chronic. *Menssana in corporesano*—so the mind and the rain too become diseased. You can well understand what kind of a life it is for a chronic sufferer with health like this.

How does this picture impress you? True, religious counsel is that which we learn by observing the conditions of our own selves and of those around us. The lessons we learn at times from birds and bees is far superior to mere book learning. The lesson Newton learnt from observing an apple fall was not to be found in any book in the whole world. I have been able to give this picture of our social condition by thinking of the condition of this dulhin-begum.

So I was very sorry for her and thought: 'Her life in this world and the next, both are ruined.' If God asks, 'what use have you made of the mind, the brain, the eyes, etc. that I had given you?' What will she say in answer? I asked one of the girls of that family, 'What explanation will you give God for not doing any work with your hands and feet?' She said, 'What you are saying is right', and told me that she does not waste her time and walks about all the time. I told her, 'Just walking about is not enough. Do some running about for at least half an hour every day.' There was some laughter at the idea of running. I was pained and thought 'Mary, Mary, quite contrary—they do not have the ability even to learn about anything. Progress is very far indeed from us, God help us.'

The sun does not enter our bedrooms and likewise our minds are not visited by the light of knowledge, for there are hardly any schools or colleges for us. Men can study as much as they like but will the doors of the storehouse of knowledge be ever fully open for us? If a generous and great soul ever comes with outstretched hands to lift us, there will be hundreds to put up obstacles in his way.

One person cannot progress against a thousand. So a spark of hope is reduced to ashes in the darkness of despair before it can brighten into a flame. There are many who are so prejudiced against women's education that the minute they hear the word they shudder at the thought of its many evil results. Society easily forgives a hundred faults of an uneducated woman, but a slightly educated woman? Even if she has committed no misdeeds society will discover some faults, magnify them hundred-fold, and blame it on her 'education'. They ironically declare: 'Salutations to women's education.'

These days most people regard education as but a means forgetting a job. It is impossible for a woman to take up a job, so they think education is entirely unnecessary for a woman.

Some native Christians might, for the sake of arguments, say that woman's thirst for knowledge is the cause of the Fall. The Genesis tells us that it was because our primal mother, Eve, ate the fruit of the Tree of Knowledge, both she and Adam were expelled from Paradise.[12]

Any 'education' does not mean blind imitation of a certain race or sect. It signifies the development of God-given natural faculties by exercising them. It is our duty to put them to good use, and misuse of them is a sin.[13] God has given us hands, feet, eyes, ears, mind, and brain. If we strengthen our hands and feet through exercise, do good deeds with our hands, observe well with our eyes, hear attentively with our ears, learn to think more keenly with our brains—then that is true education. 'Degree-getting knowledge' is not true education. Let me give an example of developing the faculty of seeing:

An untrained eye sees only dust and clay where the scientifically trained eye can see many delightful things. We dismiss clay as something made of soil, sand, coal-dust, and water. But a scientist will analyse and find the following four objects in it. On analysing sand he will get white stones such as opals, clay will yield material for porcelain or sapphire, coal-dust will lead us to diamond, and water will give us dew. See, my sisters, an educated eye finds jewels like diamonds where an uneducated eye finds clay. What, oh, what can we say to God in justification for keeping such eyes eternally blind!

Suppose you hand your maid-servant a broom and tell her, 'go and clean such and such a house of mine'. The maid, thinking the broom to be a gift from you, wraps it carefully in costly cloth and puts it away, never using it. Your house gets dirtier and dirtier and becomes uninhabitable. Then when you take an account of what the maid has done, what will you do when you see the miserable condition of your house? Will you be pleased if she cleans the house with the tool you gave her, or be pleased that she reveres your gift so much?

Our conscience has shown us our degradation, now it is our duty to develop ourselves. We should open the door to our development with our own hands. I have said earlier, 'God help us', but one should remember that even God will not pull you out by the hand unless you stretch out your hand. 'God helps those who help themselves', after all. Unless we worry about ourselves, no one else is going to worry for us, and even if they do, we are not going to benefit from it to the fullest extent.

There are many who think that women tolerate the mastery of men because they benefit from man's hard-earned money or wealth. This, to a certain extent, is true. May be it is because woman was reduced to use the money earned by others because she could not do much physical labour. That is why she had to bow down. But now we can see even the mind of women have become enslaved. Even in cases where impoverished women have to bring up their families by charring or working as seamstresses, the useless man is still the lord and master. And what about the man who does not earn himself but marries an heiress and lords over her? Nor does the wife object to it.[14] This is because for a very, very long time all the higher faculties of women have been nipped in the bud, so that their outer and inner personalities, brain, heart, everything, have become 'slaves'. We no longer have self-dependence or force in our heart, nor is there any desire to obtain it. That is why I want to cry out: 'Wake up, wake up, my sisters!'

It is not so easy, at first, to wake up. I know society will create no end of trouble. The Muslims will condemn us to death and the Hindus will arrange for the funeral pyre.[15] I also know that my sisters do not want to wake up. But they have to wake up, for the good of society. Have I not said that no good work can be easily done? When Galileo was released from prison he had said, 'But nevertheless it (Earth) does move'. We shall have to endure all tyrannies and wake up. I am giving an example—that of Parsee ladies. Here is a passage from an Urdu newspaper:

> The last fifty years have seen many changes among Parsee women. They have acquired western civilization, which formerly they did not know even by name. They too, like Muslim women used to be behind the purdah. They did not have the right to use umbrellas for protection against the sun and rain. When they could not bear the heat of the sun they used their slippers for protection. Curtains were there even when they sat inside a carriage. They could not speak to their husbands in front of others. But these days they have left the purdah behind. They go about in open carriages, talk with men and run their own business concerns. When the first few gentlemen had brought their wives out of the purdah there had been an outcry. White-haired wiseacres had said, 'Now the world is going to face destruction'.

But why, the world has not been destroyed! So I say, once, once only, all of you together, go forward in the name of freedom; time will make us get used to everything. Freedom means the progress and the developed condition of males.

You might ask, how to regain the lost treasure? How can we be worthy daughters of our country? First of all, one has to have the will or the determination to walk side by side with men in our domestic, everyday life, and, of course, one will have to have faith in the fact that we are not a race of slaves.

Let us do all that has to be done to gain equality with men.[16] If we get freedom be freely earning our own living, then we will do that. We will become, if and when needed, lady clerks, lady magistrates, lady barristers, lady judges—anything and everything. Fifty years later we will become Lady Viceroy (or, if you prefer it, Vicereine), and turn all the women in this country into queens! Why will we not earn our living? Do we not have hands or feet or brains? What do we lack? Can we not spend the same labour over our own business concerns as we do over the domestic chores of our 'masters' (swamis)?[17]

If we cannot enter the field of government jobs, we will enter that of agriculture. Why lament over our daughters because grooms have become difficult to get? Educate your daughters and let them go out into the world to earn their own living. In the field of jobs, too, men earn more money, women labour is cheaper. A low-class man gets Rs 2 per month and for the same work women get Re 1. A domestic servant is paid Rs 3 per month while a maid-servant gets Rs 2. Sometimes, however, the woman is paid more.

If you say we are weak, ignorant, and silly, then whose fault is that? Ours and ours only. We do not exercise our intellectual faculties and so they have become dulled. We will hone our intellect into keenness by exercising it. The soft arms that have become weak through idleness—cannot they become strong through work? See if this dull head does not become keen and sophisticated by the acquisition of knowledge.

Lastly, let me assert, we constitute half of the body politic. If we wallow in mud, how can society stand erect? If you tie down one of the feet of a man, how far can he travel on limping feet? It is not that the interests of men are different from those of women—they are the same. We have the same aim in life as they. A child needs both the parents equally. Whether it be in religious life or in worldly life, we should have the qualities that will make us progress side by side with them. At first they progressed rapidly along the path of development and we lagged behind. Now they feel lonely because they do not have fit companions in this world. So they have to stop and look back while proceeding along the path of ultimate development. Instead of being burdens on them we should help them by becoming fit companions in life, in work, in religion. We were definitely not created for spending an idle puppet-life.

I hope my able sisters will think about this. Even if they do not want to make a stir they will ponder over all I have said carefully.

(First published in Sen, Girish Chandra ed., *Mahila*, Baiśākh, Jyestha, and Asarh/1310, in three instalments entitled 'Ornament or Badge of Slavery'. Rept. Syed Imdad Ali ed. *Naba-Nūr* Bhadra 1311, revised, under the title 'Our Degradation'. Later still, revised version under the name 'The Degradation of Women', included in this book.)

Addendum

(This is the first published version of *The Degradation of Women*. In between paragraphs marked * had been omitted later.)

Ornaments or the Badge of Slavery[18]

(The first five sentences are the same as in the foregoing essay—Transl.)

My sisters ... abolished for us? We used to be subjugated to men and we still are. Our grandmothers used to say that it was God's will that woman should be subjugated to man. He created man first and later woman was created in order to serve him. But I have doubts about this because our grandmothers learnt this from men and they will naturally say that women were created for man's comfort and peace.

I do not know anything about primitive times but I believe that in prehistoric times when there was no civilization nor social rules, we were not slaves. As man became more and more civilized, took to wearing clothes instead of painting his body, he started to lord over women in physical strength and mental keenness. But God is not so partial as to make one race the slave of another. If that had been so then why has He given men and women, both, two hands, two eyes, etc.? Do you have a two-headed man or a noseless woman in any country? You cannot see such anomalies anywhere, so how can we say that God is partial? It is society which has created the king and his subject, distinguished between a constable and the Governor—it is that society which has subjugated woman to man. With the help of his physical strength and cunning man has won over wild animals, made horses pull his carriage, put chains around the legs of elephants, has put the noble lion inside a cage. And he has made use of the same strength and cunning to tie woman up in the bondages of slavery.

We have become used to slavery through long usage. Men have gradually enslaved even our minds. We are not able to distinguish any longer between slavery and independence. What terrible degradation! Men, from being the lord of the manor, master of the family, have become our own masters. We have gradually become their pets, like domestic animals and pet birds. Now we are the prisoners of society.

And these, our treasured ornaments ... the symbol of slavery! (Transl. two paragraphs in the foregoing essay are the same in this)

Alas, there is no end to our degradation. The Hindus forbid a married woman to cut her hair. Have you ever thought about it? It is because when the husband gets angry he can take her by the hair and beat her. Have you seen a bear dance? At times when the owner of the bear is defeated wrestling with him he pulls at the nose-rope of the bear and the bear, pained, lets him go. In the same way if a married woman tries to escape the husband pulls her by the hair. Now I do not say that the long hair of all women is used in this manner, but the opportunity is always there, readymade, for the husband. Oh, shame on us. We take care of this hair right from our childhood. Really what a fine idea of beauty do we have!

Some of my sisters ... put up obstacles for him.

(About three pages are the same as in the former essay)

Now one might ask, 'Why did you allow yourselves to be enslaved?' I will say only this in reply, 'O men! Why have you allowed foreigners to sit on the throne of India?' The same reason that made them lose their independence to foreigners (*pradhan*) has made us lose our independence to men (*naradhin*).

Now my sisters, try to understand your own rights. I know that the centuries-old chains of slavery cannot be broken in just one day. But a few minutes' earthquake can reduce an edifice made with infinite labour to rubble. A cannon destroys a fortress built over many days. So I hope that in about thirty years' time this centuries-old fortress of slavery will also be brought down by the use of force. After all, had we accepted slavery in just one day? Definitely not.

* * * 19

We cannot raise our heads against slavery, because whenever one of our sisters has tried to lift up her head, at once her head had been battered down with the weapons of religious and scriptural rules. That which we had not accepted easily has been accepted later by thinking it to have been ordained by religion. These days it has come to be, 'You wretch, you have been a slave, you will remain a slave'. So our very souls have become slaves.

* * *

When a child is being put to sleep by force, he will often raise his head and look here and there. The mother will say, 'Close your eyes and go to sleep. Look, the terrible "juju" is there'. Frightened, the child will at least close his eyes even if he is not feeling sleepy. In the same way when we look at the past and the present with uplifted heads, society says, 'Go to sleep. See, there is hellfire for you'. We keep quiet even though we may not believe it.

* * *

Men have declared these scriptures to be 'God's commands' in order to make fools of us. I do not want to go into the inner meaning or the spiritual significance of any religion; I want to discuss only the social rules and regulations in our religion, so the pious may rest easy. Whenever in ancient days a man gained fame through his own talents, he tried to control barbaric men by declaring himself to be the messenger of God or a God himself. As the intellectual faculty of men developed our heaven-sent prophets have become more and more intellectually developed.

The greatest god of all once wrote a book about religion in Sanskrit. He taught the Hindu woman:

> The husband's the lord of a woman
> He is the real god for her.
> The husband's her wealth, except for him
> None can give salvation to her.

The ignorant, hapless woman accepted all that was said.

Then, as men's brains became more and more sophisticated, clever and talented men saw that people no longer believed in God's 'messengers'. So great Jesus Christ declared himself to be the Son of God, and created his own Gospels. It is written there, 'Woman is entirely subjected to man—the husband has full rights over her property', and women, foolish women, accepted this. Then a rule was made that women will always be dependent on men, on the father or the brother before marriage and on the husband after marriage. Where there is no husband she will be dependent on her son, and women, stupid and ignorant women, bowed their heads down to this rule.

* * *

My sisters, you can see for yourself that these religious books are nothing but rules fabricated by men. The ancient sages have said all these things. Had there been a woman sage you might have seen the opposite. All the religious books were not God's commandments. Had God sent a messenger to control women then such a messenger would not have been limited within Asia only. Why was not the command of God 'Woman will be the slave of man' heard in countries like America, the countries spread out between the North Pole and the South? Can God be God over Asia only? Did He not rule over America? The air and the water given by Him are there in all the countries, so why have his messengers not spread everywhere? The uncivilized barbarians had believed this thing in primitive times and so do the civilized and sophisticated men of today. Then what is the difference between civilization and barbarity? Anyway, we are not going to bow down to man's tyranny in the name of religion any longer. You can also see that the stronger the rule of religion is, the worse the tyranny over women. The Suttee custom is a proof of this. Wherever the hold of religion is a bit loose, the more freedom do women have, almost equal to men. By religion I mean the social rules given by religion.

* * *

Some might say, 'Why bring in religion when talking of social customs?' I would say, 'It is "religion" that has made the chains of our slavery stronger and stronger. Men are lording over women in the name of "religion".' So I have been forced to bring religion in. Let the god-fearing and the pious forgive me.

We should open the door ... by the acquisition of knowledge.

(About two and a half pages of the foregoing essay have been repeated)

The saga of our misery is indeed an endless one. We are quite helpless in this wide world. This earth was made by God and every creature has equal right to dwell here. But men, clever men, rational men, have divided the world among themselves. This one is the Lord of Kabul, that one the Lord of another country—as though the earth were his patronymic. But the other creatures of the earth have not given up their rights just because man has divided it up. All creatures, the king of beasts as well as the most insignificant insects, all dwell in it. We are the only ones who have given up their rights on this earth. We do not have even a hut to call our own. 'Our home' means the house of our father, husband, or son. If we leave the house of our father or our husband then we do not have any place even to stand up in. If a father disowns a bad son then the son makes a living for himself somehow. But if a daughter is driven out by her guardian then this sunlit world turns dark for her. She thinks, 'Let the earth split and swallow me up'. Why? Is not there any place on this earth for us? It is a wonder that we still exist after such humiliation at every step.

And I say to men—'Brothers, you will not be free till we too are. Know this for sure: You will remain slaves for as long as we do. You tyrannize over us, and see, another race is tyrannizing over you. For God is just. The God in whose name you have written rules of tyranny over women in your religious books is not so partial that He will tolerate your mastery over us. We have tolerated you without a word of protest, but He has not. His compassion is for everyone. You tyrannize over the world in His name and we spread love throughout the world in His name. You have pleased Him with your prayers and meditations, but you have not been able to make him angry with us. You belong to God and so do we. Give up your vanity and hand our rights back to us. We do not want tax-free land from you. We just want to be your equals. If you say you honour women, for example worship goddess-figures like Sita and others, pay homage to Hazrat Fatima, the daughter of the Prophet (P.B.H.), and to Mother Mary, the mother of Jesus Christ, that will not satisfy us for you never forget that you are men. That word "man" itself indicates your inordinate pride. As the white-skinned people treat the "native" gentlemen with politeness so do you show respect for us. Are we so stupid that we cannot understand your tone and your attitude? You threaten us with hellfire at every step just as we make cowards of our children by frightening them with a non-existent "juju". So you too cannot lift your head against slavery. You are being paid in your own coin.'

If, instead of making us continue to live like a clawless, toothless pet tiger, men send us to their imaginary hell by condemning us to death, we are ready for it. At least we shall not have to bear the burden of this enslaved life. I do hope that the religious books have ruled: If women refuse the tyranny of man, send them to hell as a punishment.

I hope my intelligent and learned sisters will discuss all this, will reduce to rubble the fortress of slavery with the earthquake of protest. Even if they do not rebel or protest, let them ponder thoughtfully over the subject.

Mrs R.S. Hossein

(Published in Sen, Girish Chandra ed., *Mahila*, Baiśākh-Jyestha-Asarh, 1310 and taken from Md. Shamsul Alam's *Rokeya Sakhawat Hossein: Life and Literary Works*)

Notes

1. Some might say that women should be subjugated to man—this is God's will, for He had created man first, and woman had been created later to minister to him. But, for the present, we are not going to plunge into a religious discussion but writing about only what is apparent to and comprehensible to a person with common sense. In other words, I am only expressing my personal opinion.

2. The writer has actually used the word 'enslaved' (added by the translators).

3. This entire passage has been given in English including the words in paranthesis for which no explanation or reference is given (added by the translators).

4. 'Although the Japanese wife is considered only the first servant of her husband, she is usually addressed in the house as the "honourable mistress". Acquaintance with European customs has awakened among the more educated classes in Japan a desire to raise the position of women.'

(This entire passage has been given in English and then translated by the authoress. [added by the translators])

Many ladies may object to the word 'slave' (*dasi*). But I ask, what does the word 'swami' mean? If someone who gives something is called 'giver' then the one who takes must be called the 'taker'. In the same way if one is called 'husband', 'lord', 'God', then what can you call the other but a 'slave'?

If you say that the wife has become the servant of the husband through love, then no one will object to such servitude. But I ask, has not man also taken on a likewise servitude of looking after the wife with love? A poor day-labourer gets a few coins after a whole day's toil, goes to the market and instead of satisfying his own hunger with that money, buys rice and gives it to his wife. Then she cooks the rice and he is satisfied with what she gives him. This is true sacrifice. Yet, instead of calling a married man the servant of love (*prema-dasa*), society calls him 'swami' (lord)—why?

Another important matter comes to my mind. Those ladies who object to the term 'slave' and tell us about Sita and Savitri at every turn, do they know that in today's Hindu society there is one (or more) class of '*kulins*' who buy their wives? If you buy somebody with hard cash, then what can you call her except a slave? One may talk of money being paid to bridegrooms but no one ever says, 'the groom is sold'. It is the groom's qualifications (degree) which are sold, not the groom himself. But I cannot say this of the bride. A girl child of 8–12 years does not have any particular qualifications or degrees which can be sold. It follows, therefore, that the girl herself is sold. Conversing with a Brahmin lady of a good family, I had asked, 'Cannot they get kulin families like themselves that they have to buy girls?' The lady's answer was, 'Yes, of course they can. But such buying and selling is their custom. This man has bought this girl to marry her, and likewise someone else will buy his sister and marry her.'

I had not wanted to mention any sect or any definite faults, but I was forced to do this, for there are many who argue in such prejudiced manners. I had to present proofs of slavery or, as they are called, 'devis'. We are sorry for this, but it was an unavoidable duty.

5. Mr Zakaullah (a *Shams-ul-Ulama* or 'Sun of the Scholars', from the West) says, 'The nose-ring is but a version of the *nakel* (a rope to pass through the nose of animals)'.

6. Wearing ornaments is the same as wasting money in the ways I said. But I hope that instead of wasting money in that way people will use it for good purposes.

7. 'Aerial body' is a phrase in English used by the writer (added by the translators).

8. I saw in an Urdu newspaper of last 9th April that the women of Turkey have petitioned the Sultan: 'We have nothing to do except stay within the four walls of our house. Please give us this much education that we may protect our houses and the city in times of war with guns and cannons like men.' They have given the following advantages of such a procedure in the petition:

i. First of all, many soldiers are used to protect the city so there is scarcity of soldiers in the battlefield. This will be avoided (for the 'helpless' will protect the city).

ii. The children will become familiar with fighting from their childhood. If both of the parents are soldiers then the children will not be timid or cowardly.

iii. They will prepare a special uniform for themselves which will fully cover the body except for the eyes and the nose.

iv. Keeping the honour of the purdah in mind it has been decided that the male members of each family will give training in fighting to the female members for three years at least. After this the trained women will go from house-to-house to train others.

The ladies have also written, 'We will not trouble the government to spend money on the uniform. We hope to get only the guns and other arms from the government.' Let us see what the Sultan is going to say in reply in this petition. How far the news is true depends upon the newspaper. But we think it quite possible for the ladies of Turkey to have this desire. History tells us that they used to fight formerly. If we take any old Islamic book and turn its pages that while fighting:

'Princess Zaigun was taken prisoner
As all other Arab soldiers were.'

Our social leaders are shocked at the idea of 'lady clerks', and what about those who cannot imagine women doing anything more laborious than dressing dolls or weaving garlands—what will they do when they hear of 'women soldiers'? Will they faint or what?

9. This was the estimate in 1310 (1903) (added by the translators).

10. Half seer is approx. 500 gm, 1 tola is 11.664 gm, and 80 tolas is 1 seer (added by the translators).

11. Sometimes a nosering can have a diameter of 6′ and a circumference of about 19′; its weight can be 1 *chatak* (1 chatak is about 80 gm. Our authoress is nothing if not thorough! (added by the translators]).

12. European Christians believe that it is true that Mother Eve was cursed, but Christ has delivered women from that curse. They say, 'Through woman came curse and sin and through woman came blessing and salvation also'. The same sentence is then translated into Bengali [added by the translators]). No man fathered Christ, but the woman is glorified by being His mother.

Here we have a feminist interpretation of the Immaculate Conception (added by the translators).

13. Cf. 'The Parable of Five Talents' in the *New Testament* (added by the translators).

14. The freedom which certain women belonging to certain sects claim is not true freedom—it is just 'airy nothing'.

15. The reasonable men of society may not condemn us to death, but the 'unreasonable' women (who do not bother with logic) will, for sure, arrange for brooms and hatchets.

16. I am saying 'equality with men' in order to signify progress. What else can I compare it with? It is the state and status of males that has become a standard for our progress. What we want is the same kind of equality as there exists between a son and a daughter in a family, because men are the sons of society and we are its daughters. Not that we say that girls should have the same kind of headgear as men. We would rather say: 'Spend as much money and care over the head-veil of a girl as you spend over the headgear of a boy.'

17. But why should we do it? Why should the zamindar plough the field when there are the *ryots* to do it? Cannot we do anything higher than government jobs? Clerk, etc., are mentioned just as examples. If you describe heaven you say, 'There is no winter there nor summer, there is eternal spring. Diamond flowers blossom there on emerald vines.' So how can we express our high ambitions except by talking about Lady Viceroy (Vicereine)? Let

me also say, in Bengal the idea of ladyclerk is shocking, but not so elsewhere. Lady clerks and barristers are not rare in America. Time was, when in the Muslim society of other countries women-poets, -philosophers, -historians, -scientists, -orators, -doctors, -politicians, all were there. It is only in Bengali society that such ladies do not exist.

18. Obtained from a lady of an aristocratic Muslim family of Bhagalpur.

Many paragraphs of this essay are the same as those in the foregoing essay. Such passages have been indicated, but not translated. The phrase 'badge of slavery' is the authoress's own (added by the translators).

19. This and the following paragraphs preceded by an asterisk had been omitted in the published version (added by the translators).

The Inoffensive Bengali

We are Bengalis—the weak and inoffensive Bengali. What a soft and delicate impression is made by this word 'Bengali'. Ah, which god had created this honey-sweet Bengali? The delicacy of flowers, the serenity of the moon, the sweetness of honey, the fragrance of jasmine, the silence of sleep, the stability of mountains, the softness of cream, the flow of water—in a word a Bengali is made up of all the beauty and soothing quality of the world. Our name is softly musical and likewise our activities are similar and straightforward.

We are the poetic embodiments. If you think of India as a big mansion then Bengal is the drawing room and the Bengalis are the things decorating it—the drawing room set. If India is a lake then the Bengalis are the lotus in it; if India is a novel then Bengal is the heroine. In the male-dominated society of India, Bengal is the 'she-man'.[1] So we are poetry in palpable human form.

Our foodstuff—the stalks of spinach, drumsticks, curry of little fish—all are very softly toothsome. The other things we eat like ghee, milk, curd, paneer, cream, sandesh, and *rasogolla* are extremely tasty. The main fruits of our country, mango and jackfruit, are juicy and sweet. So our food has three qualities: tasty, juiciness, and sweetness.

The body receives its nourishment from the food that is eaten. The drumstick is full of seeds and our stomach is layered with fat. Cream is very soft and our nature is very timid. There is no need to talk about our physical beauty, let us talk about our dress.

Our nice body is smooth as cream with oil and our dress is the equally soft dhoti and *uttariya*. It does not impede ventilation. At times, for the sake of civilization, we do use coats and shirts, for men can endure everything, but our better halves do not imitate us and use the shameless clothes of Englishwomen (chemise, jackets, etc.). They are such delicate darlings, such touch-me-nots that they wear very soft and delicate '*haoa*[2] saris'. Everything Bengali is beautiful, delicate, and easily obtained.

It will take wells of ink, unending reams of paper, and a tireless pen to describe the characteristic qualities of Bengalis, but surely, a few of them can be put down here.

There are two ways of increasing wealth, trade, and agriculture. Trade is our main business. But we do not, like Sinbad the Sailor, float our ships on the limitless ocean in hopes of uncertain profit. We have made trade easy and labour-saving. That is, we have eschewed the hard labour that trade involves. So our shops do not have the things that are really needed. Only cosmetics like hair oils, medicines that increase your diseases, ornaments made of brass, rings and buttons of artificial diamonds, etc., are available. Such business does not need physical labour. We do not keep silver, gold, or precious stones because we have no money. And, this too is there—these days everything can be counterfeited.

As soon as someone is industrious enough to invent a 'oil for long hair', we quickly find a 'short hair' oil. If someone sells 'black-hair' oil, we quickly find a 'blonde hair' oil. '*Kuntaleen*' sells side by side with '*keshaleen*'.[3] You can find 'medicine for a cool brain' in the market and also 'brain-warmers'. In other words, all imitations and unnecessary things are available. We do not bother with rice and such because that requires labour.

Another business of ours is to sell degrees. The seller of degrees is called the 'groom' and the buyer the 'father-in-law'. Do you know how much each degree fetches—'A princess and half a kingdom'. The Master's degree is an inestimable treasure, not everyone can buy it. Even if it goes dirt cheap it will cost a princess and a whole kingdom. We are idle, frivolous, labour-saving, delicate Bengali, so we have decided that instead of earning our living with labour it is far easier to take everything that old fool, the father-in-law, can give.

Let us look at agriculture—it increases our food products. But, we have thought it out: brain-culture is far easier than agriculture. It is easier to produce money by learning by rote than by ploughing the land, and far easier to pass the MRAC exam than to show expertise in agriculture. It is far more difficult to gain knowledge in agriculture than in law. It is far easier to loll in an armchair under the fan and read the 'Famine Report' than to wander over cultivated land in summer under an umbrella. So instead of producing food we try to produce money. We do not lack money, so we are not going to starve. Let the moneyless wretch die of starvation, what does it matter to us?

We do a lot of other easy work, such as:

1. It is easier to get the title 'Rajah' than to found a kingdom.

2. It is easier to pass BSc and DSc than to learn any craft.
3. It is easier to spend money after a title like 'Khan Bahadur' or 'Roy Bahadur' than to gain fame by doing some good work by spending a little money.
4. It is easier to become a member in a 'memorial service' of a big foreigner than to sympathize with the sorrows of an impoverished neighbour.
5. It is easier to beg from America than to take steps to stop the famine in our own country.
6. It is easier to put our lives in the hands of doctors and their medicines than to take care of our health, and not to ruin it.
7. It is easier to try to become beautiful by rubbing Kalydore, milk of rose, and Vinolia powder on our cheeks than to gain beauty by being healthy and cheerful through good health.
8. It is easier to file a defamation suit if one is struck than to demand satisfaction by fighting then and there.

Then again, we are the very embodiments of idleness and our housewives are in the lead in this matter. There are some who ask the ladies to do their own cooking. But let me say, if we ourselves cannot stand the light of the sun then how will our better halves bear the heat of fire? We are ourselves soft and they are even more so, we are readers and so are they, we are writers and so are they, so how can they be cooks unless we are chefs? So the wretch who tells these goddesses to do their own cooking should be punished in three ways—(1) burn them at the stake; (2) sacrifice them by beheading; and then, (3) hang the wretch.

We are all poets, dealing more in pathos than in heroism. There are more poetesses amongst us than poets. So the waves of poetry bear a lot of tears shed without any cause. Is there anything we leave out when armed with the poetic pen? 'Broken platters', 'moth-eaten blankets', 'worn-out slippers'—nothing is left out. And look at the new words we have coined—'pearl-white blue sky', 'tear-filled weeping eyes', etc. Bengal is slowly sinking into the tears of lamentation of our poetesses. So, you see, we are all poets.

But how long can I blow my own trumpet? Let me bring it to an end.[4]

(First published, *Naba-Nūr*, Māgh 1310)

Note: The words 'healthy and cheerful' and the names of the cosmetics have been given by the authoress herself.

Notes

1. I have not gone against grammar by using the word 'heroine'. Many use the '*bechara*' (poor or pitiable) for Bengali men. In Urdu a man is called 'bechara' and a woman '*bechari*'. So if we are bechari what is the harm in 'lotus', 'heroine', and 'she-man'?

2. These were transparent silk saris made at that time. 'Hāvā' means air. The saris were extremely delicate. The translator Ratri Ray has worn them in her teens.

3. The first was a well-known oil during the first decades of the last century (added by the translators).

4. 'The Inoffensive Bengali' had been written in 1310. But, luckily, Bengalis are not 'she-men' any longer this year. Who could have known that such a change for the better will take place in the last five years? Thanks be to the Almighty, we are now the Brave Bengali.

The Better Half

One should know the disease before one treats the patient. So, before I can find a way for the development of women I would like to present the woeful picture of their degraded condition. I have told my sisters in the essay 'The Degradation of Women' that we are suffering from the disease of slavery. The causes of, and the state from which this disease has developed, have already been analysed to a certain extent. Now we shall try to show how this disease has disabled our society. Steps for the treatment of the disease will be suggested later.

It is necessary here to tell the observers of the purdah a few things. I am not raising my voice against the custom. Anyone who sees nothing in my essay 'The Degradation of Women' but my hatred of the purdah, then I shall be forced to think that I have not been able to explain myself adequately or that he has not read the essay with the right attitude.

That essay was about all women. Do the women of societies lead an imprisoned life? Or have I called them fully developed just because they do not observe the purdah? It is mental enslavement that I have discussed.

Whenever something new is introduced trouble is created by society, and then one becomes used to it. I have given the example of Parsee ladies and their changed condition in this context. They did not have even the right to use umbrellas formerly, and then they progressed beyond all these limitations but no dire destruction has resulted. At present their purdah-slavery is gone, but has their mental enslavement also vanished? No, certainly not. The fact that they have come outside of the purdah does not prove their intelligence or wisdom. Their men have brought them out only as a step in their imitation of the West. This does not prove the life and the energy of their women; they remain the same living luggages that they had been earlier. They used to stay inside the house when their men kept them there. Now that the men have pulled them out by their nose-rope they have come out. Where does bravery lie in this? That kind of purdah-fight is not worthy of praise by any means.

Was Columbus not called mad when he decided on his voyage of discovery? So what is the fact that woman wants to claim her rights and establish equality with men but an equally insane project?

No, we are not satisfied with the respect granted to women by men. People are afraid of terrible goddesses like Kali and Sheetala and worship them—true enough. But in the same way, do not 'goddesses' like tigresses, lionesses, she-serpents inspire fear and are worshipped? So who is it who gets the homage, the woman Kali or the terrible one who wears skulls for a necklace?

Our elders hold up Sita as an example when they want to teach women. But, then, she did not lurk behind a purdah. She was the true better half of Rama, his beloved, his companion. And what about Rama—he was pious, the ideal lover, everything. But the way he treated Sita shows that his relationship with her was almost that of a little boy with a doll. If the boy wants he can love the doll intensely, can become agonized on parting from her, can lose his sleep at night, can detest the man who stole the doll, can dance with delight on getting the doll back, and also, mark this, can get angry without any reason and throw the doll into the mud. But the doll cannot do anything, because, though she has got hands and feet it is but an inanimate thing. If the boy wants he can throw the doll into fire, and when she gets burnt can roll on the floor and lament loudly.

Rama has given full proof (and more) of his masterhood (*swāmītva*) and Sita? She has just shown that she has a will of her own by insisting on accompanying Rama to the forest. Rama was like an immature lad, he did not want to recognize Sita's willpower because if he gave it recognition and acted accordingly then he could not have lorded over her to the fullest extent. Her pure heart could not have been trodden down as it was with lack of faith.

All right, let us accept the dictum of our country and our time and say with the poet that we are not the slaves of our husbands—we are the other half, the better half; that we are their housewives at home and followers even unto death (or at least to the place they are posted at), a sure companion 'for richer, for poorer', their shadow, etc., etc.

But has anyone thought about how much disabled men have become with a half like us in these unregenerate times? It is a pity (or maybe all the better for our 'lords') that I am no painter or I would have painted a picture of the strange spectacle they present with such a better half attached to their bodies.

Grey-haired wise men tell us that our domestic life is like a carriage with two wheels, one of which is the husband and the other the wife. That is the reason why in England they are being continually called 'partner', 'the better half', etc. But the duties to be performed in life are arduous, not easy ones.

Difficult domestic life
Who can manage with smoothness?
Ministering to a kingdom
Is hidden in it with deftness.

Perhaps ancient scholars had imagined domestic life as the head and declared the husband and wife to be the limbs. Now let us see what it is like at present.

Now imagine a big mirror that gives you a full-figure reflection. Your right half is male and your left is female. Now stand in front of this mirror. What do you see?

Your right arm is long (30′) and muscular, and your left is short (24′) and slim. Your right foot is 12′ and the left quite small. The right shoulder is five foot high and the left only four. (So the head cannot sit firmly on the neck, it is leaning a little to the left, and because of the weight of the right ear, leans a little to the right too.) The right ear is big like that of an elephant and the left long like that of an ass! Look well, and look long—how do you appear to others! If this picture does not find favour then let me show how a two-wheel carriage goes. A carriage with one big wheel (the husband) and one small (the wife) cannot travel far. It goes round and round in one place (at home). That is why India cannot go forward on the path of development.

Social customs have separated us from men. Their joys and sorrows are different from ours. I am forced to quote here a few lines from Babu Rabindranath Tagore's *Dialogue of the Newly Married*:[1]

He: 'Why are you crying, darling?'
She: 'I've left my pet kitten behind.'
He: 'What are you doing in this lovely bower?'
She: 'I'm eating ripe berries.'
He: 'Shall I bring the moon and the stars for you?
    Oh tell me what can I do to please you.'
She: 'Pluck me a few more berries.'
He: 'How to spend the hours of separation?'
She :'I'll celebrate the marriage of my dolls.'

This shows clearly enough that the bride has not been taught how to be a fit companion to her husband. Our lords can educate themselves endlessly, but the wives are taught the three rupees only, if that.

While the husband is measuring the distance between the earth and the sun and the stars, the wife is measuring a pillow in order to sew a case for it. While the husband is walking the galaxies in imagination, measuring the cubic weight of the sun, finding out the orbit of a comet, the wife wanders about in the kitchen, measuring rice and pulses, finding out the orbit of the cook. Sir Astronomer, where is your better half now? If your wife wants to enter the corona of the sun with you, she will melt into thin air before even reaching it. It is better that the housewife does not go with you!

There are some who say that higher education is not necessary for women. If they can cook well, stitch well, read a few novels, then that is enough; there is no need for more. But doctors say there is need; therefore sons are born with the mother's attributes as well as her inherited qualities. So you see many boys of our country, well-caned, pass the FA, BA exams by rote-learning, but their minds remain in the kitchen with their mother. This can be easily found out by putting their knowledge to the test.[2]

A friend of mine was explaining the cardinal points of compass to his student. Finally he asked, 'If your right arm is in the west and the left in the east, then in which direction will your face be?' The answer was, 'At my back'.

Those who think physical exercise unnecessary for their daughter still want to see their grandsons as strong and stout, veritable wrestlers, do they not? Do they not want their grandsons to return a slap with another at fisticuffs? If they want this then they want a tender rose-creeper to produce a mighty jackfruit! If they want that their grandsons will not be strong but that, beaten with a slipper will bow down and say, 'Don't beat me, it hurts', and later standing at a distance threaten the taskmaster, 'Why did you beat me? I'm going to complain', then I am quite unable to make them understand my ideas.

There are opportunities enough for women's education in Christian society, but even there women do not enjoy all their rights. Their minds, too, are not emancipated from slavery. Husband and wife do tread the path of life together to a certain extent, but the better half cannot become one with the partner by uniting her life with his. While the husband is worrying about how to get rid of his debts, the wife is thinking of a new bonnet. She has been taught to be like 'poetry embodied', that is what she wants to be. She is unable to understand prosaic things like being in debt.

Let us have a look at Muslim society. According to this theory we are but half a man. That is, two women are equal to one man. If we put two brothers and a sister together then we have two-and-a-half persons. You will see in the 'Prophet's Laws' that a daughter should get half of what the son gets of the father's property. This law however is only limited to the books in which they are written. If you take the trouble to see the division of a rich Muslim's property or go over landed property then you will see that actually the daughter gets nothing, or very, very little.

Let me talk now of material wealth but of abstract ones, like the love and care of the father, etc. Here too there is partiality. Does a man who keeps four tutors for the son have two governesses for his daughter? Do we get even half of paternal love or care? His son might get three degrees (till BA), but does his daughter get even one and a half (Entrance and a failed FA)? You cannot count the number of boys' schools, but are there any schools for girls at all? The brother might get the title Shams-ul-Ulama but does the sister get the title Najamul Olama?[3] There are many Najamannessa and Shamsannessa in the sky of domestic life, but we want to see Najamul Olama in the literary sky.

The means of imparting education to us are like this—first the Arabic alphabet is taught and then reading the Koran. But the meaning of the words are not explained, you have to repeat them in parrot-fashion from memory.[4] If a father cares even more then he would want to make his daughter a '*Hafiz*'. A Hafiz is one who knows the entire Koran by heart. That is as far as our knowledge of Arabic goes. If Persian and Urdu is to be taught then you begin with '*Kareema be bakshaeber hale ma*' ('Oh Merciful, show compassion at our condition') and '*Banat un Nash*'.[5] These do not have vowel signs, and, moreover, the girl had not been taught to read any easily readable book before this. Not much progress can be made. Life as a daughter is over for many girls even before they finish these books. When she gets married she thinks, 'At least I won't have to study now'. Some girls are good at cooking and needlework. In Bengal, too, girls are not educated properly in the Bengali language. Some girls learn to read Urdu but do not ever learn to hold a pen. Their learning extends at most to embroidering with sequins, knitting gloves and socks, etc.

Suppose the Prophet (P.B.H.) asks you, 'How have you treated your daughter?'—what will you say?

The history of the prophets tells us that whenever men have indulged too much in tyrannizing, a prophet has come to save the good and punish the evil-doer. Women were being tyrannized in Arabia. They were killing their daughters. At that time the Prophet (P.B.H.) stood up as the saviour of women. It is not that he rested content with just giving out laws; he showed by his own example how to bring up a daughter. His life had been washed by his love for Hazrat Fatime, which shows what a treasure a daughter is! That love is unrivalled in the world.

But oh, he is no longer there and that is why we are so wretched. Come my sisters, let us say together: '*Kareema be bakshaeber hale ma*'. God will definitely have pity on us. Striving leads to results, if we try for the pity of *Karim* (God) then we are sure to get it. We are not 'half' to our mothers and to God. Had it been so then when the son gets ten months, the daughter will get half the amount of milk from the mother of what the son gets. But nothing like that is actually the case. We get the same amount of love and care that our brother gets. There is no partiality in the mother's heart. Then how can we say that God is partial. Is He not more compassionate than a mother?

Let no one think that I am against cookery and needlework from what I have said about these two accomplishments. Food and clothing are among the necessities of life, so both of these have to be learnt. But life should not be limited within the four walls of the kitchen.

I acknowledge the fact that women depend upon others because of their physical weakness. But that does not mean that men should become 'lords' over us. We can see that everything in the world takes help of some kind from another; one cannot go on without the other. If plants want water then in the same way the clouds want plants. A river depends upon rains and the rain-giving clouds depend on rivers. So is the river the 'lord' of the cloud or vice versa? Setting this example apart, when we turn to human society and the rules therein we see the same thing.

One is a carpenter, another a weaver. A barrister wants the help of a doctor, and a doctor takes the help of a barrister. So shall we call the doctor the master of the barrister or the latter the master of the former? If none of them acknowledge the other as master ('swami') why should the ladies think of their life-partners as their masters?

We are the better half and they are the worse half. We constitute half of the body and they, the other half. Women have the magic wand that is the secret of the life and death of society. India cannot wake from sleep till the women of India open their own eyes. The bravery or timidity of the lords depends upon the mothers. But let not the purblind brothers claim superiority merely on the score of physical strength.

We are lagging behind because we have not had the same opportunities of education and training that men have. Would not we have excelled if we had had the same opportunities? We have been belittled right from childhood, so we blindly acknowledge the superiority of men and belittle ourselves. Many are the times when we excuse them by saying, 'After all he is a man', and give them undeserved praise. This is what is wrong with us.[6]

I wish all my sisters well. I do not want to break their religious or social ties in order to bring them out into the open. There is no need for Hindus to forsake Hinduism and for Christians to forsake Christianity in order to bring about mental development. The mind can be set free while still preserving the distinctive feature of each group. I want, myself, to understand and make others understand, that we are bowing down today, that we occupy a humble position, only because of the lack of proper education.

Maybe there are some who have got alarmed, thinking that a revolt of wives is being arranged. Or maybe they think that hordes of women will drive men out of government posts and usurp these themselves, taking the appurtenances of legal professions for themselves. Or perhaps they will march in a body to the fields, drive away the peasants and take their fields over, take their cattle and ploughshare. There is no need to be afraid of that, let them rest easy.

We have become inefficient because men have deprived us of education. In India the two classes of the beggars and the rich are idle and the ladies do much less work than they should. We have become comfort-loving to an inordinate extent. We do not make proper use of our hands and feet, our eyes and minds, and other faculties. If 10 women gather together they gossip, praising or belittling each other or each other's husbands. They quarrel also, if need be!

I hope from now on, instead of husbands or masters, the phrase 'the other half' will be used.

(First published in *Mahilā*, Śrāvan, Āśvin, and Kartik 1310
Reprinted *Naba-Nūr*, Āśvin, 1311)

Notes

1. This essay had been published in 1310 (1904). Begum Rokeya's being able to quote Tagore this early, shows how very well-acquainted she was with contemporary literature (added by the translators).

2. I cannot resist giving here a few questions and answers from the periodical *Dāsī*.

(The questions and the answers given are in English [added by the translators]):

Q. When was Cromwell born?

Ans. In the year 1649 when he was fourteen years old.

Q. Describe his continental policy.

Ans. He was honest and truthful, and he had nine children.

Q. What is the adjective of ass?

Ans. Assansole.

Q. Who was Chandra Gupta?

Ans. Chandra Gupta was the granddaughter of Asoka.

When the sentence '*Kala jhalsaite lagilo*' had to be translated one student wrote, 'roasted some plantains'; another wrote, 'roasted some plantagenets'; and another wrote, 'roasted some plaintiffs'. Let no one think these answers are imaginary ones. They are only too true.

3. The first title means 'The Sun of Scholars', and the second 'The Moon of Scholars' (added by the translators).

4. And what is so surprising in this? Let not the Anglophile feel smug. Did not Milton teach his daughters to read Greek and Latin but did not teach them the meaning of the words? When questioned by a friend, he replied,'One tongue is enough for a woman'. True, this was in the seventeenth century, but then it was Milton! (added by the translators)

5. This reminds me of a ten-year-old girl. In villages many families employ a woman thresher. This girl used to find this work easier than reading about the temper of Hussain Ara in *Banat un Nash*. So she used to run to the threshing room and spoil a few kilos of paddy. You could not get good rice from those. It used to be a mixture of husk and rice, rather like whole-meal flour. No doubt it is good for the patients whom the doctors tell to each such bread.

[The names of these two books are: *Kareema be bakshaeber hale ma* ('O Merciful, show compassion at our condition') and *Banat un Nash* ('The Daughters of the Corpse'). This phrase signifies the constellation, the Great Bear (added by the translators)].

6. This makes me remember the Urdu lines of a great soul who was a well-wisher of women. He had written in a periodical in 1905: 'The world has denigrated you to such an extent that finally you too have come to believe the world and think "we are really not worthy of education", and you got ready to experience all the evils of ignorance with bowed heads.'

How very true this is! May God grant long life to this poet.

The Good Housewife

I had tried in my essay 'The Degradation of Women' to present a picture of our true condition, but truth is always somewhat unpalatable and many readers had not liked that essay.[1] Next, in my essay entitled 'The Better Half' I had tried to show that men and women are parts of one individual whole. The two arms of a human being or the two wheels of a carriage are the same and both are needed to make one entire object; so, the one cannot develop without the other. A one-eyed man is half-blind.

Anyway, if women do not understand my words about spiritual equality then let us not talk about high ambitions or any elevated things at all. I will ask today: 'What is your aim in life?' Probably you will reply in unison: 'To be a good housewife'.

All right then. I hope all of you want to be a good housewife and try, as far as you can, to learn how to acquire the qualities of one. Yet many of you have not been able to be one such. The reason for this is our lack of knowledge about certain specific things. Society thinks it unnecessary to impart higher education to us. Men acquire knowledge in order to earn their living; what would we, women, gain by doing so? Many think we do not even need much intelligence as we do not have to worry about appeasing our hunger or fight in the Lower Court to protect our property. We do not have to beg for certificates to get a job or flatter white-skinned masters to gain titles like Rajah or Nawab. Nor shall we ever have to appear in the battlefield in order to protect our country. So why should we get higher education (or mental culture)?[2] I would say good education or mental culture is necessary for becoming a good housewife.

It is necessary to have intelligence in order to do the daily domestic chores efficiently. If you think about it you will realize that they are the real upholders of society, the real mistresses, the mothers, and sisters of society.

Domestic chores could be categorized as mainly these:

1. To keep household things in a clean, systematic manner;
2. To manage the family within a certain income;
3. Serving meals;
4. Needlework;
5. Taking care of relatives and others; and,
6. Bringing up children.

Now let us see how these works are actually being done in our country and how they should be done. We will leave out the wealthy and the poor and take up the middle class.

One needs intelligence in order to keep the house clean and well-arranged. The housewife will have to show her taste (*salike*) in the very beginning when the house is being built.[3]

The kitchen, the gardens, etc., should be situated according to her will. If it is a rented house then discrimination should be used in apportioning different rooms to different functions. For, she is the goddess of hearth and home. But let me ask, how many housewives are there who have the ability for this? We are such housewives who do not understand the first thing about houses. Our tree has been cut down at the very root itself.

After the house is built, one needs furniture. Discrimination is needed in arranging them. One should know where each piece of furniture would look the best and where it will not. There is a feminine adage:

'Paddy and rice in the house
The wife keeps all, in a chaos.'

You can often see cobwebs decorating the store-room like awnings. Tamarind and rice are mixed up and so are different spices. It takes an hour to find sugar. As the room is kept entirely closed you get a stuffy odour the minute it is opened. The housewives are used to it.

Many ladies look for the cutter (*janti*) only after they have sat down to prepare betels. When they have found the cutter they find that the betel leaves have not been washed. At times lime mixes with other ingredients to produce an odd mixture. May be the leaves are kept in a '*ghaṭi*', areca in a '*saji*', and another ingredient in a box for clothes.[4] But a '*sāhebeysālikā*' ('lady with discrimination') does not act like this. All the ingredients of betel are kept in their proper places by them.

Some use a teapot for keeping fish. A colander is used for keeping vegetables. Tamarind pickle is kept in brass bowls. Formerly, Muslims used to keep a *mukaba* (a certain container in which things for hair-dressing are kept). These days many have a dressing table. These ladies keep many things in their mukaba or dressing table that have nothing to do with dressing the hair.

It is an important requirement in a housewife that the domestic expenditure is kept within a certain limit. Many wives do not consider how much labour is done by the poor husband to earn a few rupees, how they earn money by the sweat of their brows. They quarrel with and abuse their husbands, if they do not earn money, but do they have any sympathy? They will spend that hard-earned money extravagantly in the daughter's marriage or in the son's rice-eating ceremony, or fill the goldsmith's coffer by buying ornaments. The poor husband goes from door to door asking for certificates to get a job. Then he gets a poorly paid job after facing a lot of trouble and gives the wife the hard-earned money. Most of that money is changed to anklets on their daughter's feet, sobbing with their tinkling sound. Ah, young lady, you do not understand how much of your father's blood, sweat and tears have been spent to make those anklets!

To spend in accordance with the husband's income—that is good economy. European ladies' words have more value, so I am giving you the words of a Countess: The first point necessary to consider in the arrangement and ordering of a lady's household, is that everything should be on a scale exactly proportionate to her husband's income.[5]

How can we learn the proper use of money unless we get education? I do not say that the wives do not love their husbands. They do love them better than life itself, but cannot give them true sympathy because they lack in intelligence. The poet Sa'adi said that an intelligent enemy is better than a stupid friend. Many are the times when the blind love of the wife does more harm than good. On the other hand some turn into misers because of excessive economy. This too is not right.

Nobody denies that wives should know how to cook. It is said that the wives' cooking depend on the taste of their husbands. The very lives of the members of a family depend upon the food cooked by the wife. Very often ignorant wives prepare *korma* by mixing curd in non-enamelled copper vessels and that is little better than poisoning. Muslims often suffer from lack of appetite and stomach troubles, etc., and what except the diet can be held responsible for that? Here is what the Countess says on this issue:

> Bad food, ill-cooked food, monotonous food, insufficient food, injure the physique and ruin the temper. No lady should turn to the more tempting occupations or amusements of the day till she had gone into every detail of the family commissariat and assured herself that it is as good as her purse, her cook and the season can make it.[6]

So the housewife should have some elementary knowledge of medicine and chemistry in addition to cookery. She should know the property of foodstuffs, how long it takes for different things to be well cooked, which person should take what kind of food, etc. If the cooking is not properly done how would the body get nourishment? People do not entrust their children to inefficient nurses; likewise, is it proper to entrust the cooking of an entire family to an inefficient cook?

If the place around the kitchen is muddy then that mud gives off unhealthy exhalations and that is taken in by the family members with their food. Nor should the place for eating be dirty, and the housewife should be careful about the atmosphere of the place also.

Many persons like vegetables. Vegetables grown at home are far better than these found in markets. The housewives often grow pumpkins, cucumber, beans, etc., at home. If they have some knowledge of horticulture then would not these pumpkins, etc., grow better? She should at least know something about the soil—which place is good for cucumber and which for chillies.

There are many who have domestic animals at home like goats, hens, pigs, etc., but do not know how to look after them. There is no place meant specially for them and they wander about the entire house. It is not too much to say that such a house is a zoo or lavatory for them. The housewife should be careful about their health so that they do not fall ill, and also about cleanliness. The places where they are kept should be clean and airy. No good comes of eating a sick animal.

So you see, learning to cook involves botany, chemistry, horticulture, and the theory of heat.

Clothing comes after food. But no, man puts it even before food. The housewife should keep the clothes ready according to the weather—summer or winter. Earlier they used to spin out the thread themselves. Now, as factory clothes are easily available, the stitching is done according to one's taste. One should get good education about this too. Perhaps you are thinking that what I am saying is rubbish. Ignorant tailors have been stitching clothes all these years—what does it have to do with education? It is true that education is not directly relevant to tailoring but all the same it is indirectly related to it. You cannot read the instructions for a sewing machine unless you know how to read, especially English, and unless you understand the instructions you will not be able to use the machine efficiently. You do not have to read if you stitch by hand, but compare hand-stitching with machine-stitching—which is better? Besides, machines can stitch more in less time and with less labour, so it is better to learn how to use a sewing machine. Besides, who does not want to have canvas shoe, woollen socks, shawls, etc.? This kind of needlework cannot be done without English, books about knitting and crochet, and one can become an expert at these without a teacher merely by reading these books. The garment will come out well. Tailoring too needs intelligence. If you know how much wool to buy, then you can prevent wastage by not getting wool for three pairs when you need just for one pair.

Another duty of the housewife is to take care of the family members. It is the duty of women to give up their own petty interests for the sake of the well-being of others. This too needs training. Usually housewives, instead of bringing comfort to others, spend their times quarrelling with them over trifles. They spend their days slandering the sister-in-law to the mother-in-law and vice versa.

Nursing the sick is a very important duty of housewives. One cannot do this well unless one knows nursing. Many ailing people die in our country from lack of nursing though they might not lack medicine and diet. In many cases an ignorant nurse makes the patient drink the medicine meant for massage. Some keep the medicine in improper places so that children drink it up. This kind of mistake makes you burn with remorse for the rest of your life. Some waken the patient from much needed sleep to give him medicine. Some, out of too much care, give three or four doses instead of one. Such cases are not rare in our country. Does anyone deny that the nurse should have adequate medical knowledge? Nursing a patient without knowledge about medicine is the same as doing the work of a cobbler when one is trained as a goldsmith.

But whether one has the medical knowledge or not, one has to nurse the ailing. Is there a daughter who, washing her mother's feet with tears does not think, 'All my efforts have gone in vain. If only I could save her in return for my own life.' Is there a sister who does not sit beside her brother without taking any food? Is there a wife who does not become half dead herself with worry about her ailing husband? Is there a mother who has not spent a sleepless night with her sick child in her lap? One who has not nursed the ailing has not learnt to love. You cannot learn to love unless you weep.

One should keep one's head in times of danger. Many of us do not have this quality. We just know how to lament, perhaps hoping that Death will have pity on the tears of women. It can often be seen that the patient is thirsty and the nurse is sitting lamenting (in various rhythms and tunes). Is it not far more necessary to give the patient a little milk at such a time? Time is wasted in lamenting instead of giving milk and the condition of the patient becomes worse.

I remember the story of a devoted wife. Once her husband got chest pain in the night and she spent a wakeful night. In the morning the doctor said, 'His condition is not very hopeful. If a little oil had been massaged on the chest it would have been much better.' The wife spent a sleepless night but did not massage oil because she simply did not know. Three evils resulted from her ignorance: (1) her husband's condition became worse; (2) she herself spent a sleepless night which weakened her; and, (3) money was wasted on a doctor's visit because a massage would have cured the pain and there would not have been any need to call in the doctor.

Now if I say that a Women's Medical College is needed, perhaps it will not be unreasonable.

Childcare—this is the most important of all. The child is taught when he is being brought up. A doctor has said, 'Childcare should be learnt before one becomes a mother. Let no one become a mother without knowing the duties of motherhood.' But when a girl has to become a mother at thirteen, a grandmother at twenty-six, and a great-grandmother at forty, when will she learn the duties of motherhood?

A child inherits the mother's good qualities and bad ones, her diseases and training—everything. All the great men in history are mostly sons of good mothers. At times, of course, a good mother's son is a bad one, and a bad mother's son a good one. That happens because of specific reasons. Usually, however, an apple tree gives apples, not cherries. A child loves the mother the best and believes implicitly in her. He imitates whatever she says and does. The emotions of the mother enter the child with every drop of milk. This is how the poet puts it:

'When you suckle your baby, O mother
Sing of the heroes of the past.
Let him thrill to hear, O mother
And his veins echo to the trumpet-blast.'

Yes, it is true, only a heroic mother can give us a heroic son. A mother can make her son brave, courageous, and noble by nourishing his innate instincts properly. Many mothers teach their sons to conceal the truth and tell lies, and as a result such sons turn out to be frauds and tricksters. A bad mother beats the child without any reason and thus lowers his spirit. So they grow up to bear the kicks of their booted masters without protest. A certain Englishman had broken his new shoes by beating a labourer but did not make him pay for it, and the labourer had praised him thus: 'He beat me with a new shoe, but did not take the price of the broken shoe from me.' I need not say, many 'gentlemen' too might face the same situation.

So you need a little learning and intelligence to bring up children, for the mother is our first and real teacher. Her health has to improve first so she can give a strong and healthy child.

One cannot spend sixteen or seventeen hours working all the time. One needs to rest at times. Is it not better to spend those hours of leisure in harmless pleasure instead of playing cards, quarrelling, or scandal-mongering? One should learn painting and music for that. The lady who wants to be an expert at these will have to learn to read. A book can carry within itself the colours of paintings and the description of brushes, and the words and notations for music. It is also good to spend one's leisure reading good books or writing poems, etc.

I think I should say something about one's duty to one's neighbours. The Arab race was noted at one time for its hospitality to guests and friendly behaviour to its neighbours. There is a story about how rats infested an Arab gentleman's house and a friend of his told him to keep a cat. The gentleman said that if he kept a cat then the rats will leave his house and invade those of his neighbours, which is why he did not keep a cat.

Most of the time we are busy thinking of our own comfort and never think of the comfort of others. On the other hand we think first how a person's misfortunes may benefit us. If someone is forced to sell a certain thing then the buyer thinks that it is good opportunity to get it cheap. This petty self-seeking is not very nice in an educated society. Or it may be that someone has got suddenly angry and has driven away a good maid-servant. At once another housewife will try to get that dismissed maid. But the ideal housewife will try to reinstate that maid in her mistress's service. You should regard your neighbour's misfortune as your own.

Also, there should be a wise interpretation of neighbourhood. We should take the word 'neighbour' to mean not just those who are near our own doors. While talking of the neighbours of Bengal, one should include Punjab, Ayodhya, Orissa, and such places. It may be that a group of men are working in a factory. They have to go on strike because they have failed to tell the authorities of their troubles even after repeatedly trying to do so. Let not people from Orissa or Madras gleefully treat that strike as an opportunity for getting jobs for themselves. A good housewife will not let her son take on a job at such a place. One must also remember that we are not just Hindus or Muslims or Parsees or Christians, or that we are Bengalis, Madrasis, Marwaris, or Punjabis—we are all Indians. We are Indians first and then only Muslims or Sikhs or anything else. A good housewife will spread this awareness in her family. Then gradually petty jealousies and selfishness will disappear, and her home will become like a temple and the family members like gods. Is there an Indian woman who would not want her home to become a temple?

We should help the poor women of our neighbourhood. Buying their needlework and clothes woven with charkha thread will be of great help to them. In these and many other ways they can be helped. There is no need to talk about it at length.

I forgot to say, the children should be trained to be kind to the servants. Usually the boys of rich families are very proud and consider servants to be quite insignificant. Children, who have impressionable minds, should be made to understand that though the servants are paid servitors, they are human and have self-respect according to their posts. Many housewives cannot see any fault in their children; they scold their servants quite uselessly. It is wrong to indulge children in this manner.

The Urdu book *Banat un Nash* shows Hussain Ara, the princess, had been so spoiled and had become so undisciplined that the servants, cooks, etc., used to be terrified of her.[7] We should take care that the children are modest and quiet.

Finally I want to say that whatever you want to be—a lover, a pious man, or an atheist, everything will need mental culture.[8] If you want to be a lover, you will have to learn how to be reliable, just, and self-sacrificing for the beloved. Otherwise, if you are stupid, friend you will not be able to do any good to anyone. If you want to be a god-fearing, religious person then too you need proper education and training, for God cannot be known unless one has knowledge. There is a proverb that says, 'The worship of the ignorant is the same as the sleep of the learned'. So, even the duties that have been kept especially for women need intelligence. Just as men need mental culture to earn a living so do women need the same to manage a household.

A household managed just anyhow, as is done by the lower classes, can just be allowed, but the housewife cannot be called a good housewife in such a case and nobody expects that the sons of cobblers and sweepers will ever become holder of titles like 'Vidyasagar', 'Vidhya Bhushan', 'Tarkalankar', etc.

I have come to the end now. It falls upon you to gain success through striving. If it is the aim of your life to become a good housewife then arrange for the education and training of women.

(*Naba-Nūr*, Baiśākh 1311)

Notes

1. Some have proudly declared in refutation: 'The entity worshipped by Hindus is a female one, they worship women.' All right. But is there anything they do not worship? Animate matter and inanimate, trees—which of these can you leave out? Is not a monkey or a cow also worshipped? But do we say that these animals are superior to 'worshipful man'?
2. 'Mental culture' is the writer's own phrase (added by the translators).
3. The urdu word 'salika' means manner, taste, efficiency, etc. There is a Bengali equivalent of this word but it does not express the full meaning of this word. So I want to include this word in the Bengali language. Words like *ārjee, tahbil, māśul,* etc., are already there, well-established. Let 'salika' also be used. 'Sāhebeysālikā' means—a person of taste.

This word has been translated here as 'discrimination' as it has a more active denotation than 'taste' (added by the translators).

4. All the receptacles are inappropriate ones (added by the translators).

5. These sentences have been translated into Bengali by the writer (added by the translators).

6. The sentences have been translated into Bengali by the writer and given after the quotation (added by the translators).

7. The description of Hussain Ara as a character is quite entertaining. Let me give an example. Hussain Ara was not afraid of anyone, be it her parents, elder brothers or sisters, or anybody. She used to tyrannize over the entire household. It happened one day that her aunt Shahzamani Begum had come on a visit. The maid-servants thought: 'It is useless to appeal to the young begum (her mother). The elder begum has just come, maybe Hussain Ara will be a bit quieter on seeing her.' The minute the elder begum got down from her litter some complaints were laid before her. Nargis, shedding tears, said, 'Look, the Little Princess threw stones at me. It is a wonder that I have not been blinded.'

Sasan said, 'The Little Princess said to me, "Show me your tongue", and the minute I opened my mouth she struck at my chin so hard that I bit my tongue'.

Gulab sobbed, 'Oh she bit my ear till the blood came'.

The cook shouted from the kitchen, 'Just look, the Little Princess has poured a handful of ashes into the curry'.

After listening to all this, the elder begum called, 'Husna, come here'. She came at once, but instead of bowing to her aunt she embraced her with both arms which were dirty and soiled, as was her feet. She said in a very loving manner, 'Husna, you've become very naughty'.

Then, looking at the assembled maids the girls said, 'Oh is it this witch Sambil who has complained to you?' Then she leaped up from her aunt's lap and caught the blameless maid by her hair and started beating her. The elder begum tried repeatedly to control her, but she did not pay any attention.

Hussain Ara was later sent to a girls' school where she received good training. The writer has shown by this story that even an undisciplined hoyden like her can become a good girl if properly educated. We regard education as the stone that turns everything it touches into gold.

8. This term, used repeatedly here as well as elsewhere, has been used by the writer herself (added by the translators).

The Burkha

I have heard many times that is the 'accursed purdah custom' which has prevented our development. Many highly-educated sisters tell me to give up the burkha when I meet them. Tell me, what, after all, is development? Is it to be found only outside the burkha? Shall I then believe that fisherwomen, female sweepers, etc., have developed more than us?

We however, believe that there is not much of a quarrel between the purdah and development. It is true that higher education is needed for development. Some say that in order to get this higher education one will have to come out of the purdah and attend university classes to get FA and BA degrees. Not a bad idea. But why? Is it that impossible to have a separate university for us and women examiners? Till we get that, well, we can do without these degrees.

The purdah custom is not a natural one; it is a moral one. Animals do not have it. Man, as he became civilized, learned many things that are not natural. For example, it is natural to travel on foot, but man has invented carriages, litters, etc., for the sake of convenience. It is natural to swim across a pond but man has invented many kinds of boats, so that you can cross the seas if it so happens that you cannot swim. The women's quarters inside a house are the outcome of such an 'unnatural' civilization.

The uncivilized natives of the world live half-naked. History tells us that much earlier in uncivilized Britain men used to live half-naked. Before that they used to paint their bodies. As they grew civilized they learnt to wear clothes. Now the European ladies and our Brahmo Samaj sisters, proud of being civilized, go out everywhere, covering all but their faces. The sisters in other Muslim countries have perfected the burkha by attaching another veil on the face when they go out. Those who do not use the burkha put a veil over their heads.

There are some who object to the burkha because of its heaviness. But a comparison has shown us that the burkha is not heavier than the huge hats of English ladies.

Purdah, for us, means concealment, covering the body, etc., and not merely staying within the four walls of the women's quarters. '*Be-purdah*' means inadequate covering of the body. Those who wear dresses that cover them when going out in the marketplace observe purdah quite adequately.

Our European sisters have reached the very limits of civilization these days, but who can say that they do not have the purdah? No one can enter their bedrooms or even their drawing rooms without permission. Is this custom a bad one? Certainly not. But the sisters of our country, who in imitating Western civilization, have given up the purdah, do not have either bedroom privacy or the privacy of the burkha like us.

Some have said, 'covering the body with an ungainly veil like the burkha, covering one from head to foot and turning one into a strange monster is a ridiculous thing, as whoever has seen it can say', etc., etc. That is true but we believe that no woman of a good family would want to attract the notice of people while standing on a railway platform. So it will not do any harm to excite the contempt of people by turning into a strange and ridiculous monster. Ladies of good families will think it worse to attract people by showing off their beauty.

English etiquette also tells us that ladies should wear simple, unostentatious dresses. This is especially applicable to walking dresses. When going out on a walk they should not wear shining and gorgeous dresses.[1]

While going out on an invitation, ladies usually put on beautiful clothes and costly ornaments. A simple burkha is needed when getting out of the carriage to hide such costume from the eyes of coachmen and footmen. Burkha and veils are also needed when travelling by train to protect oneself from public gaze.

At times the European sisters say, 'why don't you break off purdah?'[2] Oh, what a botheration it is! Can one really leave the purdah? What they mean by the purdah is just sitting inside the house. If they realized that they too cannot live without purdah (privacy) then they would never have said this. It is not that their privacy (purdah) is fully protected by their dress, the evening dress being particularly objectionable. Even then, it is preferable to wear just the one thin sari that many women drape around themselves.

Then there is the question of leaving the women's quarters—we fail to understand what good that is going to do, how it is going to bring development. Those other free ladies too have their bedrooms which is a version of women's quarters.

We can see that all civilized people have some kind of purdah or the other. If there were no such custom then what would be the difference between men and animals? We cannot understand the attitude of those who call this pure custom a 'monstrous' one.

In a way it is civilization itself that has increased the observance of the custom in the world. Formerly people used to just fold their letters before sending them. These days civilized people cover their letters with an envelope. Peasants do not cover the plates they eat from. Civilized people put their food in three or four bowls on a tray and then cover the whole thing with another tray. Those who are even more civilized cover each bowl separately. More examples can easily be provided—covering the table with a table cloth, the bed with bedcovers, pillows with pillowcases, etc.

Our sisters walk barefoot while their own enlightened relatives cover their feet with civilized shoes and socks. Then, gloves have been invented to cover the hands. It is clear that there is no conflict between civilization and the purdah.

But, then, there are certain limits. In this country the purdah has become rather too strong. For example, unmarried girls have to observe the custom even with women. A nine-year-old girl cannot go out in the courtyard because a lady from the neighbourhood might suddenly turn up. Their health suffers because of this cloistered life. Second, their education also suffers. They never see anybody except very near relatives, then, from whom will they learn anything? The custom is taken to unjustifiable lengths with newly married girls. They have to live dressed up like animated dolls for two or three months after marriage. Only the person who has gone through it knows what this artificial blindness and dumbness makes one suffer. It is said that once a scorpion bit a bride on the back and she bore the pain silently. On the third day at the time of the '*cauthi*' bath the women were shocked to see the bite mark on her back. The old wives of today hold her up as an example. Probably the scorpion was not very poisonous.

These excesses of the custom will have to be moderated. In many families the women do not visit any others except close relatives. They do not meet other women and thus grow into the proverbial frog in the well. The interaction between women should be increased. Men interact with other men of different classes and we should do the same. But we should mix with those we know to be decent people, whatever their religion might be (Jews, Hindus, whatever)—no harm in that. At present we observe the purdah with women of other religions and this will have to be given up. Our religion is not all that fragile, why should we think that our religion will suffer if we meet ladies of other religions?

We shall give up unnecessary and unjustifiable observance of the purdah and keep what is necessary. If need be, we have no objection to go walking under a veil (or burkha). If we travel to the mountains for the sake of our health the burkha can go with us. It is not difficult to walk about under a burkha though it needs a little practice. But then, what work can you do without any practice?

Usually burkhas are quite coarse to look at. It will have to be made finer. Just as clothes and shoes have been gradually refined so a refinement of burkhas is also desirable. The burkha has come to us from the far-off Arabia. Shall we reach the apex of civilization just by rejecting it?

These days we have become narrow-minded, timid, and feeble, but this is not because we observe the purdah—it is because of the lack of education. Our faculties have become more and more limited because of the lack of education. The timidity of women has spread to young boys. When a five-year-old boy sees his mother fainting at the sight of an insect, will he not think that an insect is a really terrifying thing?

Let me mention here that we are not alone in fainting at the sight of insects. The highly civilized Englishwomen too are not free of this fault. You can read in *Gulliver's Travels* that when Gulliver was walking about, terrified, in the country of the Brobdingnagians one of the men took him up in his hand and showed him to his wife. The Brobdingnag woman screamed on seeing him just as an Englishwoman would scream on seeing an insect. The huge woman had taken him for one such.[3] So, you see, even without the purdah, the fear of insects remain.

To rid ourselves of the fear of insects we need the enlightenment of true education—that which will make our brains and minds cultured. Society can never make any progress unless we receive good education. It is futile to hope for development till we are ourselves mentally and intellectually the equals of men. We shall have to acquire knowledge of all kinds.

We have become unfit for freedom only through lack of education and we have lost freedom because we were not fit for it. Men, narrow-minded and without any foresight, had deprived us of education because of their own petty selfish interests. Now our far-sighted brothers have come to realize that they themselves are being harmed because of this. So they are busying themselves in trying to awaken and uplift us. I have said this before: 'Men and women, both are needed to make up anything in its entirety. One cannot develop without the other.' I still say the same, and will go on saying it—hundreds of times if need be.

Now I will tell my brothers—the money they spend in decking their daughter up in silver and gold, platinum and diamond had better be spent in decking them up with the ornament of knowledge. One gets an ineffable pleasure from reading a book which is a storehouse of knowledge, and even one per cent of this cannot be got by wearing ten ornaments. Instead of decorating their bodies with ornaments, ladies should be eager to acquaint the ornaments of knowledge which are priceless:

Thieves cannot steal the treasure:
Relatives cannot distribute it
Knowledge is the treasure of all treasures
Giving away cannot decrease it.[4]

I would add a few more lines to it:

Fire cannot burn this treasure
Water never can drown it
Eternal priceless is it
Lifelong stays this treasure.

I would say, arrange for girls' schools with the money salted away for ornaments. But I do not think that my sisters are going to give up their ornaments in order to gain knowledge. Sad it is to relate—my sisters are looked upon as chattels. One decorates the table with flowers, one makes the curtains beautiful with flower-wreaths, beads, etc., and in the same way the housewife thinks it necessary to doll her daughter-in-law up with a lot of ornaments. At times our brothers mock us by calling us 'a stand for keeping silver and gold.' But will we listen?

The purdah, however, is no obstacle on our way to knowledge. But we lack women teachers. If this deficiency is filled up with separate schools and colleges then higher education can be obtained even after due observance of the purdah. I do not think any Muslim will come forward in the field of education if we discard as much of the purdah as is necessary.[5]

I hope that our enlightened sisters have realized that the burkha is not so bad after all.

(First publication, *Naba-Nūr*, Baiśākh, 1311)

Notes

1. We can, in this dictum, hear the echo of a sentence by Sura Nur in the 18th paragraph of the Koran: 'Tell the faithful women also to keep their eyes downcast (that is, not look here and there) and not to show their ornaments to anyone except a special few.'

2. This sentence is given in English (added by the translators).

3. The relevant sentences are: 'There he called his wife and showed me to her; but she screamed and ran back as women in England do at the sight of a toad or a spider (added by the translators).' (*Gulliver's Travels* Book II, Chapter 1)

Yes, indeed!

4. These couplets were not written by the authoress, she has quoted well-known lines. The later stanza is by her. The original stanza is in couplets, which makes it very mnemonic. I am sorry to have used the Tennysonian stanza (added by the translators).

5. I saw the speech entitled 'The Purdah of Ignorance' delivered by His Excellency the Governor Sir Andrew Fraser only after writing this essay. He has said:

> Let the efforts of the educationists be first directed to the instruction of our girls *within the purdah*, and let woman begin to exercise her chastening influence on society in spite of the system of seclusion, which only time can modify and violent efforts to which can only arouse opposition to female education, instead of doing any immediate practical good in the direction of emancipation of women.

(Quoted from the *Telegraph*, 8 March)

Home, Sweet Home

Home suggests a place of peace and comfort to which a man comes after the day's labour in hopes of rest. Home protects the owner from the sun, rain, and snow. Animals too have their own homes; they too think their homes to be safe places. Listen to the poet singing:

Home, sweet home
There is no place like home
Sweet sweet home.

One does not truly appreciate water till one is thirsty and one cannot appreciate one's home till one has left it and stayed elsewhere for some time. Union is made sweet by separation. Even though men do not always leave for foreign land yet they like to come back home after spending the whole day outside in the world of work and labour. They breathe easier when they come home.

One can see two parts in a house of which one part is the shelter and the other is the domestic life or Home. Building a home is natural and instinctive. A pair of birds builds their nest together. Even a fox digs out its own lair. Those nests and holes can be called houses but they are not homes. But let it be—this is not the topic to be discussed here.

Now I want to say a few things about our homes. If we look at our society we will see that most Indian women are deprived of the comfort of having a home of their own. For those who live under the thumb of other people, those who have no right to think of their guardian's house as their own—home is little but a prison for them. One who is not happy in her domestic life, one who does not dare to think of herself as a member of the family cannot think of her home as a haven of peace. Married, unmarried, or widowed—everyone faces the same wretched condition. I am going to give a few examples as proof. No doubt my brothers will be pained to no end when I show them the true condition inside a home. But what to do—an ulcer needs an operation. The patient has to endure it, however, painful it might be. How can I show the injury inside except by lifting the covering of the skin? So I want permission for lifting the purdah from certain parts of the women's quarters.

Now, I do not say that there are no good features in our society. There is much that is good, but likewise there is much that is evil. Suppose a man has one good arm and tumour in the other. Should not the diseased arm receive treatment because the other is whole? But one should have knowledge of all the details of the disease if one is to treat the patient.

Today we are going to discuss the diseases afflicting our society. The good part of it may rest easy. There are many happy families in our society. We are not going to talk about them. Let them sleep in peace. Come, my reader, let us have a look at the inner rooms of the iron-walled women's quarters.

1. I have already said that unless you go outside you cannot appreciate the comforts of home. We have once gone to some town near Jamalpur where a friend of ours had a house. The men of that family were friendly with the men of ours and so we went to meet the ladies of the family of Mr Sharafat, the advocate.[1] We saw that the ladies were extremely polite, though of rather limited vision. Mr Sharafat's wife Hasina, sister Jamila, her daughter and daughter-in-law, and others were present. When we requested Jamila to come to our house she said they had never left the house—that was the family tradition! I do not remember whether she said 'yes' or 'no' when asked about riding in a litter. When, in great surprise, I asked, 'Then how do you go to your husband's place after marriage? How did your sister-in-law come here?' Jamila said, 'She is the daughter of a relative. In this locality you will see the houses of our family side by side.' She took me to another room and said, 'This is my daughter's house, now come and see mine.' She took me along a narrow lane which had a high wall on one side and houses on the other. She showed me all the rooms and it seemed as if the sun never entered them. Then she opened a door and I saw Hasina's daughter-in-law sitting there! Jamila said, 'see, my brother's house is on the other side of the wall, and on this side mine. The daughter-in-law stays in that room so we keep this door closed. So now you understand why we do not need any transport.' All the houses can be reached in the same manner. As we did not want to inspect the entire locality we came back to our own house which was like a home to us. Jamila has said she will shortly go to Mecca; she does not want to stay in this sinful country any longer. We hope she will experience the happiness of returning home when she comes back from Mecca.

Does the reader, by any chance, think that either Hasina or Jamila are staying in their own home? No, of course not. Being incarcerated within the four walls of a tomb is not staying at home. Here, the room in which a newly married couple spends the night is called '*kohbar*', but it should be called a '*khabar*' (the grave).[2] The house belongs to Mr Sharaf. There are many goats and hens and a gaggle of geese in it and likewise a gaggle of women. Or you can call the women 'prisoners', for they do not have a family life. Think of your own home, then you will understand Hasina's position.

2. You can say this of many families—there is a lot of outward show, as if the husband has seven thousand soldiers under him ('*haft hāzarī*'), and, in the inner quarters the wife is starved. There are drawing rooms, stables and many things outside, and inside the house there is no place for the wife even to sit down for prayers (*namaaz*).

3. Now we shall show you the diseased part—the women's quarters. Usually the chief male of the family thinks, the house is 'my house' and the family members are his dependents.[3] We have gone quite a few times to a certain family in Malda. We have never seen the wife of Mr Kalim, the master of the family, with a smiling face. Her sad countenance silently attracts our sympathy. The reason is this—Mr Kalim had quarrelled with his cousin (wife's sister's husband) a few years ago so his wife cannot meet her own sister. She cannot exert even a little bit of strength and, say, 'My sister must come to me.' Woe, alas! The house belongs to Mr Kalim. It is for him to say who should come there and who should not. Likewise the other house is Selim's where Kalim's wife cannot go.

Needless to say, Kalim's wife does not lack for food, dress, and ornaments. Tell me, can ornaments take away an orphan wife's pain at being separated from her only sister? I heard that she was not free of the pains of a co-wife either. Does her home appear as sweet home to her? Does she not sigh in private and think, 'There is no one so luckless as I?'

4. There is a quarrel between two brothers. Name one of them Ham and the younger Shem. After the quarrel, Ham says to his daughter, 'Hamida, you must not write letters to Shem's daughter Zubeida while you are in my house.' She cannot disobey her father. But it is not easy for her to forget her cousin whom she has loved since her childhood. Her heart aches. The two girls who have played together in their nursery days, who are joined together even though while staying apart have been parted and Ham has proved the powers of owing the house and the family. He expresses his strength by treading down the hearts of two helpless young girls. Needless to say, Zubeida cannot write to Hamida either. If they do manage to send letters to each other then Shem intercepts the letters of Hamida and Ham that of Zubeida. Their unshed tears, their heart-breaking sighs vanish behind the curtains. I have heard that the law does not allow the father to intercept the letters of minor girls, but this law does not enter the precincts of women's quarters. It is all right for the poet to say:

You sit in one corner of the world
And go on loving. You do not know out there
Material life is roaring neath the sky.[4]

So there you are: the law exists, but does it mean anything to Hamida or Zubeida? Who is going to count how many such letters get intercepted by brothers-in-law and such others? The widowed sister-in-law treasures the letters of her brother and sister but if the brother-in-law in whose house she stays gets annoyed then she will not get her letters. Who can help such helpless girls except God?

5. We have known Romāsundarī for a long time. She is a childless widow. Her husband has left a lot of property and two or four good houses. Her brother-in-law is the owner of all that now. But he balks at giving her shelter and a handful of rice. We said, 'Perhaps she quarrels with his wife.' Then a person who has known her for fourteen to fifteen years said, 'Roma can do everything except quarrel. She knows how to make other people her kin. She does not know how to turn away those who are her kin.'

'Why then, being so good, she still does not stay with her brother-in-law?'

'That is her ill luck.'

Oh you helpless women! You ascribe your own faults to your misfortune, but you yourselves are the only ones to suffer through your own faults. Your fault lies in your ignorance, your weakness, your inefficiency, etc. Romāsundarī said, 'I live because I have to; I eat because I have to. Our custom of *suttee* was a good one. The government has increased the troubles of us widows by abolishing it.'

Does not God hear her words? Then what kind of a merciful God is he?

6. We had visited a royal palace. We had gone when the Rajah was not there. He was a Rajah by title. The annual income from his estate was nearly Rs 5,00,000.

The palace was a consecration and a poet's dream. The drawing room was shining with many expensive things. Five or six silver chairs were scattered here and there. A ray of sunlight had fallen on a mirror and, reflected by the crystals of the chandelier it created a world of light. In one room the Rajah's silver bed was waiting for him, furnished with bed-curtains and other things. The reader might say, 'why does the Rani not use it?' But then the visitors would not have been able to feast their eyes on this bed costing lakhs! After looking at the outer rooms we went to the Rani's quarters.

Her rooms also were furnished with tables and chairs, etc. But they were covered with dust. It did not look as though the Rajah ever visited these rooms. A few Bengali books were carelessly scattered beside the bed.

I was grievously disappointed with the Rani. The image I had had of her after seeing the drawing room was the very opposite of what I saw. She was an extremely beautiful girl of sixteen to seventeen years, wearing a simple English dhoti with red borders, and very few ornaments—only three pairs of glass bangles. Her hair was unkempt—it looked as if it had not been oiled for fifteen days. Her face was so sad that it would not have been an exaggeration to say that she was the very embodiment of sorrow. It is said that the eyes mirror the heart. I cannot describe the heart-breaking expression of her eyes.

The Rajah was always wandering abroad or in Calcutta, where he had got nymphs, etc. by the score. The Rani was left all alone here. There were servants, gods, and priests—no lack of anything. Sounds of merriment also could be heard. It was only the Rani's heart which was desolate. The house was like a prison to her. It was as if she was condemned to solitary confinement in company with a host of servants. One of the ladies in our group murmured, 'How does a man with such a splendid house and such a beautiful wife spend his days away from home?'

The Rani knows Bengali. She occupies herself by reading books. She does not talk much, but the little she said was very nice. One of the elderly ladies in our group asked, 'You are a queen, then why are you dressed like this? Come, let me dress your hair.' She only said, 'I do not know what sin I had committed to become a queen.' Very true. Yet people lust after the honour of being a queen, a Rani.

What can I call these diseases to be found in the women's quarters except ulcers and tumors? Are not there any medicines for these? Widows want to die on the funeral pyres of their husbands; what will married women long for?

7. We can, according to 'the Prophet's Laws' inherit our father's property, we can have our 'own houses' too. But so what—the real masters are our husbands, sons, sons-in-law, brothers-in-law, and such. If there is no one like them, then the seniormost steward is the master. The mistress of the house is but a puppet in his hands. Whatever he tells her, she has to believe, because she is stupid and illiterate.

Here is Mohsina, the mistress of the house quarrelling with her son-in-law and going to the house of her distant relative, her brother-in-law Kasim. This house was the property of her father. So it is her 'own' property. Her only daughter is dead. But her son-in-law, along with two or three granddaughters, stays with her. It can be said that he is one of her dependents. But look at the ridiculous situation. When she came back the doorman told her that she cannot enter the house. Very angry, she said, 'What, I cannot enter my own house? Arrange for a curtain, I'm coming out of the litter.'

DOORMAN: I can't arrange for the curtain, the master will not allow it.
MISTRESS: Who's your master? I'm the only master you have.
DOORMAN: Please forgive me. Can my lady protect me from his kicks? My lady is always behind the purdah, we know only Jamal Mian. You are the mistress, as the world well knows but take pity on me and go back. If you get down here your servants will suffer. There is the possibility that my lady too might be insulted.

So the mistress went away. She asked Kasim, 'Is there no such law as will let me take possession of the house?' He said, 'Yes, there is.

You file a complaint and I will help.' Jamal, coming to know of this, came and met Kasim. He told Kasim in honeyed words, 'If you help my mother-in-law now, you will be helping a woman. If you yourself ever face this kind of situation and somebody helps the woman of your family, will you like it? Think it over—is it a good thing to happen? Why make enemies?'

Kasim came inside and told Mohsina that fighting cases is a troublesome procedure. Better not go into all that. The unfortunate woman silently bore her anger and insults.

Many more such examples can be brought forth. There is Khādijā, a rich heiress. Her husband Hasim, though poor, is an aristocrat and educated. He has managed to usurp all her property. She is penniless. Sitting in her own house Hasim married two or three other wives and made her undergo the torture of having co-wives. Well, if he did not do all this, how would he prove his manly strength? If Khādijā protests even a little then the old wives will criticize her lack of respect for her husband. One of them will point to a worn-out book and say, 'One should not cry even if the husband cuts off your head' and another will chant:

The husband's the mentor, the husband the crown
You worship the husband, let this be known.

There is no one even to sympathize with Khādijā. What can this be called but torture in Hell? A certain maulvi had said, 'women are guilty of sin. Hazrat Miyaraz had seen that in most places in Hell it is women who are being tortured.' But we can see that the ladies are suffering the tortures of Hell on this earth itself.

8. Who does not know the despicable ways and means adopted for depriving women of their patronymic? No brother will say it openly because that will be indulging women.[5]

So we will have to tell the tale. In many cases a drug-addict, illiterate and chronically ailing old man, who cannot get back his lands by fighting in the court is still given a daughter in marriage. Or, even before the sister is married she is made to write a '*la-dabi*' (denial of property) or they are kept unmarried throughout their lives and the sister-in-law treats them like servants. If a family does not have a son but only daughters (a dozen or half a dozen) then the lucky husband of the eldest daughter tries to keep his sisters-in-law unmarried. This is the ulcer in society. Ah, Father Mohammed (P.B.H.), you have given us the right on our father's property, but your cunning followers are ruining girls in many different ways. Alas, 'the Prophet's Laws' are but so many ink scribbles in books. The one who has money and power has law on his side also. Laws are not meant for helpless females.

Saudamini, widowed recently, is staying with her brother with two sons and a daughter. After about nine or ten months her sons die. Saudamini possessed Rs 10,000. At the time when she was still dazed with grief (a month after the death of her two sons), her brother Nagendra asked her to keep the money in his name. He said, 'There might be trouble if the money is kept in a woman's name. After all, I'm your own brother, not a stranger.' She was not able to think properly and wrote what her brother told her to write, thinking, 'My sons are gone, what will I do with money. He will arrange for Pratibha's marriage. I do not want to live, in any case.' Nagendra gradually married off two or three daughters of his own, but did not bother about Pratibha. When she was twelve, Saudamini got worried about her marriage. The more she prodded Nagendra, he only said, 'Grooms are not that easy to get'.

Pratibha came to be fifteen and yet she was not married. Does the reader believe that you cannot get a groom with Rs 10,000? The neighbours started criticizing him, 'Shame on him, what sort of an uncle is he?' Nagendra did not care a jot. The slander brewed in a village dies within the cornfield around the village. The huge jute plantations hide big boars, can they not hide these slanders?

Saudamini saw that her husband's hard-earned money is gone in enriching Nagendra. His daughters got married and her own Pratibha remained unmarried.

The poetess Mankumari Devi, sister mine, has said:

Weep, sad sisters, and I will weep
If nothing else then a few tears
For you, my sisters, and I will weep.
Whenever I see an 'old maid' free
Wandering unmarried, I will weep.
Whenever I see a girl not free
Of other co-wives, I will weep.
Whenever I see married girl begging
Others for food, I will weep.
This humble life I'll gladly give
For you, my dears, and helpless sigh
But I can weep, and weeping die.

Not so will I. I will not weep with her. My dear sister has spent all her strength in 'weeping die'. That is all. It is because of this weeping in solitude that we have become so weak.

On reading this essay my brothers and sisters might think that I am wielding the pen just in order to present brothers as wolves in sheep's clothing. It is not that. I have never used a harsh word for them. Have I called any of them wretches, devils, accursed, cruel, etc.? I have just brought to light the wounds in a woman's heart. It has been said, 'Talking about your own misery means slandering others', and that is what has happened here—the description of the sister's misery has reflected on the brothers. Fortunately enough, there are many brothers who maintain their sisters in happiness. But it must be said, not that I am happy to say it, that many brothers give evidence of unjust mastership (domestic tyranny) in their own houses.

Perhaps the good brothers will realize that I have not made a mistake in saying 'we have no shelter in this wide world'. Every word of that sentence is true. Wherever we are, in whatever condition, we are in the houses of our guardians. It is not that our masters' houses always protect us from the sun, rain, or, snow even then.

When there is no straw on the roof, when the last thatch of the peasant's cottage is blown away by a hurricane, when we are drowned in a heavy downpour, when we are dazzled by the lightning, when the earth shudders at the thunder and we tremble, when we die with every thunderclap—even then, dear reader, even then we are in the house of our guardians.

When, as a princess or the wife of a prince, we dwell in a palace, then too we are in the house of our master. When the same palace is reduced to rubble by an earthquake, when coming down the stairs we break our arms or legs, when we take shelter, muddied and bloodied, in the cowshed—even then we are in the house of our guardian.

Or, as middle-class wives and daughters, we might be living in a large house, and when on a spring night of new moon, evil men start the '*Lanka-dahan*'[6] in our master's house, the rooms and everything in them burst into flames, we, with only the clothes on our back run to a tree a bit far off and stand trembling—even then we are in the house of our master (I do not know, maybe when we are in the grave, perhaps even then we are in the house of our master!).

My use of the word 'home' is in the English sense of the word. The condition of the Rani, Romāsundarī, Hamida, Zubeida, and the others as have been described above—do they signify that these ladies are enjoying the domestic bliss of their own homes? Home is where there is physical comfort and mental peace. For a widow the house of her late husband becomes almost uninhabitable. The luckless woman has to fall back upon her father or her brother for support and for shelter. The story of poor Saudamini illustrates the pitiable experiences they have to undergo when they are in such a condition. There is a very appropriate proverb in Hindi which means:

My house was burnt and I went to the forest
The forest was also burnt.
Poor forest, what can it do, in faith
My fate itself got burnt.

That is the reason I say, we do not have even a humble hut of our own. No living creature is so shelterless as we are. Everyone has a home; we are the only ones who have not any.[7]

Notes

1. The names given are imaginary ones. They have been given for the sake of convenience.
2. There is an untranslatable play on words here which can be seen from the words used: 'Kohbar' and 'Kabar' (added by the translators).
3. We are not aiming at any specific person or event. A general picture has been painted by gathering true facts from here and there. Let no one think the painter inconsistent because one side of the river presents flowering mango trees and the other snow-laden trees as are found by the side of the Niagara—all, all are true, river, mango trees, and snow-laden firs.

4. These three lines seem to be in blank verse, and have been translated as such (added by the translators).

5. An article dealing with the miseries of women had been given to an Urdu newspaper. The editor dared not publish it. He wrote: 'Male readers will take offence if such an article is published.' Fortunately enough, Bengali papers have the necessary courageous honesty. Otherwise we would not have had a shoulder to weep upon.

6. Lankāpurī or Ravan's palace was burnt by the mokey god Hanuman. Here it means wanton destruction.

7. This essay has not been written for those of our sisters who enjoy domestic bliss in their own homes—it is meant for those who do not have a home of their own.

Part II

Dedication

Dear Sister mine,

It was your love that encouraged me to read *Barnaparichay* in my childhood. The other relatives, though they did not object much to my learning Urdu and Persian, were dead against Bengali. You were the only one who wanted it. It was you who had been afraid that I will forget Bengali after marriage. The fact that even after living in Bhagalpur for fourteen years, without a single person to talk to in Bengali, I have still not forgotten it and this is only due to you. Then I came to Calcutta and have been managing this Urdu school for eleven years. Here too everyone—the maids, the students, the teachers—speaks Urdu. I am talking in Urdu from morning till night. Even after all this I have not forgotten Bengali because your blessing has always supported me. I dedicate this book to you to signify my love and respect. Bless me by accepting it. The book contains your favourite *The Murder of Delicia* also.

Foreword

As the first part of *Motichur* had been highly appreciated by the readers, men as well as women, we are publishing the second part on earnest requests from them. The flaws of Part I have been corrected as much as possible. Those that still exist are the result of the writer's own lack of knowledge and experience. It is to be hoped that the discriminating reader will excuse them.

THE AUTHORESS

Advertisement

The essays published in Part II had been published formerly in well-known periodicals like *Naba-Nūr*, *Bharat Mahilā*, *Al Islam*, *Saugāt*, and *Baṅgīya Mussalmān Sāhitya Patrikā*. I cannot remember hearing any objections raised against them by the readers.

In this edition some of the essays have been edited and enlarged. *Delicia Hatya* and *Nur-Islam* have been translated from English and Urdu respectively. *Sultanar Swapna* had formerly been written in English. *Nari Sristi* is a piece partially translated from English. It has been translated here in Bengali on the earnest request of those of my sisters who have not been able to read in English. *Muktiphal* was written after the breakup in Congress in 1907 and has been enlarged.

The Light of Islam

One feels really elated on reading Mrs Annie Besant's essay titled *Islam*. Please do not be alarmed at hearing the name of Mrs Besant joined to the word 'Islam'. I too was alarmed at first, thinking that perhaps, while spreading the light of her Theosophy she had wiped her hands on our only treasure Islam. But reading the speech corrected my mistake. Let alone casting a doubtful glance, every page and every line was found to be instinct with sweet devotion like a ripe grape. The way she has given a bright picture of the light of Islam can hardly be rivalled by anything else, so much so that I cannot resist the temptation of writing down the main ideas of this essay in my favourite language, Bengali.

The thing is, not everyone has the ability or the knowledge for translation—and for a person like me to try to do it! On top of that, I have not been able to procure the original English speech though I tried my best. So I have to depend on the Urdu translation. The respected translator has used a language of a very high order, impregnated with Sufi attitude. So if I, when translating this translation, occasionally express my own feelings in my own inadequate language, I hope it will be forgiven.

Another thing, whenever Mrs Besant mentions the Prophet (P.B.H.) she does so, not with ornate honorifics but with the simple devotion of a devotee. The translator Maulana Hasinuddin has also done the same. For example, now Mohammed did not remain just Mohammed but was declared as the Prophet. Afraid of spoiling the natural beauty of her language and sentiment I too have followed the principles of the translator. Besides, you do not need a candle to show the bright effulgence of the sun, you do not need ornaments to enhance the beauty of flowers. I hope I will not be blamed for not using grand honorifics and high rhetoric.[1]

Now please listen with attention to what Mrs Besant is saying:

Gentlemen,

Religion is at the root of everything that makes a race progress on a natural, moral, and spiritual level. Man cannot get moral or spiritual upliftment or be civilized without religion. If there exists a country in which all the inhabitants follow the same religion, worship God in the same manner, call Him by the same name, and the attitude of everyone is woven together, then such a country without doubt, is extremely fortunate. But I think that a country in which people call God by different names, worship the same God in different ways, pray to the Almighty in different languages and yet think: we are all travelling to the same goal by different paths, and there is unity in this diversity, if there is such a country (but whether such a very fortunate country exists is not known)—then I think such a country would be the leader in the matter of religion.

There are many countries with different religions and people of different faiths, but India is a unique example of this idea. India can be compared only with herself. So many different religions are there and people of so many different faiths that it seems as if it is a place exhibiting all the religions of the whole world. This is that country where the ideal aspects of religion—which, as I have said earlier, is eminently desirable—is to be found in mutual friendliness, sympathy, and unity.

You might remember that three or four years ago I had talked about four great religions: Christianity, Buddhism, Hinduism, and Fire-worship, but three had remained undiscussed: Islam, Jainism, and Sikhism. These three too are included within the seven religions of India, differing from each so much that they thirst for the blood of each other and this difference in religion has become a very great obstacle to the development of friendly relationship among them.

What I want from the bottom of my heart is that in a country like India if people would take off the blinkers of prejudice and superstition from their eye and think with justice and fairness in mind, they see: we are all actually worshipping the same God in different ways, calling upon the same God in different languages and with different names:

'Give us, give us our heart's desire.
Upon whom is calling for even
The language without any words?'

—Dr R. Tagore

'Everyone calls upon Him
Whom I too call upon
The rosy down calls
With the young sun at her breast

The dusk, a young lass, calls
Shining with evening darkness.'
—Mankumari Devi

We have all come from the one and the same place and we are all going to go back there. This means that people will be able to mix and mingle with each other with true sincerity and brotherliness. One's sorrow will make the other sad—all Indians will earn the right to be taken as one race. The mighty powers of the world will accept all Indians as one and the same race. When Hindus and Muslims, Parsis and Christians, Jains and Jews, Buddhists and Sikhs will embrace each other with love in their heart I will think—this is the triumph of religion, and the name of the Almighty has brought peace on earth.

Today I will say a few words about Islam and tomorrow and the day after about the other two religions, and then discuss the true meaning of all religions which is Theosophy (*Ilm-e-Ilahi*) which contains within itself the essence of each faith. It has equal rights over all religions and no one can claim it to be only his own religion or that of a particular sect. Any man of any faith, be it the opposite of any, can say: this is my religion. On this anniversary of this Society I pray that the holy souls of all the religious leaders of the world may gaze upon us with blessings so that their followers may love each other. Amen.

Islam

When analysing any religion, we have to consider four things; first of all, the origin of that religion which secretly influences that religion. Second, its outer expression (branches and leaves) with which people are acquainted. Third, the philosophy of that religion which is meant for the educated and the intellectuals. Fourth, the deep and inner significance with which the ordinary man's self or identity wants to mix and mingle. I want to examine Islam against this touchstone so as to show you what the state of Arabia, Syria, and Iran had been in the beginning.[2]

During the sixth century the hurricane of barbarism and superstition was sweeping over Arabia, Syria, and Iran; battles and bloodshed created abysses between clans and the anger was so strong that a quarrel carried on for generation. For example, suppose someone quarrels with another over something, then, even after a hundred years the grandson of one of them would kill the grandson of the other just because 'the grandfather of this man was the enemy of mine'. This was that Arabia where people would fight each other because 'why did your camel cross in front of mine'. Blood will flow and corpses pile up for something as trivial as that. This was that Arabia where a cruel father will snatch a baby from its mother's arms and bury it alive. The mother will silently die a thousand deaths in her maternal heart. She did not have the power to protest against this brutal tyranny of her husband—and all because she was a woman. Girls were killed so that there will not be any sons-in-law. It was that country where idol worship had been carried on with different idols in different houses and each idol the enemy of the other. Human sacrifices to the idols were everyday occurrences, the place where luxury and selfishness reigned instead of love and consideration. If a powerful man killed his neighbour for little or no reason there was no one to restrain him or even to protest against.

Those days Arabia was full of luxury and licentiousness. One man would take numerous wives, just like goats and rams. They used to take pride that such a man was so rich that he had so many wives.

Women, who are God's creatures, were so much in the bondage of slavery that they used to spend their days like helpless domestic animals. There were hardly any despicable sins and faults that could not be found in the Arabia of those days.

It was in such a poisonous atmosphere of selfishness and tyranny that a baby boy was born in a Quraish household (a thousand reverent blessings on that holy child). His father had passed away a few weeks before his birth. He had been a man who had been meant by his father for human sacrifice to an idol and was saved by the pity of a female attendant of the temple.[3]

This child was born to such a luckless and miserable woman as was widowed before his birth and a few months later, unable to bear her widowhood, she followed her husband, leaving the suckling babe. So the orphan was brought up by his maternal grandfather. But, sad to relate, his grandfather too passed away after a few years and the child stayed with his uncle Abu Talib till he became an adult. One can easily guess that the boy, being an impoverished orphan, was deprived of all education—it was but natural. That is what had actually happened. Neither did he remain acquainted with the alphabet, nor did the air of moral training and discipline touch him. Yet his childhood was the ideal of a very holy life. His pure life had all the noble and desirable qualities of human beings—pity, courtesy, love, patience, modesty, humility, endurance, etc. He became the favourite of everyone because of them.

He left childhood behind and reached adolescence. Now he took a job in the house of a widowed relative in order to earn his living. This lady, Khadija Bibi, used to send him to Syria with a lot of merchandize for trading. Khadija Bibi found him to be pious, just, economical, and very trustworthy. Later she married him.

Let us remember, this young man's name was just Mahomet, he had not yet become The Prophet. His wife was not of the same faith as he. He himself was a young man and his wife was double his age. But they led a life of such conjugal bliss after marriage that it is doubtful whether any comparable example can be found and it was so for twenty-six years. After that Hazrat Khadija passed away. The activities and the character of the Prophet remained exemplary after her death. The children playing in the lanes of Mecca used to cling to his legs when he passed along those narrow lanes and he always spoke to them lovingly, patting their heads. He was always ready to help those in trouble. No one has ever heard of him breaking a promise. Consoling widows and orphans was his daily task. The neighbours used to call him '*Amin*', which means 'trustworthy'—such a noble title can be won from the world only by the highest of the high. Now please stop a while and think: what is the inner life of such a person like, whose outer life is of so much good to the world, giving so much comfort and peace. Ah, the urge for knowing the Truth used to make him wander disconsolate in forests and deserts. He spent many a day in dangerous caves, without food and sleep. It is difficult to describe how he used to search for God in a totally self-forgetful condition, lost in meditation. Only those who have dedicated themselves utterly to God can understand all this.

Gradually Hazrat Mahomet's meditations reached such intensity that he used to leave human habitation and go away to far-off forests, dwelling for more than a month in dangerous caves. There he would bow down, and weep and lament. He spent fifteen years like this. Then came the sacred moment when a heavenly Voice said, 'Arise, say aloud the sacred name of God'. He did not understand what Voice it was, whether it was really a heavenly Voice or not. This was because he was uneducated. He thought it might be a mistake or mere self-deception; maybe it was his own ego making those sounds in order to deceive him. Possibly it was not the heavenly Voice which the other prophets used to hear from God Himself and called 'Ilham' or 'Ahi'.

Then, when one day when he was thinking deeply of God, suddenly the whole place lit up with an unearthly light and a glorious figure manifested himself and told him to say the True Name aloud: 'Go, say the True Name'. Then he took courage and asked, 'Whom shall I worship?' Then the angel taught him about the oneness of God, the mystery of the angels, the creation of the world, and the existence of mankind. He also told him about the noble and heavy responsibility of the Message for which he had been born. That is, the angel told him that he had been given the work of being the religious guide and adviser of the world. Then the angel vanished.

When the angel vanished Hazrat Mohammed, who from now on will be known as the Prophet of Arabia, returned home in a very restless and awestruck condition, and fell on the floor in a half-conscious state. Hazrat Khadija took care of him and asked the reason for his troubled state. Then the Prophet told her everything and said, 'Perhaps this is but a symptom to be followed by my death'. The loyal and loving wife gave him courage by talking soothingly and said, 'No, no, you are truthful and trustworthy—you are "Amin"; you also always keep your promises, give love to the fatherless, consolation to the widows and the ailing. God will never let you die an untimely death. Now get up and do as the heavenly command—the true heavenly Voice—said.'

This pious lady, who was the first to believe in the Prophet, encouraged him with such life-giving words that he who had been sitting as if defeated and reduced to the inanimate in his weakness,[4] stood up, lit with enthusiasm and courage. He was no longer the Mohammed that he was; he had become the mighty Prophet. He took an uncivilized, anarchic country and turned it into a peaceful one. He took a desolate peninsula and turned it into a great empire. His disciples took the light of religion and knowledge to Europe where both of these things were lacking. His followers laid the foundations of a great empire. His companions sank into such deep contemplation of the Lord that it is doubtful whether any such example can be found in any other religion. When you stop and think you will find, in all fairness, that there is no such religion in which such honest belief in Truth can be found. They have obtained this faith and knowledge from the Prophet.

If we accept what some gentlemen say about one's behaviour being pointers to one's religious faith as truth, then you should observe the followers of that religion and think: how the words of the Prophet are clearly imprinted on the heart of the disciples. The training the Muslims have received from the Prophet of Arabia is such that it has made their faith strong enough for there to be no room for any doubts. A Muslim, even if he is surrounded by people who are mocking at him and showing contempt for his Prophet, does not feel ashamed to bow his head for namaaz.[5]

Then think again, they have so much faith in the *Shafa'at* (grace) of the Prophet that they are not afraid of death at all. Can anyone show me anything equal to the courage of the hermits of Africa? They used to come so happily to line up in order to face the cannon that it was as if they were accompanying a bridegroom to a marriage. Moreover, they would go on getting killed till some of them would reach the enemy soldiers. What is that heroic enthusiasm that took them to the very jaws of death? It is only the greatness of the Prophet, the Koran, and love of Islam. I truly believe that their faith will remain unmoved in future and will shine brighter then than now (Amen).

Gentlemen! Now I will present to you an example of the Prophet's love of truth. The first to believe in him was his wife who knew everything about his daily life and as she was his nearest relative, knew his nature right from his childhood. If you think of this then you will find burning examples of the Prophet's adherence to truth. You yourself know that a good orator can go to a conference and persuade his audience to believe in him by speaking eloquently for two hours—because at that time people see him on the stage and know nothing about his personal life. But it is very difficult, indeed impossible, that one's wife, daughters, sons-in-law, and other such close relatives would give a certificate for honesty and truthfulness unless he is really pure and truthful. This is what Prophethood means to me and, to tell the truth, even Jesus Christ did not get such a triumph.[6]

Among the relatives of the Prophet it was his uncle Abu Talib who was the only person who, because of his obstinacy, did not believe in him openly. He was the leader of the Quraish clan and thought it would go against his honour to forsake the religion of his forefathers. His behaviour, however, said it clearly, that he had completefaith in the Prophet. He had told him: 'O, you who are devoted to your uncle, do your duty without any hesitation. No one will be able to look askance at you while I live.' Then came a day when Abu Talib asked his son, 'What is your religion, and what do you think of Mohammed?' Hazrat Ali replied, most respectfully but with great enthusiasm, 'Father, I consider Allah to be the only one to worship, and believe Mohammed to be the true Messenger sent by Allah, and I'm not ready to give up the company of the Prophet'.

There was every possibility that the father would go angry at such an answer, but that did not happen. Instead he said, 'O light of my eyes, I permit you most willingly to be his disciple and follow him. I'm perfectly sure he will never lead you astray.'

After becoming the Prophet (*Nabiyat*) he went on doing his work silently, without any pomp and circumstances for three years. There were only 30 men at that time who believed in him. After that he delivered a public oration and described the oneness of Allah in wonderful language and also spoke against human sacrifice, luxury, and drinking, making people realize the contemptibleness of these things. His speeches lit the flame of faith in many hearts and the number of his disciples increased. But almost instantly many obstacles arose against him in the whole country. An ordinary man could not have endured the insults and humiliations that he had endured at the hands of the opposing party.

His enemies killed his faithful followers wherever they found them. They used to torture some of them. They would chain up some, make them lie down on the hot sand of the desert with the sun in their eyes, put a stone on their chest and tell them, 'Deny the Prophet and his Allah'. But even then they would recite the Prophet's principles and be martyred willingly.

Once there was a man who caught a Muslim and cut off pieces of his flesh and said, 'If you had been staying happily with your family, and instead of you, your Mohammed had been writhing, blood-stained, on the ground, then that would have been the best'. But that loyal and true Muslim went on saying till his death, 'Let my house, son, and wife, my happiness and comfort, let everything be dedicated to my Mentor. Let not a thorn prick his feet while I live.'[7]

Finally the enemies started torturing the Prophet and his disciples so much that he directed them to migrate to another country. When a group of his followers went to Abyssinia the enemy followed them there and requested the King (who was a Christian) to surrender the

Muslims to them. The King then called these unfortunate foreigners and asked them about their condition. They said:

> Your Majesty, we had been wallowing in the filth of ignorance and stupidity, we were contemptible idolators, our life was like that of brutal savages, murder was a daily occurrence with us, we were blind, atheistic and irreligious. We had no notion of goodwill and love towards each other. Hospitality to guests and neighbourly duties, were unknown to us. We knew no laws except 'might is right'. While we were in so terrible a condition Allah created a man whose honesty, truthfulness and simplicity got imprinted in bright letters in our heart. This man taught us, 'There is only one God, free of all blemish. It is our duty to worship only Him. We will have to follow truth and give up falsehood, keep our premises, have love and care for all creatures, do our neighbourly duties by others, treat women with respect, not usurp the property of orphans, and not neglect daily worship and fasting.' Oh your Majesty, we have faith in this religion and we have accepted these rulings.

Gentlemen, the faith and the loyalty of the disciples of the Prophet were of such a high order that they walk with their life (which is a treasure) in their own hands. I will tell you of another event as proof of the truthfulness and the frank open-heartedness of the Prophet.

Once the Prophet was talking with a certain wealthy man when a blind beggar called out to him, 'O thou Messenger of God, show me the way. I've come to you in the hope of finding the true path.' The Prophet was busy talking and did not hear him. The beggar again called loudly, 'O Rasul, hear me and show me the path of religion'. Then the Prophet, a bit irritated, signed to him to wait and the beggar, disappointed, went away. The heavenly command (*Ahi*) that came to the Prophet the next day, which is written in the Koran and which will thus remain written forever, was this:

> A blind man came to the Rasul whom the latter neglected and did not pay attention to. How do you know that he will not be cleansed of his sins, listening to your teaching and not benefit by them? You are treating the rich with respect. Even if he had not been faithful (*imandar*), you would not have been blamed. But you neglected one who came in all simplicity, in search of Truth and Liberation. Let such a thing not happen in future.

This Heavenly Command shook the Prophet. It had such an influence on him that whenever he saw the blind man after this he would say, 'The arrival of this man is a good omen, for it is because of him that Allah has chastised me'. He used to show much honour to and care for this man and had twice appointed him to a good post at Medina. As a matter of fact, the Prophet did not merely give advice to others but used to keep himself ready at all times so that his own soul may receive advice.

As has happened with other prophets, enmity against the Prophet went on increasing. New dangers threatened the Prophet and his disciples on account of religious enmity. Things came to such a pass that he told all the Muslims to flee and save themselves. Only one person still remained with him. The Prophet, however, went on doing his duty without any fear. The enemy conspired against his life. Abu Talib, his uncle, could not bear it any longer and calling him, said with great love, 'O you who love your uncle so much, listen to me. Don't lose this priceless life of yours. The thirty blades of the Arabs are being sharpened for you. Stop while there is time. Stop delivering your speeches.' The courageous reply that the Prophet gave to his uncle is worth serious consideration. He said:

> Dear uncle, I'm helpless. I myself don't do anything. Somebody else is making me do all this. If these unbelievers were to give me the sun and the moon in my hands and say, 'Now leave off doing your work', even then you can be sure I'll not stop my work till God wants. Or, I'll give up my life for the sake of my work. But if you are afraid for yourselves then you have only to tell me and I'll go somewhere else—my Allah will always be with me.

Then, with tearful eyes he prepared to leave. The uncle's heart overflowed with love and he said, 'Dear one, I'll never let you go. I'll save you from your enemies. Go on doing your work without any fear.'

But, gentlemen, this loving uncle was not able to stay long with the Prophet. He passed during this, the darkest possible time. In the same year his devoted wife Khadija Bibi too left him forever. This was a time of trial, of great grief and danger for him. His enemies were stronger than ever. (Misfortunes never come in single file but in battalions.)

Things came to such a pass that the Prophet prepared to leave Mecca. Then Hazrat Ali and Abu-Bakr Siddique were the only ones with him. On a certain night the Prophet, with Abu-Bakr, left for Medina while Hazrat Ali lay down in his bed so as to deceive the enemies. Then in due time his enemies came there and found Ali, not him. They did not say anything to him; instead they proclaimed a reward of much value for the Prophet's head.

While the Prophet was travelling with Abu-Bakr as his only companion, the latter very anxiously said to him, 'O my lord, there are only two of us!' He answered, 'No, no, there are three of us—one of whom is very powerful; He is one against the whole world'. Abu Bakr, greatly surprised, asked, 'My lord, whom do you mean by this third person?' The answer was: 'Allah, who is omnipotent, is always with us, protecting us.' That took away all worries and anxieties from Abu-Bakr.

The Prophet reached Medina and received unexpected welcome and honour there. Hundreds of social leaders invited him and became his disciples. His other disciples too, who were scattered about here and there, gradually reached Medina. But his enemies did not allow him to stay there in peace. They gathered an army together and attacked the Prophet. Then the Prophet, in sheer self-defence, took his small army outside and prayed aloud:

> O Father, Thou seest and knowest everything.
> If today my small army is destroyed then there
> will be no one to spread thy true name. I firmly
> believe that Thou wilt help the cause of Truth.

Finally the bloody battle—famous as the Battle of Badr—was over. Whereas a thousand soldiers of the enemy died, the toll rose to barely a hundred in this army. It is quite clear that some unknown force was helping the Muslims and so he won the battle very quickly. This was the first bloodshed in the Prophet's life which he was forced to do as there was nothing else to be done. He was so kind and loving that daredevils used to say he was timid and a coward.

Muslim-haters tried a few more times to defeat him in battle and the Prophet, in self-defence and to save his disciples had to fight them. Since he was always supported by Truth and God, he went from triumph to triumph and obtained unsought for mastery. He became the free monarch of the entire Arab peninsula.

Now there was a clear rift between the past life of the Prophet and the present. Formerly when people tyrannized over him he used to pray for their welfare instead of revenging himself upon them. Now, as every emperor must, he had to keep an army and be prepared for battle. He had to punish criminals also. But here too he has left high ideals of justice and mercy for us.

Before his birth, during the time which is known as the time of ignorance, prisoners of war were treated with such cruelty as is difficult to find even among barbarians. But in the Prophet's own time the prisoners were treated with so much kindness and courtesy as will be difficult to find even these days in civilized countries. Once, while going towards a battlefield there was a group of prisoners with them. It became known that there was not enough flour with them. The Prophet ordered that the prisoners should be given bread and the free soldiers eat dates (what nobility!).

Another such incident is this: Once after winning a battle, the treasures and other things were being shared out and the Prophet did not allow his own dear companions to take their share. They became hurt and angry and started to discuss this among themselves. The Prophet came to know about this and, calling them to him said:

> My friends, you know yourselves how miserable you used to be. Allah has saved you from all that. You thirsted for the blood of each other and instead Allah has given you brotherly love for each other. You had been imprisoned in the darkness of irreligiosity. He has lit up your minds with the pure light of faith. Have you not received these favours and rewards from Him?

To which all of them said in unison: 'Very true, that is what our condition had been like and the mercy of Allah and your kindness have given us peace and prosperity'. He stopped them and said, 'No, no just say that God took pity on you. If you had said all this then I could have been your witness. You can say about me that you had fled to this place and I gave you shelter, you were burdened with sorrow and care and I consoled you.'

They did not say anything to this. Seeing them silent, the Prophet again said, 'O my dear friends, do you not want me instead of the goods obtained from the battle? By God, even if all the kingdom of God stood against him, Mohammed would always be with his followers, for they are enduring all hardships without any self-seeking, just for the sake of God.' This speech of the Prophet overwhelmed the followers, and they who were fearless in death and lion like in war started shedding tears and said, 'O my lord, we are fully content with our present condition'.

My Hindu brothers! Actually you do not know anything about this Arab prophet. You cannot see the supernatural power that has made thousands of his followers endure torture and face death, which has generated love for God in millions of breasts. Just consider the self-sacrifice and the humility of the Prophet. He taught his followers that nobody should think of him as a god or a supernormal man. He said repeatedly, 'I'm a man just like you. There is only this difference that I'm His messenger; I take His teachings to you.' What more proof is needed of his humility and simple-heartedness? At the time when he was an emperor, even then he had sewn patches on his old clothes himself and mended his torn sandals. His servant has said about him, 'I have been with him for ten years. Let alone say a harsh word to me, he never even addressed me as "*tu*".' There is no use of the word 'tu' anywhere by the Prophet. Brothers, that was how simple and unceremonious was the life of that emperor who could have kept more than a thousand servants for his own comfort.

When the mission for which he was born was fulfilled, the dreaded day came when, a day before his death, he was brought to the mosque for prayers in a seriously ill condition. When the prayers were finished he lifted his voice as high as possible and said, 'O Muslims, proclaim this among the people that if I have ever done any injustice to anyone, let him come and be revenged on me today, let him not postpone it for the after life. If I owe anyone anything then I'm giving him my house to repay that debt. I'm ready to answer any charges today.'

One person said the Prophet owed him 30 dirhams and was paid then and there.[8] This was his last visit to the mosque. On 8 August 634, the Prophet left his earthly body behind so that he might ascend to the higher spheres and protect his religion. Such a life was of a very high and pure kind, fit for the Prophet of Allah. (It was, of course, impossible for an ordinary man.)

Gentlemen! Now I am going to tell you about the unjust charges levelled against the Prophet. These are the results of ignorance, lack of a sense of justice, or just superstition. First of all it is said that he had married nine women during the last stage of his life. It is true that he had married, but will anyone tell me that a man who, till he was twenty-four, did not know anything about women, then married a woman years senior to himself and spent twenty-six years of his life in great happiness with her, is it possible that such a man will in the last few years of his life, when vitality is running low, marry just for the sake of pleasure? Look at it in all fairness and you will at once understand the reason. First we will have to see from which level of society these ladies had come and why the Rasul needed them. There were some of them who facilitated the spreading of 'Nur Islam', and there are some who had no means of support or protection except marriage. This explains why the Prophet married them.

Another charge levelled against him is that he favoured bloodshed and ordered the killing of non-Muslims with or without any reason. Now listen to me. When two parts of any law are more or less of the same kind, that is, one is conditional and the other is not, then the unconditioned law is always taken as being a conditional one.

Muslim scholars have always honoured this fact and the sayings of the Koran (Qu'ran) also support this. That is, in one place it is said, 'Kill the heathen' and in another, 'Kill the heathen if he obstructs your worship'. I am now giving you a translation of the Commands given to the Rasul. I am not going to say it in my own words or you will think I am indulging in propaganda for the Muslims. Now listen:

> If they stop opposing you then forget whatever has happened. But if they come to attack you then let them be punished in the same way that the enemies of earlier prophets have been punished. So fight them till they stop opposing you for the sake of protecting their idolatry, and disobedient to the religion of God, continue fighting. And if they are obedient, then know for sure that Allah observes their activities. But if they are enemies of the true religion then God will help you. He is the greatest guardian and helper.

Another thing given in the Koran to advise and guide the Prophet is this:

> Call men to follow the path of Allah's religion and advice, with logic and in humble and soft language. Argue with them with solemnity and patience and kindness, because Allah knows which of them follows the true path and which of them has gone astray. If you revenge yourself then be careful that it does not exceed the wrong done to you, following justice. If, instead of wreaking revenge, you just endure it, then it is even better for him who endures. So the best thing is to endure the tyranny of your enemies with patience. But remember, your action will succeed only if God's grace is in them. Do not feel hurt by the behaviour of the heathen, do not be distressed by their cunning and deception, for God helps only those who are honest and just and fear Him.

Listen to another teaching: 'Do not tyrannize over anybody in the matter of religion. If a man accepts Islam then think that Allah has shown him the True Path and if he does not accept, then what to do—your duty was just to spread the religion and to advise people.'

Listen further to how the Prophet has described heathens: 'Those are heathens (*kafir*) who do the opposite of justice. The sinful are those who are not Muslims.'

This makes it quite clear that the principles of Islam are not so narrow as to remain limited to the disciples of the Prophet.

In another place the Command says: 'If they turn against you, but do not quarrel with or fight you, and are friendly towards you then it is against God's command to kill or try to enslave them.'

Dear sirs, you who are patiently listening to me, will it not be but just and fair to pay attention to these peaceful utterances of the Prophet which had been said in those days at times full of strife and tyranny and to those sayings that had been addressed to a small army facing a large one in order to encourage them. Would any leader or commander have done better than him?

Now take up those peaceful messages which are exemplified by the Prophet's own deeds. You will see that there is hardly any injury which was not inflicted on the Prophet but he forgave it, no such torture perpetrated upon him that he did not forgive. My brothers, if you want to know the real condition of any man you should see him just as he really lived, not through the glasses of superstition.

Each religion has some fault or other in it, the activities of all honest people have something or other wrong with it, misunderstood by heathens and stupid followers. When you want to judge any religion then take up the best and the most devoted follower. It will be unjust to take an ignoble and low man as an example. Then only shall we learn to love each other like brothers and stop regarding each other with contempt as savages do.

I am sorry that I have not been able to say anything about the two sects, Shia and Sunni, because of lack of time. I am sure you would have liked it, but I have not taken it up because it is not necessary.

Each religion has a philosophy behind its outward aspect. We might be finding a lack of this at present in Islam (and there is not much harm in that) but if we consider the time when the light of Islam first manifested itself, then we will not be able to find words to describe it properly.

Think for yourself, what the Prophet had said one thousand and three hundred years ago about the advantages of education: 'Acquire education. He who is educated develops purity in his nature, he who is educated prays to God and he who seeks knowledge performs worship (*ibadat*). The one who teaches, worships also. Education shows the right path, it is a true friend in solitude and exile, consoles us in forests. It leads us to development and gives sympathy in times of sorrow. Among friends it is like an ornament and among enemies a weapon.'[9]

The servant of Allah, when in danger, finds in education the best fruits of piety.

I feel overwhelmed when I read these sayings of the Prophet: 'The ink of a scholar is more precious than the blood of a martyr.' Dear brothers, what better glorification of education can there be if not this?

Hazrat Ali was the favourite son-in-law of the Prophet and about him the Prophet had said, 'Ali is like a door to the knowledge of Islam'. He is the one who first started to spread *Ilm-e-Ilahi.* One should read the speeches delivered by him about the necessity of education. Even at the time of battle he would read religious speeches on the battlefield itself.

I am quoting a few of the sentences of Hazrat Ali in praise of education:

> 'Education is the bright jewel that illuminates one's heart. Truth is its goal, Ilham is its guide; the intelligence accepts it. Man's words can never ever praise education properly.'

While the Muslims were busy with their duties, improving the condition of the country the disciples of Hazrat Ali were busy spreading the light of education. They carried the torch of knowledge wherever they went and as a result by the fourteenth century even children had the lamp of knowledge and science in their hands. Whenever they conquered a country they opened schools and colleges there. The famous universities of Baghdad, Cairo, Cordova, and Spain are examples of this.[10]

It is Muslims who had taught the people of England their forgotten alphabet. They had studied astronomy, translated numerous scientific texts of India, written books on chemistry and mathematics. A certain Pope who was an excellent scholar and mentor had learnt maths in Muslim school at Cordova. People called him a heathen and an imp of Satan. This shows what a darkness of ignorance clouded the Christians of that time and it was the followers of Islam who held up the torch of knowledge and wisdom.

Nor were they lagging behind in industry and invention. It was they who invented the microscope and measured the dimensions of this planet. They learnt maths from the Greeks and took music and agriculture to the farthest limits of development. They did not rest easy even then but discussed the philosophy of religion in fine detail and reached the mystery of Fana Fillah (Extinction of the self in

God). They taught that Allah is one entity and mankind is the same everywhere, there is no caste division. They explained all this in very fine language.

My Hindu brothers! If you think about these principles you will find them to be like the true Vedanta. Education had flourished for six centuries among the Muslims. If today my Muslim brothers translate these texts by their world-renowned ancestors and spread the lessons taught therein among people, I am sure they will be able to lift Islam philosophy to the highest position in the world. Everyone in the Islamic world, even little children, will be able to learn them (just as the Hindus have started to spread the teachings of the Vedanta these days). Think of how they have served their religion in order to show the world the true glory of the creation of Islam.

The Prophet, Jesus Christ, Moses, the Buddha—all dwell in the same place. They do not differentiate between one race and another. And we who are their disciples, their children, we should obtain the essence of their doctrine of universal love. They reach us with their love. The Prophet does come to his disciples till the latter has banished all harshness from his heart and has only love there.

Oh my Muslim brothers! The Prophet is as dear to us as to you. We have claims upon all the Prophets who have come in this world for the good of humanity. We love them, honour them, and bow down to them in homage. I pray to God who is the Allah of all of us—let Him give us the understanding that will stop us from quarrelling with each other in His name, whichever name we utter with our weak and childish lips. He is the only One and the God to be worshipped by all.[11]

(Published in Md. Akram Khan ed. *Al Islam*, Jyestha, Asarh 1322 and Āśvin 1323 in three issues)

Notes

1. According to Plato, poetry is the imitation of an imitation, i.e., imitation at the third remove. The present translation, being the translation of a translation of a translation, is therefore translation at the fourth remove. May God help us, because how much of Annie Besant is here, and how much of Begum Rokeya, He only knoweth. *Allah Mehrban* (added by the translators).

2. Surprisingly enough, even in these civilized times such long lasting family feuds can be seen in the Muslim families of Bengal. 'Hereditary enemy' is a phrase to be heard in Calcutta High Court. Oh, when will God have mercy on us!

3. I have some doubts as to whether the grandfather of the Prophet, Abdul Mutallib had meant to sacrifice his son Abdullah to a stone idol. If the revered scholars help resolve my doubts I will be very grateful. I have read inthe Bengali book *Amir Hamza* that Amir Hamza, the other son of Hazrat Abdul Mutallib said to his father:

'If you pay taxes to heathens
What is such a son as I am for?'

4. This is an exaggeration by Mrs Besant (Ed. *Al Islam*).

5. Are we the Muslims being described by Mrs Besant? Shame on us! We have dishonoured the name of Muslim. Are there not any convenient means to commit suicide in Bengal?

6. It is but recently that Muslim authors have started to write books and pamphlets about Islam. Before this, all the information about Islam was obtained from Christian missionary agencies. So Europe, ignorant Europe, used to shudder at the very name of Islam. What result even this recent effort has had can be seen from this speech itself. Lord Hadey, Khwaja Kamaluddin, Mr Ihaya-un-Nasr, Parkinson, and other Muslim writers have changed the attitude of European scholars. This can be found in *Islamic Review*. (Ed. *Al Islam*)

7. Here Mrs Besant has mixed up two incidents as one. This kind of mistake is excusable regarding a non-Muslim. (Ed. *Al Islam*)

8. Mrs Besant has not mentioned the story of 'the taziana of Akkas' and this, to my mind, leaves the topic of 'repayment' unfinished. The story runs thus:

One day, for some reason the Prophet had beaten a man named Akkas just once. Today that man turned up and demanded repayment of that blow. The Prophet got ready to be caned. His attendants and relatives got anxious because he could not have endured a caning (even if a just one) when he was so ill. They begged Akkas to desist or to cane them instead of him, many times instead of just once. He would not yield. They stood weeping and lamenting: 'Alas, alas, what is this cruel Akkas going to do! He will definitely kill the Prophet.' He however, remained calm and signed to Akkas to proceed. This man said, 'My lord, I had received the cane on my bare back.' At once the compassionate Prophet got ready by taking off his clothes.

Tell me, has anyone in the world been able to pay his debts like this? I think even the angels trembled to see him bare his back. Has any great man been able to show such nobility? Akkas had not come to cane him. Actually he had wanted to kiss the holy back of the Prophet. He got what he wanted; weeping and laments turned to songs of love and faith.

—The Authoress

9. It is true that good education will win over enemies. Probably that is the reason why misogynists object to educating women, because that will mean giving them weapons! I have heard that the famous zamindar of Karatiya, Marhuma Jamabardannisa Khanum had said, 'Men wield the pen now, give it but once to women'. They say 'the pen is mightier than the sword'.

—The Authoress

10. Our kind lords and masters, the British, claim that it was because they who kindly invaded and defeated us that barbarians like us have got the light of education and we too bow down and acknowledge—this is a great kindness shown to us by the westerners. But here Mrs Besant is saying that it is Muslims who were the mentors of Europe in matters of education.

11. We do not disagree with these opinions. Mrs Annie Besant is a well-known propagator and teacher of Theosophy. She has discussed Islam from

the viewpoint of her own education and religion, so it is not possible that we would agree with all that she says. Even now the true nature of Islam remains largely unexpressed. If we can present the true nature properly to the world then all just seekers of truth will give themselves to it.

All these religious leaders sent by Allah for the good of mankind are to be respected and honoured by Muslims. No one can be a Muslim unless he believes in them. There were many more prophets besides the ones named in our scriptures, whose names had not been told to the Prophet. Moreover, God's Messengers have come to every country, to every race to give people heavenly messages. All this is clearly understood from sentences in the Koran. Keeping this thing in mind we fully agree with Mrs Besant.

—Ed. *Al Islam*

The Solar System

1

Mr Gauhar Ali is sitting in a double-storied house at Kurseong, surrounded by his wife and daughters. It can be easily inferred from the way in which his nine daughters are gathered together all around him that the family is a happy and prosperous one. The youngest daughter Masuma is in the lap of the eldest Kauser and the others are sitting on little stools all around the parents. Lucky is Mr Ali, shining like the moon surrounded by stars.

Kauser is the favourite of her grandfather. It is he who has given her this name which means heavenly lake, like 'Mandakini'.[1]

The room they are sitting in his half-Muslim and half-European in its furnishing and the two styles suit it quite well. A tray with teatime refreshments are waiting on a teapoy.

Mr Ali has a book in his hands which he is reading aloud and explaining to everybody. The topic under discussion is the air—its coolness and its heat; its lightness and its heaviness; how many kinds of gases are there in it; how the air gradually changes into vapour, cloud, water, and snow, etc. The audience is very attentive and the seventh daughter Suraiya is the only one trying the patience of her father by asking all sorts of questions. At times she snatches the book away from her father to look at the pictures. The father is not at all irritated. Instead he feels amused.

The mistress, Nur Jehan, looks at the door and remains 'Brother has not come yet. The tea is getting cold.'

GAUHAR ALI (GA): 'Maybe your brother is playing with the Lepchas on the street.'

RABIYA (RAB): 'We left him after passing the second bench, and couldn't he cross this bit of the road even till now?'

SURAIYA (SUR): 'My my, you call it "a little bit"! I couldn't walk so far and the ayah took me up.'

RAB: '"My my" to you! I can easily run from here to there in one stretch.'

Mr Ali joined his daughters and said, 'All right. Do it first and brag afterwards. You should not say "I can do this" before you have done it.'

KAUSER (KAU): 'Dad, wouldn't it be about two miles from here to the second bench?'

GA: 'A bit more. Anyway, since Rabbu has said it she will have run there in just one stretch.'

AKHTAR (AKH): 'How will you know whether she has run there in one stretch or has stopped on the way to rest?'

GA (*Wide-eyed*): 'How shall I know? Let Rabbu go as far as she can. Then when she feels tired let her come back from there and say she has failed. She herself will say how far she had reached. Is my daughter going to tell a lie?'

RAB (Enthusiastically): 'No, Dad, I never tell lies and I'm not going to.'

AKH: 'I know well enough that you don't tell lies. But you might have told just a little lie to get appreciation.'

RAB (Proudly): 'Better die than tell a lie.'

GA: 'That's right. I'll feel really hurt if any of you tell lies. I do hope you all will never hurt me this way.'

Some of the girls cried out together 'we won't tell', 'We won't hurt' and such things, in a confused murmur.

Suddenly there was the sound of footsteps on the stairs. All the girls except Kauser and Masuma ran away saying, 'Uncle's come!'

Gauhar caught Nayeema and asked, 'Why are you running away darling?'

NAYEEMA (NAY): 'No … I … no … uncle …' (i.e., I won't stay, uncle will scold)

Jafar Ali entered the room. Seeing the girl running away, he said, smiling to Mr Ali, 'What disturbed the solar system?'[2]

GA: 'Because you are a comet.'

Nur Jehan started making tea for her brother and told Mr Ali, 'Now move a little, let my brother sit near the fireplace.'

JAFAR ALI (JA): 'No, I won't sit there. I'm so tired that I'm sweating all over. I'm all right here.'

Kauser put the tray of snacks in front of Jafar and wiped his brow with her dupatta. He drank one cup and giving the cup to his sister said, 'Nuru, another cuppa'.

GA: 'You made a mistake. He had to come here to get another cup and this is not right. You should have gone to him to give it.'

Nur Jehan smiled a little with bowed head. Kauser felt like laughing out loud so she left the room and sent Badr to help her mother.

JA: 'Now look, I can't stand your "English". Are you the only one who has ever gone to England?'

GA: 'Well, so have you. I feel amused to hear you scolding and so I act more British than the British. Anyway, why are you so late? Gossiping with the tribals?'

JA: 'How can I gossip with them when I don't know their language? They go on saying "*kanchhujanehh*" all the time.'

Badr wanted to show off her knowledge of the tribals' tongue. '*Janechhu*' means to go.

NUR JEHAN (NJ): 'Darling, there's no need to talk with them. You better go to Kauser.'

GA: 'Then why so late?'

JA: 'I was sitting on the bench to get some rest. You can see the whole of Kurseong from there … markets, etc.'

NJ: 'Yes indeed, the world seems small when you sit there.'

GA: 'The day they walked up to Chimney Side[3] and came down—how happy they were! Probably the Japanese were not so glad to conquer Port Arthur and the Baltic Fleet.'

NJ: 'How can the Japs be so glad? They haven't yet finished their work while we have reached our goal after walking twelve miles!'

JA: 'Ascending on a balloon has not yet been done by women.'

GA: 'Just you wait. It won't be long before that too happens.'

JA: 'When are you going to England with family?'

GA: 'As and when the opportunity comes.'

JA: 'Yes, each of your daughters will shine like a jewel after studying at Oxford. Not for nothing do I call your family a solar system. Your daughters are the planets and you are the sun. They even have the names of stars—Mushtari, Zohra, Suraiya.[4] Why have you left out Mars, Mercury, Saturn, and such?'

NJ: 'Now why do you laugh at the girls' names when quarrelling? Besides we have not kept the names ourselves, the head of the family has done so. He will give whatever names he likes to his own granddaughters. What right do we have to say anything about it?

Gauhar, to tease Jafar even more, said, 'Why just England, I want to go to America as well. Kauser wants to see the Niagara.'

JA: 'The wish of yours won't be fulfilled; you won't be able to show Kauser the Niagara now.'

GA: 'Why not?'

JA: 'She'll be out of your reach next year.'

GA: 'So what, we'll go with our son-in-law.'

JA: 'That is, if your son-in-law is a fool like you.'

GA: 'Do you know him better than I?'

JA: 'The little I know of him makes me hope that he is not quite as "forward" as you.'

GA: 'I too hope that he isn't so "backward" as you are. He will definitely show Kauser the Niagara.'

2

Badr pulled at Akhtar: 'Mummy and Daddy are quarrelling. Let's go and listen.'

AKH: 'If we go now instead of shouting Mummy will start firing at us.'

BADR (BA): 'We won't show ourselves. We'll hide in the next room.'

KAU: 'Shame Baddu! You shouldn't spy. Be careful.'

BA: 'Then what to do about the few words I've heard?'

KAU: 'What's done is done. Don't do it again.'

AKH: 'Masuma's asleep. Go Nayimu, you too go to bed.'

NAY: 'I won'th, I won'th.'[5]

AKH: 'Then I won't let you sit in my lap.'

KAU: 'Come, let's go and study. Dear Mushtari, just go and see if there's a fire in the fireplace in our schoolroom.'

ZOHRA (ZOH): 'We'll get a lot of holidays when we are at Dowhill school, won't we?'

AKH: 'First you've to get there, and then only get holidays.'

BA: 'Go wash your face at Pagla Jhora.'[6]

RAB: 'Why, Appa, why can't we go to school? The three of you are grown up and you'll go. Why won't we?'

KAU: 'I wonder if uncle will let us go.'

RAB: 'Uncle isn't nice. I feel frightened when I look at his eyes. He has come now just to prevent our going to school.'

SUN: 'I'll definitely go.'

ZOH: 'Yes, all by yourself. You're the pet of the family.'

BA: 'Rabbu, go wash yourself in the cool waters of Pagla Jhora. The three of us will get admitted into the technical school.'

RAB: 'Won't uncle prevent it?'

KAU: 'He had tried to, now he has agreed.'

ZOH: 'Appa, is there only a Nun there, no Nana?'

BA: 'No, there's no Nana there, there's a horde of Nanis.'

[Here 'Nana' is the masculine counterpart of 'Nun'. Mischievous girls call the nuns of St. Helen's Technical School as 'Nani'. They can be excused anything. This school teaches girls cooking, needlework, knitting, and such fancy works.]

Zohra caught Akhtar lovingly by the hand and said, 'Appa, knit a nice shawl for my doll, will you?'

Suraiya put her arms around Akhtar's neck and said, 'Make lots of sweets, won't you?'

RAB: 'Yes, and then you'll eat lots of sweets.' [They laugh]

Mushtari came and said the schoolroom was ready, so all of them went there. Kauser took the seat of the teacher and addressing everybody, gravely said, 'Which of you didn't understand what Dad told us about the air? Tell me and I'll explain.'

MUSHTARI (MUSH): 'Dad talked about the air. He didn't say anything about the rainbow. I'll ask him about it tomorrow.'

ZOH: 'I'll tell him to bring me one.'

SUR: 'I too want a rainbow.'

The elder sisters laughed. Mushtari said, 'You stupid, can one catch a rainbow?'

RAB: 'It's true you can't catch a rainbow. But you can catch air and fill a tube with it and examine it and it is not impossible to get a rainbow.'

KAU: 'This logic is unanswerable.' (All laugh)

RAB: 'Why, what's wrong about what I said?'

AKH: 'No, Rabbu, what you said is not so bad. The human voice can be and has been caught in machines, like the telephone, gramophone, phonograph, etc. It should not be so difficult to catch a rainbow.'

Again everyone laughed.

KAU: 'Be quiet. If Mummy hears she will say, "And this is how you study, do you?"'

MUSH (Controlling herself with difficulty): 'But Dad says nothing when we laugh.'

RAB: 'No, instead he too laughs.'

BA: 'And have you heard, uncle beats cousin Javed and cousin Huran Bubu.'

ZOH: 'Is that true? Then I'll never go to his place. If he beats his own children then he'll beat us even more.'

SUR: 'But Dad never beats us.'

RAB: 'Dad's good and so is Mummy, but not Uncle.'

BA: 'You wait, I'll tell Uncle.'

AKH: 'Has Rabbu ever been afraid to tell him anything?'

KAU: 'Enough, enough. Now be quiet.'

BA: 'Appa, why don't you ask us if we understood those things about air?'

KAU: 'Tomorrow I'll look at clouds and make you look too and ask questions. You ask me now and try to understand.'

RAB: 'Tomorrow I'll enjoy myself by putting potassium in water.'

MUSH: 'What will you enjoy by doing that?'

BA: 'Don't you remember? There will be a fire the minute it's put into water.'

MUSH: 'Yes, I remember now. I'll play with hot water and sodium.'

NAY (Rubbing her eyes): 'And I? What'll I play with?'

AKH (Smiling): 'No need to play now. Come to bed.'

RAB: 'Mushtari, my fire will be better than yours.'

MUSH: 'Why? Will the fire be brighter and more yellow if you put sodium in water?'

KAU: 'You know nothing but how to fight. This Rabbu is to blame, she is the one who starts it.'

RAB: 'Forgive and forget. Now let me say something useful. The snow on Kanchenjunga, was that also air?'

KAU: 'Yes, and can turn into vapour if it gets enough hot.'

RAB: 'Then why doesn't it melt in the sun?'

KAU: 'Of course it does. The snow becomes soft in heat and starts flowing. It's called a glacier. Dad calls it "snow-river".'

RAB: 'How nice. A river of snow must be very lovely. Let's go one day and see it.'

BA: 'Is Kanchenjunga very near?'

RAB: 'Even if it is not we are not afraid of walking. We had climbed Chimney Side the other day. That's quite far off. It isn't that easy to climb up 5–6 miles and then come down. And just the other day we went down where Dowhill and Eagle's Crag join.'

BA: 'Don't you remember how tired you were to reach that point?'

KAU: 'Rabbu had said "I can't walk any more. Leave me here. If a bear eats me then let it." '

RAB: 'If we didn't get the *dandi*[7] on time then we could not have come.'

KAU: 'Dad had arranged for the dandi. He knew Baddu's and Rabbu's heroism will show itself when we're halfway there.'

BA: But I don't boast like Rabbu that I can walk to the Kanchenjunga, or run and pass the second bench at one stretch. By the way, where did I keep the flower I brought from the forest at the joining point of Eagle's Crag? I've forgotten totally.'

KAU: 'They must have walked back to the forest.'

BA: 'That means you have kept them safely. No worry for me.'

KAU: 'What are your flowers like? Can you find them out from among those I gathered?'

BA: 'Yes I can—they are like the *bokul*.[8] They look and smell like bokul but are yellow.'

RAB: 'And the pink-and-purple veil we've seen on Kanchenjunga—where does it come from?'

KAU: 'The vapour rising when the sun has heated the ice-floods like a veil of clouds over the peak …'

AKH: 'Why, I thought the veils come from Benaras!'

Suraiya came to Kauser and said, 'Elder Appa, won't you give me a rainbow?' Kauser kissed her and said, 'Tomorrow, I'll give you a rainbow tomorrow'.

BA: 'What's that? How will you catch a rainbow?'

KAU: 'Don't you know that the prisms in the chandelier give off rainbows?'

BA: 'Oh, ho. How easy to catch a rainbow!'

AKH: 'Our Elder Appa is a Wishing Tree. Is there anything she can't give?'

KAU: 'Not a Wishing Tree. Call it a Wishing Creeper.'

3

It was teatime and Nur Jehan was waiting for Gauhar and Jafar at the tea table. Mushtari caught her veil and asked, 'Why aren't we going for a walk today?'

NJ: 'Your uncle had gone to see the Victoria School this morning. He's going to take some rest now. How can we go out and leave him alone?'

ZOH: 'Why, will he be scared? All right, you stay, we'll go with Dad.'

The minute Gauhar entered Mushtari and Zohra appealed to him and he said, 'All right, let's go, but not very far. Just to Eagle's Crag and back.'

ZOH: 'No Dad, not Eagle's Crag. There are a lot of leeches there.'

MUSH: 'Let's not go to that place of leeches.'

GA: 'You are afraid of leeches?' (hearing Jafar's steps) 'All right, be quiet. We'll take your uncle with us. He will walk in front and we'll follow him.'

ZOH (Clapping in joy): 'That'll be nice. Whatever leeches there are, will catch him first.'

MUSH: 'Hush, Uncle's there.'

Meantime Jafar has come and joined the tea table.

GA: 'Won't you come walking today?'

JA: 'No, my legs hurt.'

GA: 'But if you don't walk today then tomorrow you'll start limping. Come to Eagle's Crag, at least.'

JA: 'I won't be able to wear boots.'

GA: 'Why wear boots, wear your slippers. It isn't a stony track; you'll be walking on grass.'

RAB (Aside): 'It'll be easier for the leeches to catch him if he wears slippers'

(They all laugh).

JA (To the girls): 'Shame, why do you laugh? You all have no manners. Why can't you give them a scolding, Nuru?'

NJ: 'If you just scold them without telling them the reason they won't obey.'

GA: 'Why should they obey without any fault or any reason? What's the harm in laughing?'

JA: 'There you are, Gauhar, you've spoiled them too much.'

GA: 'All right, so you're coming?'

JA: 'No. Is the road slippery? Does one go up or down?'

GA: 'It'll naturally be a bit sloping. Where'll you get plains here?'

JA: 'Then I won't go. I don't want to roll about, huge as I am.'

GA: 'What a shame! You don't like a road of stone, don't want to roll in a sloping road, this is just womanishness.'[9]

NJ: 'I object to the word 'womanishness'. Why don't you say 'timid', 'cowardly', etc.?'

JA: 'Give a man an inch and he takes an ell. If a woman is educated she protests against them and criticizes them. Are you going to teach Gauhar how to speak?'

GA: 'If women object to our unreasonable words and take part in our conversation then so much the better.'

JA: 'You're a fool. I supported you and scolded Nuru and here you are going against me.'

GA: 'It's no use supporting the strong. It's natural that you'll support your sister.'

NJ: 'Why should you support me? Of what good am I to him? Can I advise him about his cases at the court? Can I help him by sending five or six armed men at the time when fighting breaks out in his lands?'

Gauhar smiled. Jafar changed the subject: 'Really, Nuru, won't you come with me? I had thought you'd not be able to come next year as you'll be busy with Kauser's marriage. But why not come now? Are you the one who has taught her this?'

The girls left for the fear of bursting into laughter.

GA: 'For god's sake! I've not taught her anything. Why, she used to go regularly with you every year to her father as if on a pilgrimage. As to why she doesn't want to go this year, ask her yourself.'

JA: 'Tell me, Nuru, why won't you come?'

NJ: 'I'm trying to get Rabbu and the others admitted to Dowhill School.'

Jafar started with surprise the minute he heard the word 'school'—'What's that? Getting girls admitted in a school? Muslims have as yet not been forgotten in India, the Muslim society has not been destroyed yet. Are girls going to study in a school now? And this curse is to be visited on my nieces? Ours is to be the family subjected to the first shameful downfall?'

GA: 'You've started moaning and groaning even before you have heard anything. There are only girls in this school. There are seven or eight lady teachers. Men are not allowed in. What's the harm in sending the girls there?'

NJ: 'There are no men in that school. Ayahs and maid do all the work. Only the cook and the kitchen-servants are men, and there is no contact between the school and the kitchen. Two or three servants bring the food from the kitchen. I've had a talk with the headmistress that I'll supply a few maids to carry the food and she'll send those men off. This teacher is a very lady-like person. She gives due honour to the purdah custom. I inspected the whole school. There are no men servants anywhere.'

JA: 'Yes, you talk on and I listen. And what about the boys' school next door? Boys and girls will play together during the break.'

GA: 'There's fully a mile's distance between the two schools. How can they play together then?'

JA: 'If your eyes are all right then even from the station you can see that the tops of both the schools are side by side.'

Nur Jehan could not contain her laughter any longer. Gauhar laughed and said, 'Hats off to your investigations. Did you come to know this on looking over Victoria School today?'

JA: 'I didn't enter the school.'

GA (Surprised): 'Then where were you for three hours today?'

JA: 'I sat for some time on the third bench. Then I reached the boundary of the school and found the road to be really endless. I asked one of the people on the road who said there were fifteen more turns before you reach the school (the road is not straight, so there are fifteen more turns). So I thought this road is not going to end today and so I came back.'

Nur Jehan smiled and Gauhar said, 'So the mullah can reach only up to the mosque. You've come back even before reaching the gates, you haven't even seen Victorial School and yet you are expressing your opinions on Dowhill School. Do you even know the place where this girls' school is? It is only Victoria School which has got two spires. Do you think it is an old and ordinary village school? It's a huge mansion, standing in its own extensive gardens. Why, the games field itself is five *bigha*s in extent.'

NJ: 'And Dowhill School is even bigger than that. I saw fifty beds in one of the rooms and there is a space of two feet between each. Now guess how big the hall is.'

JA: 'Is it easy or even possible to build so big a hall in this mountainous region?'

NJ: 'It may not be easy but it is possible. Haven't big mansions been built? I was dazzled by a tennis court. We cannot easily imagine how many stones have been broken in order to make such a big level space. Not only have stones had to be broken, many places have had to be filled up also. It can't be that such a big place didn't have any holes and deep crevices. You can see on the one hand the mountains of the Great Artist and on the other the manifestation of the intelligence He has given to man. How wonderful the coming together of these two is!'

GA: 'Dear brother, stay here for a few days and you too will turn into a poet. If the flower of poetry can blossom in the deserted heart of a woman who has no knowledge of poetry—'

JA: 'I'm not any less prosaic than Nuru. Both of us were famous for being prosaic.'

GA: 'But here the climate is such that—

> The dumb can speak when he sees it
> And the stupid talk in rhymes'

JA: 'But what is the good of it? Writing poetry is like a disease of the brain. No one wants our ladies to wander about in the mountains and become poets.'

GA: 'Then what does one want?'

JA: 'What one wants is this: they should do their housework well, cook and feed others, and practice namaaz and observe *roza* regularly.'

GA: 'Doing namaaz for whom?'

JA (Very angry): 'For whom? For Allah, who else?'

GA: 'All right, you're right. You know the Persian proverb—"Remember the artist while looking at the painting". And whom did she praise just now as the Great Artist?'

JA: 'The Great Artist is God, of course.'

GA: 'Then what is the conflict between religion and poetry. The more you see of God's creation, the more is the love and devotion you have for Him. How will you ever come to know God unless you study the world with the senses you have? When you stand on a mountaintop your heart fills with love and faith. Your heart echoes to the song, unknown to yourself.'

The Poet unique paints a picture unique
And hides Himself for ever

JA: 'I don't understand Bengali all that well.'

GA: 'Then say—*Jami, chaman, gul*.'[10]

JA (Stopping him): 'Let your poetry have some rest now. So the girls will go to school?'

GA: 'Of course Kauser, Akhtar, and Baddu are already past the age for schools and I feel very bad about it.'

JA: 'Then why not admit Nur Jehan too?'

GA: 'I've no objection. She too says she would like being a mutton dressed as a lamb.'

JA (To his sister): 'You could easily do it. Do you too want to make them Christians?'

NJ: 'Why should they become Christians? I can say with pride—my girls will never go astray. They are pure gold, not to be destroyed by water or fire.'

GA: 'I too say with pride: your wife's faith (*iman*) might tremble, but my wife's is unshakeable.'

JA: 'How does my wife's faith tremble?'

GA: 'Because she does not know anything about her religion. She prays like a parrot, without understanding the words. If you don't shut her up in a golden cage and let her meet a missionary Englishwoman she will at once think, "How noble Christianity is!" So be careful. Shut her up in an iron chest if you can.'

JA: 'And does Nuru know the meaning of the words of namaaz?'

GA: 'You can test her. Do you think that even in 20 years I haven't been able to make my better half a shadow-like companion for me?'

JA: 'See then, it does not matter whether she has studied in a school or not. Then why spoil the girls?'

GA: 'Our forefathers never travelled by train or sent a telegram, and did that matter to them? Then why do we send telegrams and travel by train?'

JA: 'We need all those things.'

GA: 'Whatever we ourselves need, our womenfolk need too. They are the ones who supply what we need. The wives of peasants don't know gold-thread embroidery or how to make pickles because peasants don't need these things. European women don't know how to prepare *paan* because their men don't need it. Conversely our women can't thresh or winnow paddy because we don't need it. As we are learning to eat cutlets and puddings our wives are learning to cook them. Do they lead life different from ours then? They need school and college education too, just as we do. I'm sure you'll grant that my family life is better than yours. Your wife can never understand your joys and sorrows.'

JA: 'Never mind that. She never says a word against my opinion. If I say during the day that it's night she'll say, "Yes, what a lovely moon!", and if I say a new-moon night is day she'll say, "What a terrible sun there is!"'

GA: 'How nice!'

All laugh.

JA: 'What else? If the husband and the wife don't agree then life becomes a Russo-Japanese war.'

GA: 'But this is no agreement of husband and wife. What you said expresses only your views, we never know what she herself thinks. She never expresses her own opinion. When you visit a zoo next time, say something in front of the animals and when they keep silent or shake their heads take that for agreeing with you.'

JA: 'Now let me say something important. Kauser is getting married next year and you all are gallivanting about with her in the mountains. What will the boy's party say if they heard about this?'

NJ: 'We know that they don't object.'

GA: 'The boy works in Simla. Besides, a wife will go with her husband and a daughter with father, what do other people have to say about this?'

JA: 'All right, all right. May God bless you. You have got the kind of groom you want. This means you won't give Akhtar in marriage to the boy of my choice?'

GA: 'No, she will be married to the future brother-in-law of Kauser.'

JA: 'Then why not marry off both of them together?'

GA: 'That would have been the best, but that boy is in England at present.'

4

A few people were sitting by the waterfall in a place called Tung in the foothills of the Himalayas. The youngest girl of the group said, 'Akhtar-Appa, see, this waterfall has come here from some place and is flowing away from here to some other place. Can you tell me where it has gone at the end?'

AKH: 'No Rabbu, I don't know where it has gone but it has come from inside that mountain.'

RAB: 'But how can just a stream of water break the stones of the mountain and come out? Is that possible?'

KAU: 'Not only has this fountain broken stones apart, but many huge stones have been worn into sands by rolling at its feet.'

Rabbu could not quite understand how a big stone could turn into sand. She asked her father, 'Is it really so, Dad?'

Before Gauhar could say anything Jafar said, 'Yes, it's true. Just as you all play in your father's lap in love and safety so do these fountains dance in the lap of their mountain-father. The father is immoveable. The Himalaya is patient like Gauhar. Also, the huge Ganges you see from the steamer was born from one such little fountain.'

RAB (With great joy): 'Uncle, please tell us which of these fountains is its source.'

JA: 'The source of the Ganges is not to be found here.'

KAU: 'What are you thinking of, Akhtar?'

AKH: 'I'm thinking how these thin streams are cutting deep chasms in the mountain and flowing on, singing the praise of the Creator. They flow on forever—no pause, no rest, no idleness, no negligence.'

RAB: 'Akhtar-didi, I too have discovered the source of a river.'

AKH: 'Oh yes?'

KAU: 'Tell us, what have you discovered?'

RAB: 'The Pagla Jhora of Kurseong is the source of river Pagla.'

AKH: 'Tchah! You fool!'

BA: 'But Rabbu's not so very wrong either. After all the Tista river is near Darjeeling.'

KAU: 'Really, your researches! Baddu's become quite a scholar.'

BA: 'All right, if the research is wrong then let it be. I'll tell you something amusing. Now see how the railway track has snaked across the mountain with the cliff on one side and smaller hills on the other, looking like waves. How if we call it "mountain-wave"?'

KAU: 'That will be nice. You remember the waves in the sea, don't you?'

BA: 'No didi, I don't.'

RAB: 'Uncle, may I go and touch the water of the fountain?'

JA: 'How will you go? It's not easy to climb down.'

RAB: 'If you just allow me I'll manage somehow. Baddu-Appa, will you come?'

BA: 'No, you go by yourself.'

Jafar permitted her and Rabbu started. It was a slow and difficult process and finally she was stopped short by a huge boulder. She would not be able to get to the water unless she crossed it. Kauser warned her from above, 'Be careful, don't wet your clothes'. Almost crawling, Rabbu managed, very carefully, to go past it. Then she dipped her fingers in the cool water and started playing with it.

Baddu felt a little envious. Standing by the railing she called out, 'Why Rabbu you look as if you've reached Paradise, so happy you are. Stay there, we are going.'

Nur Jehan too called, 'Come, darling, it's getting late'. They started on their way. They were all going to walk to Kurseong from Tung. Two or three tribals drew away to one side to let them pass. Gauhar said to Jafar, 'See their chivalry?'

JA: 'It's their habit. Often even women draw away to the side, leaving me to take the good part of the road.'

NJ: 'That's because they think people from "lower down" to be weak.'

JA: 'I don't own myself to be weak before a woman.'

GA: 'What's the harm in acknowledging one's weakness to one who is strong?'

JA: 'At any rate I won't allow women to be physically stronger.'

GA: 'But why not? Give the devil his due.'[11]

JA: 'But I can't give women their due.'

GA: 'Then try to race a tribal woman along a shortcut.'

JA: 'A shortcut? But people can't walk there.'

NJ: 'Then why do you feel ashamed to own your weakness to those who easily climb up and down such paths with a two-maund load on their back?'

[It is necessary here to describe these shortcuts in the mountain. They are steep mountain paths on steep hillsides, very difficult to negotiate—here a boulder, there a pit, and there a slope where you cannot rest your feet upon. The government has cut sloping but easy roads for men, horses, and carriages which are known as 'government roads' in the local language. But these are very meandering and roundabout ones, so the local Gurkhas and Bhutiyas follow the shortcuts. Where a shortcut takes five minutes the roads will take twenty to twenty-five minutes, making you take many turns.]

Nur Jehan said again, 'The chivalry of these tribals is really praiseworthy'.

GA: 'We should take lessons in politeness from them. In vain do we boast of being civilized and polished.'

NJ: 'Have you noticed another thing? They don't beg, whether man or woman.'

JA: 'That's because they don't need to.'

GA: 'That in itself is worthy of praise.'

Conversing thus, they did not feel tired while walking. When they reached Kurseong station Kauser asked, 'Rabbu, are you feeling tired?'

RAB: 'No, not at all.'

JA: 'You know, we'll have to walk one more mile.'

Gradually they reached a bench. Some Gurkhas were sitting on it. They respectfully left the seat on seeing them. Nur Jehan said, 'Let's sit down for some time'.

JA: 'No, let's go, it isn't very far now.'

BA: 'Oh, Uncle, let's sit. See how the sky is burning.'

JA: 'Look westward and it's all burning. It's as if there's fire everywhere.'

AKH: 'See, see, Appa, even the Kanchenjunga is on fire!'

JA: 'What a glorious sight! You can see two or three peaks of the Kanchenjunga from here. It's become really golden in the light of the setting sun. It looks as if the sun is going to hide in the west and the soft clouds are running after it. I never noticed the beauty of dusk. The smaller peaks are getting golden in the light of the setting sun and the light breeze is playing hide and seek with them by making the clouds sail near them.'

GA: 'Why, brother mine! And it is you who say that poetry is a disease of the brain!'

JA: 'You yourself said that the air here carries the disease. The air in East Bengal carries malaria and that of the Himalayas carries poetry.'

GA: 'Not just poetry but renunciation too, and also yoga. Sit down here and see the games the Creator plays and you'll get all that you get from the evening namaaz. One understands one's own insignificance here.'

NJ: 'To be frank our usual prayers do not have much intensity of emotion and devotion.'

GA: 'And we are impelled by social customs to deprive our womenfolk of worship like this, depriving them of the sight of the glory of God's creation—how shall we answer to the Creator for this? It is the eye's function to see and we keep them blind—shame on our civilization! My wife had not seen the light of the dawn and sunrise before she came here.'

JA: 'Maybe I too hadn't, but I don't moan and groan for that.'

GA: 'But you could have seen it if you had gone out to the meadows. You were not bound down. Also remember that it is part of religion to impart knowledge.'

JA: 'People become atheists if they acquire knowledge and so it is necessary to keep ladies at a far remove from it.'

GA: 'So the curse falls on the ladies. This is a great mistake. There is no conflict between religion and knowledge. Instead knowledge is an important part of religion.'

The conversation went on, covering many subjects, nor were the girls silent. Akhtari murmured, 'See, Appa, how lovely the tea-gardens on the hillsides are looking bathed in golden sunshine. They are covering their shining bodies with smoky veils of vapour.'

KAU: 'Right, right, sis. I too was thinking the same. How glorious God is! We bow down to such artistry.'

BA: 'Let's go home now.'

AKH: 'Why in such a hurry to go, didi?'

BA: 'What more is there to see? See, the tea-gardens are feeling cold as dusk is deepening and are covering themselves with blankets. We can't see anything anymore.'

KAU: 'I don't know if the tea-gardens are feeling cold or not, but Baddu definitely is. She has forgotten to bring a shawl.'

They started for home.

5

It is evening and Gauhar Ali is sitting in his daughters' classroom and teaching them. After the lessons are over he sits and talks to them for half an hour. He tells them about history or geography in a conversational manner. Today they are discussing the solar system.

MUSH: 'Now Dad, why does Uncle call us a solar system. Do we also wander in the sky?'

GA: 'He does so in sarcasm. But we can take it positively.'

KAU: 'Don't you know you can sometimes find a diamond in a dustbin?'

GA: 'Yes, let's try to get something valuable from that dustbin of sarcasm. Will you try, Kauser darling?'

KAU: 'You try, please, Dad.'

GA: 'I've told you that each planet orbits the sun in an orderly manner. It's the planet's duty to go around the sun and it is the sun's duty to give them light, to keep them attached by gravity and at the same time make them rotate on their axes. Everyone in this universe is doing his duty. If there is a flaw, chaos results.

'Now suppose each family is a solar system and the members of the family are each like a planet—it's the duty of the planets to travel along the path decreed by the householder according to his position and ability. The householder's duty is to attach everyone with the strong chain of love, to look after their welfare. If because of poverty there is lack of food then he should feed the children first, then his dependants and lastly eat himself. If anyone in the family is negligent in doing his duty then disorder will come and the family will suffer many evils.

'If a planet leaves its orbital path and goes away, then, free of the sun's pull, it might knock against another planet and break into a hundred pieces and endanger other planet too. Each will have to be in its own orbit and keep to it dutifully.'

At this time Jafar came in and said, 'Salaam! Now you've come to the right path. That is exactly what I say—there will be anarchy and chaos if one leaves the limits set for him. The solar system of society is fixed. There are certain limits for women and they should not cross them.'

GA: 'Please forgive me. First let me say my say. Do sit down.'

AKH (Aside to Kauser): 'Uncle doesn't even know how to talk. He makes society the "solar system" and women the planets.'

KAU: 'There you are! If society is the solar system then how does it have the power to control the orbit of the planets? That is done by God, Himself. Well, let's listen to them now.'

As Jafar sat down so did the girls. They had all got up respectfully on seeing him. Gauhar went on to say, 'It's not that disorder and anarchy comes when women leave their orbits. It can happen when men do so as well'.

JA: 'But there are no limits set to men, how can they leave their orbits?'

GA: 'No, men too can't be self-willed. They too have their duties. Can you go away anywhere leaving your family unprotected?'

JA: 'No, I can't.'

GA: 'Then how can you say your path has no limitations?'

JA: 'Even then I've a lot of freedom.'

GA: 'No one has the power to neglect his duties.'

MUSH: 'Dad, all of us do our duty, but Nayeema and Masuma don't do anything.'

RAB: 'They are too small for it.'

GA: 'Oh yes, they too have their duties. Nayeema's is to eat, sleep, and play in a systematic manner. Masuma's is to eat, sleep, laugh, and learn to run.'

RAB: 'Oh, what duties! If they don't do them how is disorder going to strike us?'

KAU: 'They've not yet learnt to be naughty like you. So they do their duties properly. If Masuma does not laugh or Nayeema does not eat then we'll know that they're ill. We'll have to get busy looking after them.'

GA: 'And if we're busy looking after them won't that introduce disorder in our own daily routine?'

RAB: 'Yes, I understand now.'

GA: 'There's another thing you should pay attention to. I said that the planets go around the sun along their orbits. There is this similarity among them—that each of them goes around the sun. But that doesn't mean that they do everything at the same time. (Looking at Jafar) They have their "personal" freedom. When Jafar says that the women-planets and the society-solar systems have no personal freedom he is making a mistake.'

JA: 'It's no mistake, it's the right thing. Women shouldn't be given any freedom. You've probably learnt these notions about freedom from the tracts on Indian Reform published by the Christian Tract Society of Madras. You take all that these missionaries tell us as gospel truth.'

GA: 'I've not read a single one of those tracts. Why should I go to the Christians to learn anything? Hasn't God given me any brains for myself? Moreover, I'm now here at Kurseong so you go and search in my house. If you can find a single one of those tracts of Christian Tract Society then I'll give you a thousand rupees.'

JA: 'Bet of a Rs 1000?'

GA: Yes, I bet you a thousand crisp new notes. If you don't get any of these tracts then you'll give me one thousand rupees.

JA: 'No, let it be like this—you pay, win or loss. Ha haha!'

GA: 'There—your heroism ends there.'

At this time Nur Jehan came and sat down beside Kauser.

BA: 'Dad, what is the personal freedom of planets like?'

GA: 'Yes. For example Mercury takes about three months to go round the Sun, Venus takes three months, Jupiter twelve years and Saturn thirty years. This is the individual difference or "freedom" they have. No one can command Saturn "You must orbit the sun in three months like Mercury". There are many other differences which you won't be able to understand now.'

KAU: 'Besides it is difficult to tell all this in so short a time.'

GA: 'Yes, it isn't possible. Just like that there are similarities and differences between the members of the family.'

JA: 'For example my eyes are similar to those of Gauhar's and our opinions are dissimilar.'

[Everyone laughs.]

GA: 'If we look at plants then there also we find similarities and dissimilarities side by side. Baddu, just the other day I showed you the similarities in the general form of different kinds of ferns and fine differences in the leaves, remember?'

BA: 'Yes, I could not find two leaves that looked the same.'

GA: 'There you are. Brother Jafar thinks that no one in the world should speak except him—especially not women. No one save he should study in a school etc., etc. This is not nature's law.'

JA: 'Do I ever stop people from talking?'

GA: 'No, that you don't, but the way you speak doesn't allow anyone else to get a word in. Your sister has been trying for three days to tell you about the girls going to attend school but you never heard her patiently. The way you interrupt the ladies to show your own eloquence is not nice in a man who has been to England.'

JA: 'If I talk a lot, why don't you talk too?'

GA: 'I can't talk so much. I'll give two hundred rupees to anyone who can defeat you in talking.'

NJ: 'It isn't only a duel in talking, but regular armed robbery.'

JA: 'Now Nuru, you too are against me.'

NJ: 'No no, pardon me, I've not said too much now, have I?'

GA: 'That's right. Anyone who can defeat brother Jafar in eloquence, wit, word-stealing, word-robbery, and word-duel will get two hundred rupees.

NJ: 'I timidly say, my brother might talk for two hours, but what he says is almost impossible to make out.'

GA: 'He talks sometimes to the left of his goal and sometimes to the right, sometimes in front of it and sometimes at the back, wandering about all over the place—but yes, he does talk. But this isn't natural. God doesn't want that everyone in his family should say, "It's a moonlit night" if he declares daytime to be nighttime. Women too have eyes and ears, they too can think. These faculties should be properly exercised. Their tongues are not meant just to repeat and parrot-fashion only what we teach them.'

JA: 'Now get up, you've talked enough for one day.'

GA: 'A few more words, please, but not about you. Just as the planets go round the sun on their orbit, so we should do our duty and that too with our eyes fixed on Truth, that is, God, with firm faith. One shouldn't leave Truth, for downfall is inevitable when you leave the path of Truth. One has to fix one's attention on the Truth at the centre.'

KAU: 'We are each a small star in the solar system and God is our sun.'

GA: 'Right. Those who lead a regular and happy life like the solar system are beloved of God.'

KAU: 'There should be unity among us as well.'

GA: 'Yes, but this unity should be based on Truth. There should be some great and noble virtue at the root of unity.'

JA: 'I'd say it'll be better if unity is based on justice or love.'

GA: 'Yes, both of these are noble attributes, but an excess of them leads to trouble. For example at times harsh justice is in conflict with soft love and often an excess of love tyrannizes over justice. A judge shouldn't be too kind, and also, innocent men get punished quite often because of lack of proof. Truth however does not have two aspects like a coin. It is pure—and transparent. That's why I say, let Truth be the basis of unity.'

JA: 'All right. It's time for namaaz, let's go to your room.'

GA: 'Let's go. You be the imam at the namaaz.'

JA: 'No, you don't concede me superiority, so you should be.'

GA: 'But remember—I'll lead and you'll follow.'

JA: 'No, that'll never happen.'

GA: 'Then follow "personal" freedom.'

JA: 'Amen. You pray in your room and I will in mine.'

After both of them had gone Badr said, 'If Uncle had not laughed at us by calling us the solar system we would never have come to know so many things'.

AKH: 'Yes. Today Dad has taken out the Kohinoor from the coal for us.'

KAU: 'Remember, we are all stars in a solar system.'

(*Naba-Nūr*, Phālguna 1312 and Caitra 1312)

Notes

1. It will be convenient for the reader if he knows the ages and the names of the girls: Kauser eighteen, Akhtar sixteen, Badr fourteen, Rabiya twelve, Mushtari ten, Zohra eight, Suraiya six, Nayeema four, and Masuma two.
2. The reader will please excuse the use of a few English words in male conversation. The translation is given within brackets.
3. Chimney Side is a certain place where a huge chimney had been built for a factory. It is thought to be the highest place in Kurseong.
4. That is, Jupiter, Venus, and Krittika.
5. Children of four or five years often lisp. We have kept that lisp for the sake of naturalness.
6. The biggest waterfall in Kurseong.
7. A vehicle like a sedan chair, carried by men.
8. A small creamish very fragrant flower.
9. The word 'womanishness' has been used by the authoress herself (added by the translators).
10. This translates as 'the world, the garden, and the flower'. The rest has not been said.
11. This expression is given in the original (added by the translators).

Sultana's Dream*

One evening I was lounging in an easy chair in my bedroom and thinking lazily of the condition of Indian womanhood. I am not sure whether I dozed off or not. But, as far as I remember, I was wide awake. I saw the moonlit sky sparkling with thousands of diamond-like stars, very distinctly.

All of a sudden a lady stood before me; how she came in, I do not know. I took her for my friend, Sister Sara.

'Good morning', said Sister Sara. I smiled inwardly as I knew it was not morning but starry night. However, I replied to her, saying, 'How do you do?'

'I am all right, thank you. Will you please come out and have a look at our garden?'

* This one is in the author's own original English. There has been no need to translate it.

I looked again at the moon through the open window, and thought there was no harm in going out at that time. The men-servants outside were fast asleep just then, and I could have a pleasant walk with Sister Sara.

I used to have my walks with Sister Sara, when we were at Darjeeling. Many a time did we walk hand in hand and talk light-heartedly in the botanical gardens there. I fancied, Sister Sara had probably come to take me to some such garden, and I readily accepted her offer and went out with her.

When walking I found to my surprise that it was a fine morning. The town was fully awake and the streets alive with bustling crowds. I was feeling very shy thinking I was walking in the street in broad daylight, but there was not a single man visible.

Some of the passersby made jokes at me. Though I could not understand their language, yet I felt sure they were joking. I asked my friend, 'What do they say?'

'The woman say that you look very mannish.'

'Mannish?' said I, 'What do they mean by that?'

'They mean that you are shy and timid like men.'

'Shy and timid like men?' It was really a joke. I became very nervous, when I found that my companion was not Sister Sara, but a stranger. Oh, what a fool had I been to mistake this lady for my dear old friend, Sister Sara.

She felt my fingers tremble in her hand, as we were walking hand in hand.

'What is the matter, dear, dear?' she said affectionately.

'I feel somewhat awkward', I said in a rather apologizing tone, 'as being a *purdahnashin*[1] woman I am not accustomed to walking about unveiled.'

'You need not be afraid of coming across a man here. This is Ladyland, free from sin and harm. Virtue herself reigns here.'

By and by I was enjoying the scenery. Really, it was very grand. I mistook a patch of green grass for a velvet cushion. Feeling as if I were walking on a soft carpet, I looked down and found the path covered with moss and flowers.

'How nice it is,' said I.

'Do you like it?' asked Sister Sara (I continued calling her 'Sister Sara' and she kept calling me by my name).

'Yes, very much but I do not like to tread on the tender and sweet flowes.'

'Never mind, dear Sultana. Your treading will not harm them; they are street flowers.'

'The whole place looks like a garden,' said I admiringly. 'You have arranged every plant so skilfully.'

'Your Calcutta could become a nicer garden than this, if only your countrymen wanted to make it so.'

'They would think it useless to give so much attention to horticulture while they have so many other things to do.'

'They could not find a better excuse,' said she with a smile.

I became very curious to know where the men were. I met more than a hundred women while walking there, but not a single man.

'Where are the men?' I asked her.

'In their proper places, where they ought to be.'

'Pray let me know what you mean by "their proper places".'

'Oh, I see my mistake. You cannot know our customs, as your were never here before. We shut our men indoors.'

'Just as we are kept in the zenana?'

'Exactly so.'

'How funny,' I burst into a laugh. Sister Sara laughed too.

'But dear Sultana, how unfair it is to shut in the harmless women and let loose the men.'

'Why? It is not safe for us to come out of the zenana, as we are naturally weak.'

'Yes, it is not safe so long as there are men about the streets, nor is it so when a wild animal enters a marketplace.'

'Of course, not.'

'Suppose some lunatics escape from the asylum and begin to do all sorts of mischief to men, horses, and other creatures—in that case what will your countrymen do?'

'They will try to capture them and put them back into their asylum.'

'Thank you! And you do not think it wise to keep sane people inside an asylum and let loose the insane?'

'Of course not!' said I laughing lightly.

'As a matter of fact, in your country this very thing is done! Men, who do or at least are capable of doing no end of mischief, are let loose and the innocent women shut up in the zenana! How can you trust those untrained men out of doors?'

'We have no hand or voice in the management of our social affairs. In India, man is lord and master. He has taken to himself all powers and privileges and shut up the women in the zenana.'

'Why do you allow yourselves to be shut up?'

'Because it cannot be helped as they are stronger than women.'

'A lion is stronger than a man but it does not enable him to dominate the human race. You have neglected the duty you owe to yourselves and you have lost your natural rights by shutting your eyes to your own interests.'

'But my dear Sister Sara, if we do everything by ourselves, what will the men do then?'

'They should not do anything. Excuse me; they are fit for nothing. Only catch them and put them into the zenana.'

'But would it be very easy to catch and put them inside the four walls?' said I. 'And even if this were done, would all their business, political and commercial, also go with them into the zenana!'

Sister Sara made no reply. She only smiled sweetly. Perhaps she thought it useless to argue with one who was no better than a frog in a well.

By this time we reached Sister Sara's house. It was situated in a beautiful heart-shaped garden. It was a bungalow with a corrugated iron roof. It was cooler and nicer than any of our rich buildings. I cannot describe how neat and how nicely furnished and how tastefully decorated it was.

We sat side by side. She brought out of the parlour a piece of embroidery work and began putting on a fresh design.

'Do you know knitting and needle work?'

'Yes, we have nothing else to do in our zenana.'

'But we do not trust our zenana members with embroidery!' she said laughing, 'as a man has not patience enough to pass thread through a needle-hole even!'

'Have you done all this work yourself?' I asked, pointing to the various pieces of embroidered teapoy cloths.

'Yes.'

'How can you find time to do all these? You have to do the office work as well? Have you not?'

'Yes. I do not stick to the laboratory all day long. I finish my work in two hours.'

'In two hours! How do you manage? In our land the officers, magistrates for instance, work seven hours daily.'

'I have seen some of them doing their work. Do you think they work all the seven hours?'

'Certainly they do!'

'No, dear Sultana, they do not. They dawdle away their time in smoking. Some smoke two or three cheroots during the office time. They talk much about their work but do little. Suppose one cheroot takes half an hour to burn off, and a man smokes twelve cheroots daily then you see, he wastes six hours every day in sheer smoking.'

We talked on various subjects, and I learned that they were not subject to any kind of epidemic disease nor did they suffer from mosquito-bites as we do. I was very much astonished to hear that in Ladyland no one died in youth except by rare accident.

'Will you care to see our kitchen?' she asked me.

'With pleasure,' said I, and we went to see it. Of course the men had been asked to clear off when I was going there. The kitchen was situated in a beautiful vegetable garden. Every creeper, every tomato plant was itself and ornament. I found no smoke nor was there any chimney in the kitchen—it was clean and bright; the windows were decorated with flower garlands. There was no sign of coal or fire.

'How do you cook?' I asked.

'With solar heat', she said, at the same time showing me the pipe, through which passed the concentrated sunlight and heat. And she cooked something then and there to show me the process.

'How did you manage to gather and store up the sun's heat?' I asked her in amazement.

'Let me tell you a little of our past history then. Thirty years ago, when our present Queen was thirteen-year-old, she inherited the throne. She was Queen in name only; it's the prime minister who was really ruling the country.

'Our good Queen liked science very much. She circulated an order that all the women in her country should be educated. Accordingly, a number of girls' schools were founded and supported by the government. Education was spread far and wide among women, and early marriage also was stopped. No woman was to be allowed to marry before she was twenty-one. I must tell you that before this change we had been kept in strict purdah.'

'How the tables are turned,' I interposed with a laugh.

'But the seclusion is the same,' she said, 'In a few years we had separate universities, where no men were admitted. In the capital, where our Queen lives, there are two universities. One of these invented a wonderful balloon to which they attached a number of pipes. By means of this captive balloon which they managed to keep afloat above the cloud-land, they could draw as much water from the atmosphere as they pleased. As the water was incessantly being drawn by the university people no cloud gathered and the ingenious Lady Principal stopped rain and storms thereby.'

'Really! Now I understand why there is no mud here!' said I. But I could not understand how it was possible to accumulate water in the pipes. She explained to me how it was done but I was unable to understand her, as my scientific knowledge was very limited. However, she went on:

'When the other university came to know of this, they became exceedingly jealous and tried to do something more extraordinary still. They invented an instrument by which they could collect as much sun-heat as they wanted. And they kept the heat stored up to be distributed among others as required.

'While the women were engaged in scientific researches, the men of this country were busy increasing their military power. When they came to know that the female universities were able to draw water from the atmosphere and collect heat from the sun, they only laughed at the members of universities and called the whole thing "a sentimental nightmare"!'

'Your achievements are very wonderful indeed! But tell me, how you managed to put the men of your country into the zenana. Did you entrap them first?'

'No.'

'It is not likely that they would surrender their free and open-air life of their own accord and confine themselves within the four walls of the zenana! They must have been overpowered.'

'Yes, they have been!'

'By whom? By some lady warriors, I suppose?'

'No, not by arms.'

'Yes, it cannot be so. Men's arms are stronger than women's'.

'Then?'

'By brain.'

'Even their brains are bigger and heavier than women's. Are they not?'

'Yes, but what of that? An elephant also has got a bigger and heavier brain than a man has. Yet man can enchain elephants and employ them, according to their own wishes.'

'Well said, but tell me please, how it all actually happened. I am dying to know it!'

'Women's brains are somewhat quicker than men's. Ten years ago, when the military officers called our scientific discoveries a sentimental nightmare,' some of the young ladies wanted to say something in reply to those remarks. But both the lady principals restrained them and said, they should reply, not by word but by deed, if ever they got the opportunity. And they had not long to wait for that opportunity.'

'How marvellous!' I heartily clapped my hands.

'And now the proud gentlemen are dreaming sentimental dreams themselves.

'Soon afterwards certain persons came from a neighbouring country and took shelter in ours. They were in trouble having committed some political offence. The King who cared more for power than for good government asked our kind-hearted Queen to hand them over to his officers. She refused, as it was against her principle to turn out refugees. For this refusal the King declared war against our country.

'Our military officers sprang to their feet at once and marched out to meet the enemy.'

'The enemy however, was too strong for them. Our soldiers fought bravely, no doubt, but in spite of all their bravery the foreign army advanced step by step to invade our country.

'Nearly all the men had gone out to fight; even a boy of sixteen was not left at home. Most of our warriors were killed, the rest driven back, and the enemy came within twenty-five miles of the capital.

'A meeting of a number of wise ladies was held at the Queen's palace to advise what should be done to save the land.

'Some proposed to fight like soldiers, others objected and said that women were not trained to fight with swords and guns and that were they accustomed to fighting with any weapons. A third party regretfully remarked that they were hopelessly week of body.

'If you cannot save your country for lack of physical strength, said the Queen, try to do so by brain power.

'There was a dead silence for a few minutes. Her Royal Highness said again, "I must commit suicide if the land and my honour are lost".

'Then the lady principal of the second university (who had collected the sun-heat), who had been silently thinking during the consultation, remarked that they were all but lost and there was little hope left for them. There was however, one plan which she would like to try, and this would be her first and last effort; if she failed in this there would be nothing left but to commit suicide. All present solemnly vowed that they would never allow themselves to be enslaved, no matter what happened.

'The Queen thanked them heartily, and asked the lady principal to try her plan.

'The lady principal rose again and said, "before we go out the men must enter the zenanas. I make this prayer for the sake of purdah." "Yes, of course," replied her Royal Highness.

'On the following day the Queen called upon all men to retire into zenanas for the sake of honour and liberty.

'Wounded and tired as they were, they took that order rather for a boon! They bowed low and entered the zenanas without uttering a single word of protest. They were sure that there was no hope for this country at all.

'Then the lady principal with her two thousand students marched to the battlefield, and arriving there directed all the rays of the concentrated sunlight and heat towards the enemy.

'The heat and light were too much for them to bear. They all ran away panic-stricken, not knowing in their bewilderment how to counteract that scorching heat. When they fled away leaving their guns and other ammunitions of war, they were burnt down by means of the same sun-heat.

'Since then no one has tried to invade our country anymore.'

'And since then your countrymen never tried to come out of the zenana?'

'Yes, they wanted to be free. Some of the Police Commissioners and District Magistrates sent word to the Queen to the effect that the military officers certainly deserved to be imprisoned for their failure but they never neglected their duty and therefore they should not be punished and they prayed to be restored to their respective offices.

'Her Royal Highness sent them a circular letter intimating to them that if their services should ever be needed they would be sent for, and that in the meanwhile they should remain where they were.

'Now that they are accustomed to the purdah system and have ceased to grumble at their seclusion, we call the system "*Murdana*" instead of "Zenana".'

'But how do you manage', I asked Sister Sara, 'to do without the police or magistrates in case of theft or murder?'

'Since the "Murdana" system has been established, there has been no more crime or sin; therefore we do not require a policeman to find out a culprit, nor do we want a magistrate to try a criminal case.'

'That is very good, indeed. I suppose if there were any dishonest person, you could very easily chastise her. As you gained a decisive victory without shedding a single drop of blood, you could drive off crime as well as criminals without much difficulty!'

'Now, dear Sultana, will you sit here or come to my parlour?' She asked me.

'Your kitchen is not inferior to a queen's boudoir!' I replied with a pleasant smile, 'but we must leave it now for the gentlemen may be cursing me for keeping them away from their duties in the kitchen so long.' We both laughed heartily.

'How my friends at home will be amused and amazed, when I go back and tell them that in the far-off Ladyland, ladies rule over the country and control all social matters, while gentlemen are kept in the murdanas to mind babies, to cook and to do all sorts of domestic work; and that cooking is so easy a thing that it is simply a pleasure to cook!'

'Yes, tell them about all that you see here.'

'Please let me know how you carry on land cultivation and how you plough the land and do other hard manual work.'

'Our fields are tilled by means of electricity, which supplies motive power for other hard work as well and we employ it for our aerial conveyances too. We have no railroad nor any paved streets here.'

'Therefore neither streets nor railway accidents occur here,' said I. 'Do not you ever suffer from want of rainwater?' I asked.

'Never since the "water balloon" has been set up. You see the big balloon and pipes attached thereto. By their aid we can draw as much rain water as we require. Nor do we ever suffer from flood or thunder storms. We are all very busy making nature yield as much as she can. We do not find time to quarrel with one another as we never sit idle. Our noble Queen is exceedingly fond of botany; it is her ambition to convert the whole country into one grand garden.'

'The idea is excellent. What is your chief food?'

'Fruits.'

'How do you keep your country cool in hot weather? We regard the rainfall in summer as a blessing from heaven.'

'When the heat becomes unbearable, we sprinkle the ground with plentiful showers drawn from the artificial fountains. And in cold weather we keep our room warm with sun-heat.'

She showed me her bathroom, the roof of which was removable. She could enjoy a shower bath whenever she liked by simply removing the roof (which was like the lid of a box) and turning on the tap of the shower pipe.

'You are lucky people!' ejaculated I. 'You know no want. What is your religion, may I ask?'

'Our religion is based on Love and Truth. It is our religious duty to love one another and to be absolutely truthful. If any person lies, she or he is—'

'Punished with death?'

'No, not with death. We do not take pleasure in killing a creature of God—specially a human being. The liar is asked to leave this land for good and never come back to it again.'

'Is an offender never forgiven?'

'Yes, if that person repents sincerely.'

'Are you not allowed to see any man, except your own relations?'

'No one except sacred relations.'

'Our circle of sacred relations is very limited too; even first cousins are not sacred.'

'But ours is very large; a distant cousin is as sacred as a brother.'

'That is very good. I see purity itself reigns over your land. I should like to see the good Queen, who is so sagacious and far-sighted and who has made all these rules.

'All right,' said Sister Sara.

Then she screwed a couple of seats on to a square piece of plank. To this plank she attached two smooth and well-polished balls. When I asked her what the balls were for, she said, they were hydrogen balls and they were used to overcome the force of gravity. The balls were of different capacities to be used according to the different weights desired to be overcome. She then fastened to the air-car two wing-like blades, which, she said, were worked by electricity. After we were comfortably seated she touched a knob and the blades began to whirl, moving faster and faster every moment. At first we were raised to the height of about six or seven feet and then off we flew. And before I could realize that we had commenced moving we reached the Garden of the Queen.

My friend lowered the air-car by reversing the action of the machine, and when the car touched the ground the machine was stopped and we got out.

From the air-car I had seen the Queen walking on a garden path with her little daughter (who was four-year-old) and her maids of honour.

'Halloo! You here!' cried the Queen addressing Sister Sara. I was introduced to Her Royal Highness and was received by her cordially without any ceremony.

I was very much delighted to make her acquaintance. In course of the conversation I had with her, the Queen told me that she had no objection to permitting her subjects to trade with other countries. 'But,' she continued, 'no trade was possible with countries where the women were kept in the zenanas and so unable to come and trade with us. Men, we find, are rather of lower morals and so we do not like dealing with them. We do not covet other people's land, we do not fight for a piece of diamond though it may be a thousand-fold brighter than the Koh-i-Noor, nor do we grudge a ruler his Peacock Throne. We dive deep into the ocean of knowledge and try to find out the precious gems which nature has kept in store for us. We enjoy nature's gifts as much as we can.'

After taking leave of the Queen, I visited the famous universities, and was shown over some of their manufactories, laboratories, and observatories.

After visiting the above places of interest we got again into the air-car, but as soon as it began moving I somehow slipped down and the fall startled me out of my dream. And on opening my eyes, I found myself in my own bedroom still lounging in the easy chair!!

Note

1. This means a lady who observes the *purdah* custom.

The Murder of Delicia*[1]

Let not my sisters be alarmed that the word 'murder' means a real murder with a dagger and a gun and bloodshed and all that! The famous novelist Marie Corelli has written this novel named *The Murder of Delicia*. There is so much similarity between the story of Delicia and that of our own women that one feels like saying:

How did Miss Corelli know
The way our women's life does flow!

Today we shall compare the social condition of England with that of our own and see which is the better expert in tyrannizing women.

* The novel *The Murder of Delicia* has been retold by Rokeya, it is not exactly a translation. It carries her comments. So the present work is not the translation of a translation but a translation of Rokeya's work with her original comments and footnotes. The footnotes are all hers unless otherwise indicated (added by the translators).

What is the life of an Englishwoman like? We think of them as being free, educated, equal with men, honoured by society—and we see many brilliant images of their happiness and prosperity in our mind's eye. But if we take a look at their homes we realize it is all a shame. So do drumbeats sound nice but only if they are in the distance. But every day hundreds of *The Murder of Delicia* are enacted in that nursery of civilization, London. Alas, even in that world, women are powerless and weak!

When we see the picture of any famous couple in the newspapers we think—Lord Someone is quite powerful and brilliant in society, but if we could look inside Lady Someone's heart we would understand what that power and brilliance is really like.

The novelist Marie Corelli is herself a woman so she has been able to portray Delicia's misery quite graphically. Women readers will understand the true meaning of *The Murder of Delicia* correctly. It is not easy to translate this wonderful novel properly, yet I cannot resist the temptation of presenting the story to my sisters.

The author has said in the 'Introduction' that she has portrayed Delicia after real events in the real world. We, too, know of many such real events. Let us name one such representative character 'Mazluma'. It seems as if every brush-stroke in *The Murder of Delicia* is painting the portrait of our Mazluma. I will paint one of hers and compare it with that of Delicia and show how much of resemblance is there between the women of England and those of India. The difference between them will also become clear.

Delicia is free. She belongs to the ruling class and is not closeted within a harem. Mazluma, in contrast, is doubly enslaved because she belongs to the class of the ruled and is imprisoned within the inner portion of her home. But how much difference is there between the two? Well, not much because both are women! Both are oppressed by society. But Delicia is educated and Mazluma is illiterate—there is this all-important difference. The well-educated Delicia is killed by the assassin her husband like a heroine in the battlefield of life whereas the illiterate Mazluma gives up her helpless life at the feet of her tyrannical husband. The courageous Delicia, revolver in hand, tells her husband, 'I'll kill you if you take a step towards me.' Poor Mazluma can never say that. She will fall at the feet of the tyrant and weep, 'My lord, what crime has your slave committed?' or 'Be kind to your slave'. She will be kicked again and again while trying to wash those feet with her tears. This is the difference between them.

Delicia has self-respect, which Mazluma does not have. Delicia too is oppressed and tyrannized, yet there is an aura of glory about her; her head is bloody but unbowed. She would rather die with her head held high than join her palms in supplication to beg for her life. This grandeur is not there in Mazluma. This is because of lack of education in women. She has been told from the day she was born, 'You have been born a slave, you will always be one.' So her very soul has become enslaved. She no longer knows her own value. She licks the feet of her menfolk even when she is being trampled by those very feet. This is the difference between free Delicia and enslaved Mazluma.

Our writers endow their women characters with many virtues. Most of them sing the praises of the forbearance of women (for had they not been endlessly forbearing and forgiving it would not have been easy to tyrannize over them). But these books do not give any instance of any self-respect in them. Now look at the story of Delicia.

Delicia had devoted herself to literature right from her childhood. Her first book was published when she was only seventeen. Her excellent books were appreciated by the readers. Thus she won fame and also earned money from the sale of her books. This earned her many enemies also. Other authors burned with jealousy. They thought writing books was the privilege only of men; women should dress well and live in luxury. If it is very necessary, then a woman who has neither youth, nor beauty, who is quite ugly in fact, can be allowed to wield a pen. But that a young and beautiful girl like Delicia should compete with them was unbearable.

Delicia got married when she was twenty-seven. The reason the lovely, rich, and talented girl was unmarried for so long was because men looked at her with something like awe, fear, and dislike. One could not think of being happy with a woman who was indifferent to her looks and always pre-occupied with writing. (We here do not have 'female writers', but women who can read or write drive away suitors.)

Mr Wilfred Carlyon was a handsome nobleman. Obedient to his father's will, he had joined the army. He was possessed of the following: a handsome physique, fully six feet high, and a long family line. His income was as nothing. He looked at Delicia and thought her fair game. First of all she looked like a rosebud, second she was rich. So the day came for Delicia—the day that comes but once in a man's life (or a woman's) that is as evanescent as a bubble that shines like a meteor but vanishes forever in a minute. That magic moment arrived in her life. She was at a dinner party and Mr Carlyon was also there. 'Delicia', whispered Mr Carlyon, taking her hand. 'Delicia, I love you.'

* * *

Quite a crowd attended her marriage. On one hand there was Mars and on the other Minerva, it can be called the union of Kartik with Saraswati[2]—one has to have a look at such a couple. Most of the flowers strewn for them were meant for Delicia.

Usually one says 'the man married the girl', but here one would have to say the opposite. Delicia was the one who took the responsibility of providing Mr Carlyon with a living. One cannot say this about Mazluma. There one will have to say: she surrendered herself to her husband with all her wealth. It came to this: it was Delicia who laboriously gathered all the honey and her husband was the drone.

Delicia wore just a spray of flowers for ornament at her wedding. All the ladies were surprised. What! The bride has no ornaments! How odd! Just like our own women. As soon as five or six women get together they start talking about ornaments. The minute a bride arrives all the women present make a thorough search of her whole body to have a look at her ornaments. The way they pull at her ears to look at her earrings! Delicia's ears were not actually pulled like an Indian girl's but her hearing was much taxed by the comments of the shrews.

The elderly women started whispering. 'Poor Carlyon is so handsome! And look at what he did—he went and married a "female author!"'[3]

Mr Carlyon told his friends that she was a natural rose. Artificial colouring, wigs (made from the hair of female convicts), perfume, cosmetics—nothing was used by her. One of his friends said, 'Lucky dog, you don't deserve such a prize.'

'Maybe not, but—', said Mr Carlyon and glanced at him. That glance of his itself completed his sentence. He had pierced Delicia's armour with just such a glance. Not for nothing had his friends nicknamed him 'Beauty Carlyon'.

The first three years of her married life passed more or less uneventfully. She did not go to parties much; the major part of her days was devoted to her literary labours. Writers like solitude. A man who has found pleasure in the life of the mind does not like to waste his time in empty pleasures. Carlyon however liked to attend parties. He accepted two or three invitations every day.

Then a spark of fire fell on her nest. She did not see it. Unknown to her, the spark started its work silently.

A few of her friends tried to tell her but she did not pay any attention. She thought, 'These people want to destroy our peace. What do they get from slandering people?' Had she become cautious in time things would not have gone so far, she could have curbed her husband. But she was blind; she could not suspect her husband at all.

Mr Carlyon said one day, 'It's a shame that literary women do not get a title … so let me give you one, Delicia. Now that my elder brother is dead, I've inherited the family title.'

Delicia laughed at this empty generosity and said mockingly: 'I'm your vassal, my liege lord.'

Will the title of Lady enhance her honour? What was it compared to her fame as a writer? Many such ladies come and go, but 'authoress Delicia' will remain.

Another day Lord Carlyon said, 'I think the old days were better.'

'Oh yes! The days when men shut up their womenfolk inside four walls, just like cattle are put in an enclosure? And they used to give them only as much food as they themselves thought fit! And would beat women if they turned disobedient! Maybe those days were better but I don't think so. I want to see a continued development. I want civilization in which both men and women would get education.'[4]

* * *

Carlyon said, 'I think progress is far too quick. I want to vote for a slower progress.'[5]

There are envious men who are jealous of other people's fame. Delicia's married life was quite a happy one. She had lost one baby once, but such a sorrow is a sacred one—it purifies the soul. Except for this blow to the mother's heart, she had no other sorrows or sufferings. She was well-established in the literary world. How could people bear such happiness? They tried slandering and tale telling. Delicia knew the world and did not pay much attention to whispers. But while trying to avoid the whispers of scandal-mongers she also neglected the cautionary advice of friends. She never thought that the husband of someone as loyal as she would ever go astray. Ah! What simple faith!

A friend of hers, Mr Paul Valdes, tried to warn her several times but Delicia got angry. He said, while caressing Spartan, her favourite dog, 'Lady Carlyon, you've but one faithful friend now'.

DELICIA: 'Are you talking of Spartan, or of yourself?'

VALDES: 'I'm talking of Spartan.'

Mr Valdes said casually that Lord Carlyon was an insignificant person. Delicia got irritated and sent him away. How can a loyal woman bear to hear her husband slandered?

It seemed as if Spartan did not like his mistress's behaviour. He went on looking at her as if to say, 'Why did you drive Mr Valdes off? He is my friend.' Delicia understood him and said, 'Spartan, he's saying things against the master. We won't let him come here anymore.' But Spartan was not satisfied.

Those whose poems and essays were not appreciated like Delicia's books became envious. Whenever a few gentlemen got together at The Bohemian they consoled themselves by slandering her. A certain poet said, 'How can a woman write so well? Most of the books are written by her husband.' Mr Valdes said, 'That's a lie. The husband is as big an ass as you.'

'You called me a liar, Mr Valdes, and an ass?'

Mr Valdes said, 'Yes, I've seen a letter written by Lord Carlyon. His words are misspelt and his grammar awful. He can't write a single sentence correctly. If you think that he can write his wife's books, you're definitely an ass. But you don't really think so. You're saying that out of sheer envy.'

After some more heated words the poet said, 'Do you know, Mr Valdes, that the pen is mightier than the sword?'

Mr Valdes laughed contemptuously and said, 'Oh, now I know. You'll abuse me in one of your halfpenny rags.'

* * *

One day Delicia had gone out shopping. She wanted to buy few things for her husband. Besides the things he wanted she wanted to buy something especially nice for him. Their wedding anniversary was at hand and she wanted to give him something. Love itself is intangible, so one wants something tangible to express it. The loyal wife wanted to express herself in the shape of a ring or a set of cufflinks. After looking here and there she found a set she liked. She entered the shop. The owner, thinking her to be a wealthy woman started showing her several ornaments. Delicia selected only those links and did not want anything else. But the jeweller would not let her go so easily. He continued to show her several attractive things. There was a lovely diamond '*jugnu*' (pendant)[6] among them. It was a diamond dove holding a scroll in its beak on which there was a motto in ruby.

She took it in her hands and said, 'This pendant is lovely. It's poetic and artistic.'

'Yes, but it's not meant for sale. It's made to order for Lord Carlyon.'

Delicia was surprised at this. She thought maybe it was meant for her. Before she could say anything the jeweller took it out so that it may catch the light and shine. He did not know Delicia and said quite openly, 'Lord Carlyon will have to pay a bit more than £500 for it. When a gentleman wants to please a lady such an expense means nothing. Of course you'll understand that the lady isn't Lord Carylon's wife.'

Delicia said, 'Why should I think that? I think it's but natural that a gentleman would have such a pendant made for his wife.'

The jeweller shook his head wisely and said, 'You think so? But we usually see that when a gentleman places an order for a certain thing it's never for his wife. We don't like that our carefully made things are never worn by ladies. Why is this valuable diamond-dove not going to Lady Carlyon but to the dancer La Marina?'

What has this jeweller said? Her head spun around.

* * *

Finally the jeweller asked her, 'Have you read the books of Lady Carlyon? She is known as Delicia in the literary world.'

Delicia said, 'Yes,—I think so.'

Jeweller: 'Well, she's a very famous lady. It's a shame that her husband never thinks of her.... It's said that the money Lord Carlyon wastes so carelessly is his wife's—he doesn't have a penny of his own. What a shame if that is true! Lady Carlyon of course pays for the ornament for La Marina without knowing.... Will you take this pair of links?'

DELICIA: 'Yes, thank you. These are fit for a gentleman.'

JEWELLER: 'That's right. These are not showy, but good. Fit for a gentleman no doubt, but (with a smile) gentlemen are getting rarer day by day.'

Delicia heard many more things from the jeweller against her will. The things she had not let her friends say to her were the very things the jeweller said, to her great mortification. What does a Bengali woman think of this? Does this not reflect Mazluma's condition? But then, what is the heroism of a man if a necklace is not snatched from the neck of Mazluma and given to a courtesan?

When she returned home Delicia found a wire from her husband: 'Don't wait dinner for me. I'll be late.'

Delicia, deeply mortified, locked herself with Spartan in her study. She said to him. 'Spartan, I feel as if I've taken poison.' Spartan looked at her with melting eyes. It was as if his glance mutely said, 'Why do you trust men? Dogs are more faithful.'

Lord Carlyon could not give her as much love as Spartan could. Delicia was thinking of many things—was it right that her hard-earned money should go for buying ornaments for La Marina, a dancer, a chorus girl?

There is a lot of difference between the money of Delicia and that of Mazluma. The money frittered away by the profligate husband of Mazluma was not earned by herself; it was inherited. In other words it was the money of her ancestors, who were males. One can somehow bear the fact that the wealth of one man is wasted by another. But it is unbearable that the hard-earned money of Delicia should be wasted like this—it is the inexcusable action of a coward. When analysed like this Delicia's condition is more wretched than that of Mazluma's. Yet the English claim to be civilized. Is this civilization? Is this chivalry?[7]

Delicia thought, 'I had a statue on a golden altar. Today it has fallen down. The statue is still unbroken, but it is lying beneath the altar.'

Her love died when the statue fell down. What a terrible irony of fate! The heart breaks at the thought—one was waiting for the festivities of a wedding anniversary and here is the funeral of love!

Lord Carlyon returned at about 1 o'clock. To his great irritation nearly all the rooms were in darkness. He had been spoilt by Delicia. Is it not an insult to him—this evidence of neglect? Every night the rooms were lit up till he returned, why were they in darkness today? He had forgotten that he had told them not to wait dinner. His attitude was—she should wait for me even if I had told her not to. He was quite annoyed at not getting any answer on knocking at her door. Was she asleep this early? She always waited for him—why this negligence today? He knocked and knocked till Spartan got up and growled at him. He was lying outside the door. If he could speak he would have said, 'Why have you come here? My mistress is asleep. Don't disturb her. Go to hell.' This growl further annoyed him. He cursed the dog and went to his own room.

Tonight he was in a bad mood—he had lost a lot of money (Delicia's money) at cards. La Marina too had not treated him well.[8] The sweetness of Delicia would have been as balm. But she was asleep!

Next morning she went out riding. On her return she heard that Lord Carlyon was still asleep. Her mind had regained its calm in the morning air. She thought of the jeweller's tale as a nightmare. One does not like to hear ill reports of a loved one. People like to deceive themselves. After all, Delicia was but a woman.

As soon as Lord Carlyon came in she smiled at him and said, 'Will, you're up! Did you come in late last night?'

Lord Carlyon did not like this. He missed something in her greeting today. He was a bit surprised—why? Why was Delicia avoiding him? Why was her smile not quite so sweet as on other days? Her manner was faultless, yet her behaviour seemed to have no sparkle in it.

He said, 'Delicia, some parts of your new book are quite objectionable. Last night someone was telling me this.'

Delicia said, 'Indeed? Who said that? May be certain parts of my book have touched a tender spot.'

Carlyon: 'It was Fitzhalf. You know him. He said he'll not let his sisters read it. He made me quite angry.'

Do not his words echo what is said in our society? Those periodicals that express liberal views are not allowed to be read by women. Not only in Bengal, in the western states too the periodicals (which are meant for women and most of which are written by them) are not allowed to be seen by women by their menfolk. After all, the menfolk are the ones who control everything! Now listen to what Delicia said in reply.

'You have read my books. Have you seen anything in them that Capt. Fitzhalf might object to?'

Lord Carlyon: 'I can't remember off hand.'

Capt. Fitzhalf had been long looked askance at in society. Delicia brought up the subject of the Captain's character. Not that his sisters were above reproach either. Who was he to abuse her books? Physician, you had better cure yourself first.

* * *

Half of the £8000 got from the sale of Delicia's new books was deposited in Lord Carlyon's account. She always gave half of what she got to her husband.

That afternoon when Mrs Cavendish came to call on Delicia she invited her to dinner and to the opera afterwards. She knew Delicia from childhood and loved her like a daughter. Delicia accepted her invitation with joy, for it is unbearable to sit in solitude with a heart as heavy as hers. She thought maybe it will help her forget.

Today is a great day, the city is plastered with posters proclaiming the performance of 'The Birth of a Butterfly—La Marina (Heroine.)' Delicia too wanted to have a look at La Marina. After all, her nest was going to be burnt because of this woman. It was but natural to want to see the cause of her destruction. She arrived at the opera in due time with Mr and Mrs Cavendish. The Empire is overcrowded tonight. Lord Carlyon is also there.

* * *

So the butterfly was born—La Marina was dancing as the butterfly. Delicia saw the dove glittering at her breast, the same dove she had seen at the jeweller's, on Bond Street. It was the identical dove with the scroll in ruby lettering. There was no scope for doubt. How can one not believe the jeweller now? The bright opera house grew dark before her eyes. Her limbs froze in sudden cold.

Mrs Cavendish, seated beside her, exclaimed on seeing her grow so pale, 'What, Delicia! Are you not feeling well?' She said to her husband, 'Take her outside, she's going to faint.'

Delicia controlled herself and said, 'I'll be better in a minute, don't worry about it. The heat here is unbearable. Don't get disturbed because of me.' Alas, Delicia, is the heat in the room burning you or is it the fire in your heart?

On coming back from the Empire she, first of all, wrote a letter to Lord Carlyon and gave it to a servant, Robson, and told him to give it to her husband the minute he came.

Then going to her bedroom she called her maid and said, 'Emily, we're going to the seaside. You finish the packing so we may leave by 10 o'clock tomorrow to go to Broadstairs. We shall take Spartan with us.'

Emily was undoing her hair. She suddenly stood up, unable to sit still. Emily was surprised, 'What is wrong, my lady?'

'It is nothing,' Delicia tried to smile, 'No need to be frightened, Emily, it is not that I'm unwell. I'm just tired. You may go now. I'll be better if left alone. Be ready for our journey tomorrow.'

The scene she had seen at the Empire was too difficult to digest, it would have been so even for Mazluma though Indian women are incomparable in their forbearance. It was like a thunderstroke for Delicia.

* * *

She could not hold her tears back any longer. She knelt down and cried out, 'O God, I've at last realized what it is I've lost! Love has engulfed me and then vanished like a dream. Oh! Oh! Only that crown of thorn, my fame as a writer, is left now.'

Alas, Delicia too, like Mazluma, wept in darkness and solitude. Were they only tears or the lifeblood wrung from the heart?

'I loved him so much—I worshipped him. This is punishment for worshipping him like a God.'

* * *

'Love! How tender it is! It dies at the least rough touch. Ambition can grow even if it is destroyed once but love! It's like the flower of aloe—blossoming but once in a hundred years. What shall I do with my life now?'

What, after all, can you do? Throw it, throw it to drown in the waters of death. You used to see your lord lit up with the radiance of your own love. He had no light of his own. A person who is bathed in light cannot see things that are hidden in darkness.

Alas! What a terrible mistake! Delicia used to think of her husband as a god above all reproach. What faith, in her simplicity, she had had in him! The idol she had placed on the jewelled throne of her heart had broken into pieces in front of her very eyes. Delicia, do not, do not pick up the shards.

When idolators worship an idol made of clay they believe that God is really there, for however short a time. When at the end of the ritual they think that god has left it, then they immerse the lifeless clay idol in water. Who would worship a mere clay idol? If the devotee came to know that instead of a god, a devil had entered the idol would he worship it? Not only that. The very idea that one had worshipped a devil instead of a god is intolerable, it is blasphemy.

How terribly has Delicia been betrayed! She had worshipped a faithless devil, taking him for a good and loving husband. She had mistaken clay for gold. The castle she had built in the air in her folly had become a broken-down ruin and she had been thrown into the debris.

That the one worshipped is not worthy of adoration, that he is but a devil in disguise comes as a thunderbolt to the worshipper. Only someone who has undergone the same experience can understand it. It is the deadly bite of a scorpion of which only the one who has experienced it can understand the intensity. The devotee was walking along a path covered with the leaves and flowers of imagination, dazed with love. Then someone awakened him and told him there was a deep and dark pit only a step further. If he took but one more step his fall was certain. Oh, what a painful awakening would that be! Why did he not die before awakening? Alas, it is the truth.

But who would want to know such a truth? Why could one not die before knowing such a truth? That one who has been trusted with gold is not worth a copper himself, that one at whose feet flowers had been offered in the faith that he is divine is no better than a beast—this discovery is unbearable.

Oh! What a cruel betrayal is this, what torture! Delicia, the god you worshipped is but an ordinary gentleman, an officer in the Army. Nothing more. But it is not right to call a traitor a beast. What beast can be so mean and ignoble? When a man is called a lion it signifies admiration for his bravery, and when a dog, it means gratitude and faithful friendliness. A horse is a noble animal. An ass may be stupid but it is not blood thirsty. Bison, rhino, boar—no, no animal is worse than man. No animal kicks a devoted worshipper.

But what does it matter to the lords and masters if a woman's heart is broken? The sighs of oppressed women do not disturb the sleep of powerful men. Yet I ask: Does devotion have no value? Do the lords of the universe lead a merry life after having lost that invaluable rare love that gods themselves seek? Mazluma cannot make her tyrant starve, she cannot avenge the wrong done to her, but she can at least withdraw her blind devotion. She need not hate her god but at least she can look upon him with pity. Is it a glorious thing for the powerful to be pitied by the powerless?

Delicia, in her pain, is feeling like a caged bird. It is as if her heart is crying out:

My love, my devotion was pure, my lord,
And a fine return have I got.

Gradually the intensity of her grief lessened and finally she fell asleep. Now Mazluma, is not Delicia's lament but an echo of your heart's cry? Are not the tortured sighs of her burning heart similar to those of yours? The difference is that the tyranny of Delicia's husband is like stealing while that of Mazluma's husband is armed robbery.

* * *

Lord Carlyon knew the law—he knew it to be in his favour. There is no legal punishment for men who kill women in this manner. Supposing Delicia wants a divorce, will she get it? No, for she will not be able to prove his cruelty. It is not legally a crime to be friends with a dozen La Marinas, let alone one. Neither is it legally a crime to fritter away the hard-earned money of a wife to please a courtesan. In order to have a divorce she will have to prove the disloyalty of her husband and that they have been separated for more than two years. 'Delicia cannot be free of me'—Lord Carlyon got real pleasure from thinking of this law. What law is this! It is made by men. It has been invented by men for the advantage of themselves only. It is not a crime to trample over the hearts of women or to ruin their lives.

* * *

Delicia was thinking of social rules and customs after she came to Broadstairs. There are laws for those who physically torture anyone or kill anyone, but there is no punishment for those who break the hearts of women, who bury love alive.

'I can sue him,' thought she, 'only if he beats me or fires at me, otherwise not.'

She was thinking of her broken idol while walking on the sea beach in the evening. The idol has been thrown down, but a few shards, like mementoes, still remain. The flower withers and falls but the stalk might still hold a few petals—the painful memories remain.

Her tears would not stop. She could not see in front of her because of tears. The sky, the sea, the beach—she could not see anything. Then suddenly Spartan barked joyfully and somebody said, 'Lady Carlyon, may I say something?' She looked carefully and saw Mr Valdes.

The day before she came to Broadstairs a newspaper named *Honesty* had published a slanderous article on her. Paul Valdes had whipped the scoundrel. He had come to give her the news. Delicia did not understand at first; she was so absent-minded. Then she understood and smilingly said, 'Aha, so you beat the man who according to the papers is a combination of Shakespeare and Milton.'

* * *

Valdes said, 'You look out of spirits, Lady Carlyon,' and she answered, 'You're right. I've lost the love of my husband.'

'Then you've heard it all?'

'What! Did everybody know it except myself? Tell me, is it possible that he has so far forgotten himself that he is not ashamed to visit La Marina openly? Has he made me an object of ridicule and pity in this flagrant manner?'

In this country of ours the wife is not put to shame when the husband is at fault. On the contrary the husband is put to shame at the least misconduct on the part of the wife. In England, however, the wife feels ashamed if the husband goes astray. This is the different between us.

Valdes answered, 'Lady Carlyon, your friends had tried to warn you. You did not listen. When I had hinted to you that your affections are misplaced you had driven me off. But I won't say that it was wrong of you. You only acted as a loyal wife. But now you know everything.'

'Yes, now I know, but what is the good of knowing? What can I do? There is nothing a woman can do about the infidelity of her husband. I cannot show any bruises, nor can I prove any misbehaviour. The law will tell me, "Go home, you stupid woman. Whatever your husband does, if he behaves politely then you cannot be separated …" and so on and so forth.' These are the words of an Englishwoman! What heartbreaking words! The same fire that burns Mazluma is also burning Delicia.

She went on to say, 'Mr Valdes, you register emotion on the stage,[9] you can show sorrow and pain, but have you ever been able to feel the intense torture that goes on in the depths of a woman's heart that is broken and silent? No, I believe even your sensitive imagination cannot reach that far. Do you know why I've come to the seaside so suddenly? I know that if the pain becomes too hideous this quiet sea won't refuse to give me shelter. But no, I'll not drown myself. Can you guess why I've come here to avoid meeting him? I'm afraid I'd have killed him otherwise.'

* * *

She was thinking, what to do now? Should she travel to broaden her mind? If continuous travelling tires her then should she stay in some little-known glen in the highlands of Scotland or should she devote the rest of her life to literature in a little cottage in some green Irish valley?

But what will society say? 'What is the reason behind Lady Carlyon's self-exile?' They will whisper, 'there must be something behind it.'

So long as you can bear the tyranny of your relatives and lick their feet you are all right. But if you show you have some self-respect, if you take legal advice to protect your own property, if you show the least independence, you are finished. According to society you have gone to the dogs. If you take a house for yourself because you cannot adjust with your relatives, then you have fallen beyond redemption. Delicia was right when she said, 'What shall I do with this my life?' Formerly Indian women would burn themselves with the dead body of their husbands to escape the accusations of society in their widowhood. Delicia too did not have to worry too much over her burdensome life. She escaped soon enough to find eternal peace in the bosom of Death.

Actually she had died on the day she had seen that pendant on the bosom of La Marina at the Empire—that is, her heart had died on that day itself. The death of her love was the same as her own death. She just carried on in order to perform but one duty.

She came back from Broadstairs after two weeks to hear a lot about her husband's doings from Robson. Her whole body trembled with anger and shame—her own servant pitied her! Robson's manner held pity and sympathy.

She went to her bedroom for a bit of rest. Looking at the bed she thought, La Marina had laid her head on this pillow! She felt as if her heart was pierced with a dagger; she fainted and fell down. Hearing the sound of her fall Emily came running. When Delicia opened her eyes she saw Emily attending to her.

Delicia had to go to Lady Dexter's party in the evening. This was before she had met her husband. There in the party she heard her husband speaking against her, with her own ears. He, of course, had not seen her. As soon as he had finished speaking she stood up and looked piercingly at him. An instant later she moved away. Lady Branswith (with whom her husband was conversing) asked in surprise, 'Who is she?'

Lord Carlyon, a little apprehensive, said, 'That's Delicia, my wife'. Lady Branswith said, 'So that's who she is—a famous writer. I had no idea she is so lovely. She must have heard what we were saying.'

* * *

As soon as Lord Carlyon came in Robson told him that the mistress was waiting for him in the study.

His heart beat loudly as he approached her. He entered after hesitating a bit at the door, as if a criminal was approaching the queen knowing that a sentence of death will be the verdict.

He began, 'Delicia, I'm really sorry—'.

Delicia's eyes sparkled with anger. She said firmly but quietly, 'Be quiet. There is no need to tell lies anymore. I know you now. Your mask has fallen, no need to pick it up.'

He was thunderstruck. He tried to smile. Delicia looked at him fixedly and said, 'This evening you said so many things against me …'

'Not against you', Lord Carlyon tried to cover it up, 'I only said that nearly all learned ladies lose their feminine gentleness.'

'Pardon me,' said Delicia, 'You said "women who write books, like my wife"—these were the exact words you had used.… All the time that I worshipped you, you had been betraying me. You've killed me with your cruelty.'

* * *

After some more talk Delicia said, 'I want to tell you—from now on we shall live separately. The reason is I don't want to pay for dressing up chorus girls. Neither do I want to pay for our generosity to Lady Branswith.'

Lord Carlyon said, 'Are you mad, Delicia? Do you really want to live by yourself? How will you manage?'

'I'll live, I won't die. Don't worry about that.'

He thought, maybe, Delicia's anger has died down by now and tried to come near her. Delicia quickly took up her revolver and said, 'Be careful don't try to come near me.'

He smiled a little, 'You are mad, Delicia. Put down that gun though it may be empty. It doesn't become you!'

'No, it doesn't become me, but it's not empty. I took care to fill it before you came. I give you my word that I'll fire it if you do not but take one step forward.'

* * *

She now stretched out her hand for the final goodbye and said, 'Goodbye, Will. I had truly loved you. Even till a few days ago you had been everything to me. That love is gone forever. But let us part in peace for its sake.'

He did not touch her outstretched hand. He was not going to take leave of her that easily. He went on trying to justify himself. But Delicia did not speak anymore. She continued to write.

'Are you listening?' said Lord Carlyon, 'I'm not going to leave you.' Delicia did not move or say a word. Only her pen moved.

Lord Carlyon said, 'The government is right in curbing the rights of women. If you got all you want then there will be no end to your tyranny. Women should be quiet and modest. If they are lucky enough to be rich then their money should be spent for the welfare of their husbands. This is the law of nature. Women are meant to serve men. Problems come up only when they don't want to do it.'

If an Englishman can speak like this then why are we surprised at seeing the meanness of a few England-returned men? It is not impossible that those who go to England to get a degree should get poisoned at the contact of a few Carlyons. All right. All that Lord

Carlyon said is very true. Now why does the government not get rid of all women by firing at them? What are so many cannons and guns for? Or, better still, one can put all the women of the British Empire in a room with the necessary amount of gunpowder and just blow them up, thereby getting rid of all troubles at one stroke. No one will be alive to write a *Tragedy of Delicia* or *The Tale of Mazluma's Murder* then.[10]

Let us be thankful that the number of Carlyons is not very high in England, only a hundred or two. There are great-hearted men like Mr Cavendish or Mr Paul Valdes too as well as men like Carlyon. As a rule, men like the former predominate. In our country too there are a few (though not many) such liberal men. Let us thank God that there are a few flowers in this wilderness of thorns.

Delicia went on writing in silence. Lord Carlyon at last said, 'I'm going to bed. Goodnight, Delicia.' Now at last Delicia looked at him and said, 'Goodnight'. This was their goodbye, their last meeting. She shut the door on him as he left.

While the fever is raging the patient has a kind of energy. The day the fever leaves for good the patient becomes extremely feeble, all of a sudden. As long as Lord Carlyon was in the room, the excitement of anger and mortification kept Delicia strong. As soon as he left she broke down. Gradually consciousness left her. She fainted.

Next day she could not get up. She stayed in her room the whole day with a broken heart and a broken body. The same morning Lord Carlyon started for Paris, leaving a letter for her. The morning mail brought many letters. When reading them, Delicia sighed, 'They (the writers) don't know I'm dead.'

What is remarkable in Delicia's character is this: though society and the law was against her she managed to free herself of her faithless husband. One has to admire her moral courage. How noble she is! She does not need the love of a man who loves La Marina. She said clearly to her husband, 'The hand which has dirtied itself by touching La Marina has no right to touch me.'

You might say that she could do this only because she had money of her own. Had she been dependent on her husband for her daily bread she could not have done it. But the idea we get of her personality, of her independent spirit makes us think that even if she had been penniless she would still have been separated. She would have left the palace of Lord Carlyon to become a teacher at a school, or a governess, or a nurse in some hospital. She did not live for long after driving away her husband. She would certainly have found some way or other for earning a livelihood for herself for the rest of her days. Where there is a will there is a way.

This attitude of Delicia, why, her very death is extremely beneficial to society. A few Mazlumas will have to meet their fate like Delicia if any reform is to be brought about in society. When has ever any good been done to the world without the self-sacrifice of a great man?[11] But in order to have such an attitude or such good taste one should have education. When, oh when, will Mazluma become a heroic woman like Delicia?

She made her will before her death. She left an annuity of £300 per month for her husband. The rest, £60,000 went to the poor. The money from the sale of her books was to be given to the poor too.

She passed away, while Lord Carlyon was still in Paris, of a heart attack.

How full of despair is this story of Delicia! She died of sheer misery in the very flowering of her life. The bud withered away unopened. Who is going to find out how many such Mazlumas die of broken heart in a dark corner inside our own homes? The rising and setting of their sun is not recorded in any almanac.

Whatever her married life had been like, Delicia had not been happy in her social life either. Why was it that she did not get the honour that was due to her? Because she was essentially a meek person. As she was a well-established writer in her own right she posed a threat to other male writers. What! A woman has so much ambition? This was not to be borne by society. So society got some satisfaction in saying, 'Most of her books are written by Carlyon.' One will have to praise the writer (the books were well-written), so let us give the praise to Carlyon instead of Delicia.

Who mourned sincerely for Delicia? It was Spartan. If he had the gift of speech he would say 'If being truthful, faithful, and devoted are good qualities then dogs are better than men. If selfishness, slyness, and hypocrisy are good then men are better than dogs.'

What do our Bengali brothers say to this? This is said by an English woman. Our native lords are powerless to say anything to her. Even if they said anything it is doubtful if their voice would reach the writer across the seas. What can you do, brother? You can but shed silent tears.

Dear reader! I know you are tired at the end of this long novel now. Even then I cannot let you go without giving you the last sentence of the book:[12]

'Not a tear, not a heartthrob of one pure woman wronged shall escape the eyes of Eternal Justice, or fail to bring punishment upon the wrongdoer!

This we may believe, this we must believe, else God Himself would be a demon and the world His Hell!'

Notes

1. The actual pronunciation is 'Dilisia' but in Bengali 'Delisia' will sound much better so we have spelt it as 'Delicia'.

2. The former is the Indian God of War, the second the Goddess of Learning (added by the translators).

3. The phrase 'female author' is the author's own (added by the translators).

4. Miss Corelli had perhaps never visited India and so she has described women being penned as an ancient custom. We do not call our home a 'pen' but does it matter? Fact is Fact.

5. It is a blessing that time and tide do not wait for the vote of men. When an Englishman thinks like this then what can we expect from an Indian?

6. The writer uses the word '*jugnu*' for a pandant. The jewelled pendant in a centre of a five-fold or seven-fold necklace is called a 'pendant' but the ornament which is actually a pendant is called a 'jugnu' in Bihar. In Bengal a pendant is not an ornament by itself. In Bihar a jugnu is an ornament. So we used the word 'jugnu'. In the translation 'pendant' has been used. (added by the translators)

In the translation 'pendant' has been used.

7. The word 'chivalry' is the author's own (added by the translators).

8. When she drank she threw the bottles at her lovers. Tonight he had got a taste of her drunken temper.

9. Mr Valdes is a famous actor.

10. *The Murder of Delicia* has on p. 282: Edward Fitzgerald, one of England's greatest poets wrote thus—'Mrs. Barrett Browning is dead. Thank God we shall have no more *Aurora Leighs*.' It is the manner assumed by men who have neither the brain nor the feeling to write an *Aurora Leigh* themselves.

11. There are some sentences to this effect in the 'Introduction'.

12. This sentence has been quoted by the writer in the footnote and translated by her in the text. Since the original is available a translation of her translation has not been attempted (added by the translators).

The Fruit of Knowledge[1]

In olden days Adam and Eve used to dwell in the Garden of Eden. They were the guests of God and lived in great happiness, lacking nothing. God had only forbidden them to eat the fruit of a certain tree.

One day Eve, walking along the saffron-strewn love paths of Paradise, reached the Forbidden Tree. She was gazing, enchanted, at the beautiful trees of the garden. Listening to the song of the birds she plucked a few fruits in an absent-minded way and ate one Forbidden Fruit.

The moment she ate it her eyes were opened. She came to understand that though they were living like kings as the guest of the King, she did not have even a piece of cloth on her beautiful body. She at once covered herself with her long tresses that came down to the knees. Her heart became heavy with an unknown pain.

At this time Adam reached and Eve asked him to eat the fruit in her hand. Eating this half-eaten fruit his mind also awoke to knowledge. He realized his miserable condition with the whole of his being. 'Is this Heaven? A loveless, jobless, idle life—is this the bliss of Heaven?', he asked himself. Moreover he understood that he was a prisoner, he did not have the power to step outside the boundaries of this garden. He has a palace made of bricks of silver and gold joined with mortar of pearl and coral dust, but he does not have anything to call his own, not even a piece of cloth on his body. What kingly luxury is this? Now the ignorance of a dream of heavenly bliss vanished—knowledge, like awakening after sleep, made everything clear. Consciousness and restlessness replaced the peaceful placidity of entrancement. He said to Eve, 'What a spell had we been labouring under! We were so happily entranced in our condition.'

Eve answered, 'Yes. This beauteous land with fragrant beds of saffron like grass, this delicate spray of diamond flowers, these trees with leaves like emeralds and flowers like rubies—all these please the eye but cannot satisfy the aspirations of the mind. The lotus-laving nectar-like waters of the heavenly lake quench the body's thirst, but not that of the heart. What do we need these heavenly luxuries for?' Both of them pined for an unknown change.

God came and saw that the couple hid behind a tree on seeing Him. He called them but they could not come near Him because of shame and a sense of injury. God, who is omniscient, understood everything. He became angry with them and said, 'So you want to be free? Go away then. Go to Earth and see how sweet freedom is.'

That was the Fall, and the couple came to the Earth. Here they went through many trials 'for better, for worse; for richer, for poorer; in sickness, in health', and came to know true conjugal life. Eve loved the daughters more and she blessed them with longevity, peaceful domestic life, and the treasure of undying love in their hearts.

Adam loved his sons more, but as his willpower was not very strong he did not grant them any specific boon.

Mother Eve's blessings made her daughters prosper day by day. Adam's sons went on falling ill because of too careful an upbringing, and died quickly. When they did not die a natural death they fought each other, injured and killed each other, threw each other into prisons, and suffered many other evils.

The half-eaten Fruit of Knowledge which Eve had thrown on the ground grew into a huge tree in the eastern part of the Earth. In due time it was full of fruits and flowers. But the people of that country did not know how to care for it. The ground below it was strewn with ripe fruits. Crows and foxes would come and fill themselves, and the rest of the fruits rolled to the banks of a river nearby and some fell into the river. The river water, mixed with the juice of the fruit, flowed into the sea, on the other side of which was Fairyland.

The people of Fairyland were very fine to look at, but they had little except physical beauty to boast of. Their land did not grow proper food either, only the tasteless, un-nourishing food, the *makal* fruit.[2] The djinns,[3] though they laboured hard, could not produce proper food in this harsh, infertile country. The peris dwelt in luxurious palaces and were surrounded by many luxuries. They were very wealthy, yet they suffered from hunger—such is God's will!

One day a few djinns, driven by hunger, drank a little sea water. At once their ignorance vanished. The problem of food that had troubled them for ages was solved in a trice. The light of knowledge made the way clear to them. That very day they decided to set sail for trading.

They filled their ship with the fruits they had and started on their voyage. After touching many countries the ship reached the Isle of Gold, inhabited by a race with golden skin.

The merchant was dazzled at the sight of the prosperous cities of this country. They used to think that there was no land as rich as theirs. But the soil of this country was extremely fertile. There were many kinds of fruit trees there, the chief of which was the mango. The highly civilized saintly people of the country lived on fruits. The djinn merchants thought, 'If only we can fool them!' So they exchanged the makal fruits they had brought for mangoes of different varieties. This went on for years. Every year they brought a cargo of makals and exchanged it for that of mangoes. But as their trade prospered there came about a famine of mangoes in the Isle of Gold.

Next year the merchants were worried at seeing the shops sparse of mangoes. They went into the villages to find more. They saw the fields glowing with golden paddy, ripe for harvest. The peasants were happily carrying bundles of rice to their homes. The merchants sighed, 'They do not suffer from hunger!' Then after a little hesitation the merchants offered to exchange makals for the grains. The peasants did not understand their language. Little plump children surrounded them and looked at their hands and faces with great interest. The merchants thought, 'What's this? Have we become objects of amusement for peasant children?'

Anyway, the merchants managed to make themselves understood by the peasants. At first the peasant did not want to exchange paddy for makals but then, his son said, 'Oh Dad, give them. They're hungry, and we have lots.'[4]

The Fairyland, highly developed in knowledge, increased its trade year by year. Now there was no lack of food so the peris did not suffer in any way any longer. From time to time they rode their magic chariots and came to the Isle of Gold. They became friendly with the women of this country who tried to imitate the peris in their costumes. Only the imitation of their wings was still left to be done!

Formerly only a ship or two had come once a year to the island with makal, but later many ships full of this fruit came there around three or four times a year, and tons of paddy were exported. The fruit was so beautiful to look at that the peasants could not control themselves. They left storing grains in granaries and started selling as soon as the grains were harvested so there was famine in the land.

At this time another significant event had happened. A wonderful guava tree had grown by the seaside. Nourished by the waters that contained the juice of the Fruit of Knowledge, these guavas had some of the attributes of that fruit. The djinns and the peris used to gather and keep the fruits carefully for themselves. But one day when the merchants were loading the ships with makals a few guavas fell into the ship. Those were brought to the Isle of Gold and sold along with the makals.

A few lucky ones ate the guavas from Fairyland and threw away the seeds. So guava trees grew from those seeds in this land too. Gradually, a hundred years passed.

The virtues of these guavas made a few gentlemen of the Isle of Gold open their eyes. What an awakening it was after the enchanted sleep of centuries! But then, they were cast into darkness when the light of knowledge opened their eyes. For, they looked about and saw how the djinns had taken away everything from their country in exchange of the worthless makal fruit. Now they were sucking their blood like leeches. Their hearts bled at the sight of the misery in their country.

The mango orchards are no longer there. Fruits do not hang upon the boughs of the trees any longer. No grains exist to be harvested. The fertile land is lying barren. Grim hunger is reigning in every home. The peasants are not plump as they used to be. They have become skeletal, wearing ragged clothes. The people have nothing now—except for makal fruits. The shops lining the streets sell makal, the village markets sell makal, and so do the groceries. What is to be done now?

But it was a blessing in disguise that along with the makals they also got the guava of knowledge; so it was not long before they found a way. They swore they will not take any more makals now. Everyone, young and old, all took a solemn vow that they would not be spell-bound by the makals anymore. They had got a new enthusiasm and great strength which would not have been possible if they had not been exchanged by makals. They thanked the djinns a hundred-fold for this unintentional benefit.

The makal-filled ships came into the port as usual. But this time the cargo was not sold. When the merchants could not get rid of the fruits, all the fruits, which were so beautiful to look at, started rotting and they sent the news to their home, the Fairyland.

The result was a lot of commotion. Even the water of the sea was stirred with this. Finally a grey-haired Ancient said, 'Go and find out why the men of the Isle of Gold do not want makals any longer.'

The merchants went everywhere in the island, listened to many rumours and came to know that those who have eaten guavas have turned against makals. The merchants sent this news in a minute to Fairyland with their magic power. That very day the leader of the merchants ordered, 'Uproot the guavas.'

The merchants informed the leader, 'It is not possible to uproot such a big tree. What are your further orders?' At once the leader said, 'Cut it down at the root.'

Hundreds of axes started raining blows at the roots of the tree. At first the people of the country were surprised, then they understood the whole thing. At first they pleaded with the merchants, falling at their feet and begging them to stop. But the djinns would not stop at any price. Then the whole country became highly disturbed. The peaceful land burnt with the fire of disturbance. Still the djinns would not desist; instead they tried to persuade the people by saying: 'You must know that God had forbidden the Fruit of Knowledge to mankind, and Mother Eve was driven out of Paradise for eating it. So this Fruit is very bad for men. It is for your own good that we are labouring so hard to cut down this tree.'

But the people of the country had become enlightened. They were not going to be deceived by false arguments. They said, 'Then why do you all eat it? Go and cut down the guava trees in Fairyland first, then come and cut ours. If our First Mother gave up Paradise itself for this fruit then we can guess its inestimable value. A fruit brought from Heaven should be treasured carefully on earth.' But this was against the vested interests of the djinns, and they did not listen to it.

A lot of argumentation went on for quite some time. The Isle of Gold discussed the cutting down of the tree in detail. Then an octogenarian scholar said, 'Why are you quarrelling for this miserable guava? It's only a transformed version of the original Fruit of Knowledge. You had better try for the primal tree planted by the Primal Mother. The scriptures tell us that it is in the eastern part of the world. Let's go and look for it.' So everyone left the present to look for the past. The Ancient, however did not go with them. He rested content after giving the advice.

The men of the Isle of Gold travelled far and travelled long, climbed hills and crossed rivers, passed through deserts and forests and finally reached a huge dead tree at the place marked out. After examining many scriptures and listening to many legends they came to the conclusion that this dead tree was indeed the original Tree of Knowledge. Their sorrow knew no bounds. Had they come, after infinite trouble, suffering hunger and thirst in strange lands, just for this dead tree? The local people said the tree had died about 200 years ago. One of the seekers said, 'Thank God that you haven't used it for fuel.'

What was to be done now? How can it be given new life? Some said, 'Water it', some said, 'wet it with tears', and some said, 'wet it with your heart's blood'.

Many proposals came forward. They would not hesitate if even the sacrifice of a few lives will bring it to life.

They started caring for it in many different ways. Neither tears nor blood was denied. But can the dead come to life? All efforts went in vain and they started lamenting. One of the men, tired with weeping, lay down at the root of the tree. He dreamt that a hermit was telling him:

> My child, it's no use weeping. The tree won't come alive whether you sacrifice two million men or three. Two centuries ago the idiotic scholars, blinded by selfishness and lack of foresight, had forbidden women to eat the Fruit. This came to be accepted in time as a social law and men monopolized the Fruit. Women were barred from plucking and eating the fruit, stopped taking care of it and, deprived of their caressing gentle touch the tree died. Now go back to your country. Take the seeds of this tree and plant them. If the djinns want to cut the tree down, let them. Don't

obstruct them but store the seeds in secret. The care of the saplings should be taken by men and women together, and you'll get the fruit you want. But be careful. Don't deprive the womenfolk. Remember a woman brought this fruit and women have every right over it.

On waking up this man related the dream to his friends, and all of them said, 'Let's go back.' A generous man said, 'Yes. Some men once crossed a river on the back of a crocodile and then didn't give it what they had promised. These people had deprived women of that which was brought by a woman. Now they have to suffer for it.'

The boys of the Isle of Gold cleared a space in the garden, then called the girls and said, 'Come, sisters! Join us. Let's prepare the soil with spades and you all plant the seeds with your own hands. What an auspicious day this is! We shall have our own tree from now.' The djinns, awestruck, stood silently. They could not throw any obstacles in the way of this holy work. Nobody, neither djinns nor giants could stop this noble work begun with new hopes, and new aims and aspirations.

Then the Isle of Gold became doubly and trebly prosperous. The people therein dwelt in happiness. They are not going to be fooled with any enchantment now, for women have become thefoundresses of the Garden of Knowledge.

'This fairy tale is a wonderful tale.
A dead man will rise up if he hears it well.'

(There is no information about the publication of this tale.)

Notes

1. Neither the Koran nor the Bible has been followed in this story.

2. The authoress has named the fruit 'Makal'. In Bengali, though it is a real fruit, the name symbolizes attractive appearance but no real worth (added by the translators).

3. Djinn: male; Peri: female.

4. Alas, alas:

> You gave away your wealth
> to another
> And you exchanged your
> wealth for hunger.

The Creation of Woman

(A few days ago I read a fine humorous story about the creation of woman in an English newspaper. I could not resist the temptation of presenting my sisters with a translation of this story. I will say beforehand that I will not give a literal translation—instead I will give the main ideas. Let not anyone be annoyed or disappointed at the disparity between this and the original.)

Colonel Ingersoll liked to tell an old legend about the creation of woman whenever he delivered the speech, 'The Mistake of Moses'. He wanted to prove how much more liberal and nobler this oriental story is than the account given in the Bible. I do not know whether, if he had read the following account in Hindu mythology he would have taken it for the best of all such creation myths.

This Sanskrit manuscript has been but lately discovered. Mr Bain, an Englishman, has translated it. After that it was published in the *Chicago Times Herald*. The story goes thus: 'In the beginning there was nothing but darkness—no sun, moon, stars, or the Earth. The Hindu god Tvasti created the universe. When, at the end, the time for creating Woman came, the creator Tvasti saw that he had used up all the available raw material in creating Man. Nothing solid or dense was left. Not able to decide anything in his despair, he sank into contemplation.'

After much contemplation, Tvasti stood up and collected the essence of certain things—the roundness of the full moon, the curving dynamism of serpents, the dependence of creepers and vines, the light vibration of grass, the fragrance of roses, the delicateness of flowers, the lightness of new leaves, the glance of deers, the brightness of sunlight, the tears of mists, the restlessness of wind, the timidity of rabbits, the vanity of peacocks, the softness of birds wings, the hardness of diamond, the sweetness of honey, the warmth of fire, the cool of snow, the cooling of doves, the chattering of magpies....

After translating this much I felt so tired that I put down my head on my left arm on the table. Probably I dozed a bit. Suddenly my room became very bright, as if four suns were shining there. I looked up and saw a very bright figure standing in front of me like a pillar of light. My eyes were dazzled and I closed them. The shining figure in front of me, in a voice of thunder, said: 'Hear me, my child. I'm the Creator, Tvasti. I'm pleased with what thou wrote about my creation of woman. I've used 33 ingredients in creating her. The Englishman, Mr Bain left out 12 of them by mistake when translating the Sanskrit book. It has now pleased me to come here to correct that mistake, for there should not be any mistake in the scriptures. I'll tell thee the names of those 12 things. Do write them down.'

Spellbound, I took up the pen and started to write slowly.

'The sourness of tamarinds, the hotness of black pepper, the flavour of salt, the sweetness of sugarcane....

Thinking that there was some mistake I stopped. Then plucking up courage I said,'O Great One, these are the spices for pickles!'

God Tvasti, smiling yet firm, said, 'Write down whatever I say'. Then, without another word I wrote down like a machine: 'The bitterness of quinine, false arguments of the illogical, the jabbering of the quarrelsome, the absentmindedness of philosophers, the mistakes of politicians, the fortitude of stones, the liquidness of water, and the entrancement of sleep'.

My sisters reading this book may have become quite annoyed by now because of this break in the story. But what can I do? You cannot act independently when translating another's writing; especially if you are writing something historical, then you have to chain your imagination too. Now let us go on with the translation. No, I had better give the list from the beginning, mixing the translation with my dream vision of the God:

> After some contemplation, Tvasti stood up and collected the essence of certain things: the roundness of the full moon, the curving dynamism of serpents, the dependence of creepers and vines, the light vibration of grass, the fragrance of roses, the delicateness of flowers, the lightness of new leaves, the glance of deers, the brightness of sunlight, the tears of mists, the restlessness of the wind, the timidity of rabbits, the vanity of peacocks, the softness of birds' wings, the hardness of diamonds, the sweetness of honey, the warmth of fire, the cool of snow, the cooing of doves, the chattering of magpies, the bitterness of quinine, false arguments of the illogical, the jabbering of the quarrelsome, the absentmindedness of philosophers, the mistakes of politicians, the fortitude of stones, the liquidness of water, and the entrancements of sleep.

The God Tvasti got these 33 ingredients together and mixed them well with an egg beater and built woman. It goes without saying he had to face a lot of trouble creating her. He had to do a lot of research work, think long, meditate deeply, and labour hard. The more trouble taken over anything, the better it is. After you have done apprentice work in making a lot of things and then finally make something, then that last thing is definitely the best. So there can be no doubt that woman is the best creature created by God. Then Tvasti gave Man this Woman as a precious gift.[1]

After eight days Man came to him and said: 'Oh Lord, the woman thou gavest me has made my life a misery. She is chattering away all the time. She doesn't allow me a moment's rest. She weeps without any reason. She's bad, she's very bad.' So Tvasti took her back.

After eight more days had passed, Man came to the God again and said, 'Oh Lord, my life has become lonely and tasteless ever since I returned the Woman thou gavest me. I remember how lovely she was. She used to sing and dance and play before me. I remember the way she glanced at me—oh by my faith, how she used to send sidelong glances to me! She was my companion to play with, my soulmate. I can't bear to be separated from her.' Without a word God Tvasti gave the Woman back to him.[2]

On the fourth day Tvasti saw Man coming to him, with the Woman. After paying him homage Man said, 'Lord, forgive me, I can't quite make out whether Woman is the cause of my happiness or of my annoyance. But there is more suffering than joy. Oh Lord, set me free from her.'

This time Tvasti got angry and said, 'Go, and do thou as thou likest'. Man cried out loudly and said, 'She will be the death of me, Oh Lord. I can't I really can't spend my whole life with her. I can't stay with her'. Tvasti said, 'But thou cannot stay without her, either'.

 Man started to lament, 'How troublesome this is! I can't shed this burden, nor do I want to keep it.'

Ever since then Woman has been a burden, as a curse to Man.

(Md. Nasiruddin ed. *Saugāt*, Paus 1325)
Rept. Caitra 1375

Notes

1. The gift was like casting pearls before the swine!
2. Woman too was a brainless, mindless puppet. She did not feel insulted when Man refused her. Nor did she feel any pride when he came to take her back. God Tvasti knew, of course, that Man deserved such a 'wooden puppet' for his wife.

Nurse Nellie*

1

My youngest sister-in-law Khuki had been ailing for three years. Finally, advised by the doctor, she has come to Lucknow for a change on her life. I have accompanied her to take care of her. By the grace of God there are many persons in our group including her husband, son, and others.

Hem Babu, a friend of ours, was in Lucknow as well. I heard that his wife Bimala was ill and hospitalized. So I went to see her. She was lying down. A nurse used to change her clothes and bandage her arm; nurses used to do everything for her. I was there for about two hours and saw about five of them going in and out on different errands. But the nurse who took away the bucket of blood looked rather odd to me.

* Based on real events.

I visited her on alternate days. It was not that I was very eager to see her; rather it was the thin and sad nurse whom I wanted to see. She was the very embodiment of sorrow. It was as if her face was very well known to me, or half known, and I felt—I do not know what I felt on seeing her. One day Bimala asked, 'Tell me, why do you stare at Nurse Nellie like that?' I hid my thoughts and said, 'I feel sympathy for her, she has such a sad face'.

Bimala replied, 'Yes, she has many troubles and I too feel bad for her. But what to do? You can't help her by giving a little money. She gets Rs 6 which is just enough to live on. At first I did give a little. But then I came to know that Sister Riva takes away everything and distributes it among all the workers in the hospital—maybe she gets a little bit from time to time. See how unfair Sister Riva is. Nellie does all the dirty work and never gets good things to eat.'

'Is she a sweeper by caste?'

Bim: 'No, she's a Bengali Christian. I've heard she had been a housewife at one time. The Christian priests persuaded her to become a Christian, and took her out of her home. They changed her name to Nellie. She knows Bengali and so she has been assigned to us, i.e., Bengali patients. They don't allow her to enter the quarters of Muslim girls as they are afraid that someone will turn her into a Muslim, and, do you know, she can read the Koran quite well.'

I felt very odd on hearing that she could read the Koran. Who knew which Muslim family she had plunged into darkness by leaving it! Oh, what an insult to the noble Koran! Christian Nellie, female sweeper Nellie, who cleans the buckets of filth with her hands, touches the holy Koran with the same hands. The work she does is that of a sweeper but the hospital authorities call her a nurse.

I used to go to see Bimala but never got a chance to talk to Nellie. She used to come to us to do different tasks, or used to look at me with her big, lovely eyes. When I looked at her she would cast them down and go away. I tried to find a way to come near her. Even if I got a chance to ask her something she would just weep. Then I got a good opportunity to be near her.

The doctors decided to operate on Khuki. But I just would not allow her to be taken to the hospital. There was a lot of argumentation with *Dulha Mian* (her husband). He tried very hard to make me realize the many benefits of a hospital, reciting logic tome and showing me the example of Hem Babu's wife. But it was a hospital which had once brought me ruin. My very soul was burnt. That injury had still not healed. But I did not say all that to Dulha Mian. Finally it was I who triumphed. Dulha Mian said, 'Blessed be woman's superstition!', and quit arguing. It was decided the operation would be conducted at home.

Next day in due time Miss Folly, a senior doctor, arrived with her retinue. There were two or three nurses with her also. We were all Bengalis and did not know a word of Hindi and so Nurse Nellie had come to interpret. After the operation everyone went away except for two nurses—Nellie and Lizzie.

Next day after everyone had taken their meals and the patients had been given food and medicine, I asked Nellie in private: 'Nurse, where do you come from?' She fell down at my feet, controlled her tears with much effort and asked, '*Bubujan*, don't you recognize me?'

What! My head spun round and I sat down on the floor. Yes, I did recognize her. Oh, what a terrible truth, what a cruel truth had I discovered! Nellie told me the history of her misery, each word bathed in tears.

2

My father lived in village—pur. When my grandfather died, my father and uncle divided the property between them. There were only three members in my uncle's family (except for the servants)—he, his wife, and their daughter, Nayeema. In our family there were five of us siblings, and then our parents, which made it a total of seven. Even then we used to hear that uncle had no money, that there were many debts, etc.

Our family was a quite well-to-do. We used to eat well, dress well, and had a lot of ornaments. There was no house like ours, surrounded by trees as it was. We had three hundred and fifty bighas of tax-free land with only our house in it. There was quite a forest outside our house, with tigers, boars, and foxes. We did not have clocks but that was no loss. In the morning different birds sang their songs to wake us and when evening came foxes told us the time for evening prayer had drawn near. At night the nightbirds would hoot and tell us the time. Our childhood had been spent in great happiness amid entirely rural surroundings.

Sometime later our aunt passed away, leaving her only child, a girl of three years. My uncle was at sea. His main problem was bringing up this daughter. My mother consoled him: 'Why do you worry so much? Nayeema's mother is gone, but I'm still here. Zubeida, Abida, and Hamida grew up in these arms and my lap has room for Nayeema now, hasn't it?' Uncle was greatly relieved. The next day he left Nayeema, along with five servants, with us and went away.

Nayeema was the youngest of us all and so we loved her very much. My father loved her the best of us all. So she was treated like a princess among us all.

We did not go in for higher education in the village. Nayeema learnt whatever little we ourselves learnt. All the domestic crafts of villages, like different kinds of needlework and many such things. Our relatives thought that nothing was quite so useless for a woman as learning to read and write.

Nayeema has been staying with us for seven years.[1] My uncle has passed away. He has wasted all the property he had inherited, except for Nayeema's mother's ornaments. These he had given to my father.

A few days ago my elder brother Jamal Ahmad has been transferred here from a foreign country and has come home after getting the post of D.M. I have come from my husband's home to meet him and a few more relatives have also come. Our house is full of relatives.

The four of us sisters were sitting and talking one day when my elder brother came there. He asked us, 'Don't you all study? How can you go on with such dark minds? Nayeema, don't you study at all?' Nayeema said, 'I've read the Koran. These days I'm learning to translate the Koran.' My brother said, 'And this is all? Don't you read anything else, a little Bengali, a little English?'

I showed off my experience of eighteen years of life and said, '*Bhaijaan*, you've learnt a lot of Bengali and English, gone abroad, and come back as a D.M. or Collector. What will Nayeema become by learning English? Where will she go as the Collector?'

Bhaijaan replied, 'If she becomes educated then she can become the wife of a Collector. She'll get a good husband, a good family.'

All of us laughed. I ran to Mummy and told her this odd whim of Bhaijaan. I said, surprised, 'Bhaijaan says that Nayeema can become the wife of a Collector if she's educated'. Mummy became a bit grave and said, 'Hm. All right, then. That will be done.'

3

Our house has the air of a festival. Nayeema is getting married to Bhaijaan. There is no limit to our joy—our doll Nayeema will become our elder sister-in-law. My youngest sister Abida is quite angry; she will never touch Nayeema's feet and do salaam to her because Nayeema is two years younger to her. All of us teased Abida crazy with this. Bhaijaan too is quite annoyed—in fact he is furious. He has been travelled to England, and is dead against child marriage. How can he make himself ridiculous by marrying a ten-year old girl? He will not be able to face the society of educated Bengalis. He is blaming me—'Zubeida is to be blamed. I said something purely as a joke and she went and told Mummy about it, and now there is all this trouble.'

Let my Bhaijaan get angry or whatever, he has one great virtue—he is obedient to his parents and other relatives. A few conciliating words from my mother and father's advice easily won his consent. Mummy said that she has brought this orphan up with great care and did not want her to go to another family. Bhaijaan did not say anything after that, but got ready for the marriage like a good boy, an obedient son.

A distant cousin, asked me, 'What, won't you put *mehndi* on the foreign-returned sahib?'

Bhaijaan said with repressed anger, 'Do whatever you like. If you're satisfied by covering me with mehndi or worse, I've no objection. I've bowed my head. Torture me as you like.'

At once I prepared mehndi and put it on his palms. I had not wanted to keep it there for long but I went away on some other errand and completely forgot all about it. Coming back after quite some time I saw my poor Bhaijaan sitting quietly with his arms on the handles of the chair. I quickly washed them and he got so angry on seeing his palms red! He has learnt a lot about botany and all, but he did not know about the attributes of mehndi. He snatched his hands away from mine and used a lot of soap to wash them in the bathroom, but the colour remained.

4

An aristocratic Muslim lady has been in the Women's Hospital for the last two months, with her six-month-old baby boy Jafar. She is being pampered no end. The senior and junior doctors and the nurses are always with her taking turns. She queens it right royally here. Her husband and brother-in-law also came occasionally with her five-year-old daughter Jamila. The patient is my sister-in-law, Nayeema. My mother did not want to send her to the hospital.

But as her condition deteriorated Bhaijaan told Mummy, 'Mummy, I've never disobeyed you till now. But now a life depends on the treatment given in the hospital, please don't stop me now. I won't be able to obey you now.' Bhaijaan has repented of this one instance of disobedience throughout his life.

Some missionary women are talking and laughing in the adjoining room. One of them said, 'Now we'll see. The wretched critics won't be able to say that we convert only the famine-struck starving beggars.'

2nd WOM.: 'Even the Bishop of Calcutta would have been pleased to have got such a prize!'

3rd WOM.: 'Oh, how clever you are—you've only made a fool of a girl of nineteen (I would call her a girl though she's the mother of two children) and converted her. What's so difficult in that, pray?'

1st WOM.: 'It may not be difficult, but ... will tremble—it will disturb the whole of Bengal. It's not a joke to catch the wife of a Collector.'
2nd WOM.: 'It's getting late. Let's go to the room of Nayeema Bibi where I'm to sing a hymn today. She'll stay here for another month. Time enough for us!'

Two or three missionary ladies used to visit Nayeema all the time. It was their first duty to look after and nurse the sick. Nayeema had been spellbound by their selfless love. They used to sing hymns in the evening, talking about the greatness of Jesus, and showing her the way to save herself from eternal hellfire. Nayeema did not know anything about the history, philosophy or science of her own religion. The greatness of Christ influenced her pure heart very deeply. Physically she improved, but mentally she deteriorated. Even the light of a glow-worm seems wonderful to one who has never seen the light of the sun. Nayeema's state of mind was very much the same.

5

Nayeema, no, my Bhabijaan, came back from the hospital three months later. But she had changed a lot. She was no longer the sweet-spoken, smiling Nayeema she used to be. Now she does not speak to others as nicely as she used to. Everyone thought that she had become irritable through long illness. Bhaijaan sent her to the country with Mummy. He thought that the healthy village air will improve her physically and mentally. But that did not happen. She had not forgotten her friends of the hospital. The rural air did not appeal to her any longer.

One day she asked her mother-in-law why she had not been given higher education? What did they lack; what obstacle was there? My mother looked at her daughter-in-law in surprise. Then she smilingly said, 'What are you saying? Have you run mad or what?'

Nayeema replied, 'So I'm talking nonsense? You've turned me into an ignorant animal. You haven't taught me to read and write so that I might sit in polite society. My husband talked about my education, and you hurriedly married me off, casting me into bondage.'

MUMMY: 'You were never such a chatterbox as this! From where have you learnt all this? I've brought you up from three years old. Why, you're a cherished treasure! I've kept you in my own family instead of sending you away to another. Do you regard that as a bondage?'

NAYEEMA: 'How can ignorance understand the importance of education? So you didn't think it to be necessary. You understood only marriage.'

MUMMY: 'Child, you show me what is what by educating your own daughter, making her pass her L.A., B.A. examinations. I'm not saying that education is bad, but we didn't have the ways and means in these rural parts. There are no schools of any kind here. We can't even get lady teachers to come and do the teaching. If you can educate yourself in the town, well and good.'

So that was what happened. There was no good arrangement for educating girls in the village and even if there were one or two Muslim girls' schools like oases in a desert, good families would not send their girls there. Besides, what will the people of suburbs do? So, a few missionary ladies were employed by turn for Jamila. They, following their own rules, would start with a story from the Bible and then move on to other things. This too was not at all convenient.

Finally an European governess was employed. She gradually extended her influence far enough to become my sister-in-law's companion, Jamila's teacher, and the mistress of the family. Miss Lawrence became everything in this family. She had cast a spell over the entire family with her sweet words.

6

There is a great deal of hullabaloo. The court is full of people. Almost all the people of the district are present there. What is the matter? The matter is this, Mrs Nayeema Khatoon, the wife of the Magistrate Mr Jamal Ahmad, has fled to the Lal Kuthi Mission House with ornaments worth Rs 2,500 and Rs 17,000 cash. The case has been going on for a whole month. This is the day of the verdict.

The reporters of different newspapers are also present; their papers will become very popular if they publish such sensational news.

There is a group that has come just for the sake of vulgar entertainment. Some have come just to jeer. Some have come in order to deliver speeches against women's education. Some just slander women's education. Some add insult to injury by congratulating Mr Jamal Ahmad on educating his daughter, saying that she had been brought to the highest peak of education. Some genuinely grieved, have come to sympathize. Some have come to console. A few have become alarmed at the thought that it will be difficult to guard the womenfolk at home. If the wife of a Collector has left her home because of the missionaries then what about us?

Nayeema herself declared that she has been converted to Christianity at her own will. She had not wanted to leave her home as she had no complaints against her husband and her mother-in-law. But the baptism could not have taken place at home and so she had come to the Mission House. She had left her husband, son, daughter, and home only for the sake of religion, for the sake of Christ.

The judge had tried to reach a compromise by saying that now that the baptism was over and done with she could come back home. But Miss Lawrence described the miserable condition of the women's quarters in the houses and especially that of Nayeema in a long speech, holding the audience spellbound. She had been in and out of the households in Bihar and in Bengal for ten years and knew everything about the women's quarters.

Finally it was decided that the cash and the ornaments Nayeema has brought with her will remain with her and the children with their father. Nayeema had tried quite hard to get the custody of her son and failed.

7

Nayeema is staying at Lal Kuthi with the missionary ladies. She is being petted and pampered. They cannot treasure her enough. What intense love for religion; what noble self-sacrifice! Can it be praised enough! She is the ideal woman in the Mission House. She is the jewel in the crown, the light of their eyes. Her head has been turned by too much praise and flattery. But why is she so sad after so much adulation?

Self-sacrifice for Christ was very attractive while she was still in her family. Then when the trial went on at court, when no hope was left of meeting her husband and children in this life, her happiness vanished. She started repenting even as she returned in triumph from the court. She fainted the minute she left the litter. The missionary women said, 'It's the heat', and started fanning her. Oh yes, heat was there, the heat of a burning heart was leaping within her in a conflagration.

As soon as she regained consciousness she cursed herself. She uttered the words of faith again and again, and called on Allah. But all this was useless now. Waking at night she would think, 'Let me run away and fall at the feet of my husband'. But she did not know the way. How far was the Collector's residence from Lal Kuthi? In which direction did it lie? Who will tell her the way? Alas, there was no one.

The missionary women petted her for as long as they did not get her money and ornaments. Gradually they took everything. Now she *owns* only two glass bangles and a coarse dhoti from England. These days they tell Nellie to walk to the church, which she will not do.

Finally they found it a burden to feed her. In this place everyone works, going from house to house, spreading the light of Christianity. Why should Nellie sit at home? Finally they sent her to the hospital to do nursing. But thinking it inadvisable to keep her in Bengal they sent her to Lucknow.

Nayeema had brought the Koran with her, thinking she will show the hollowness of Islamic religion by annihilating each of the sayings in it with logic. Those flights of imagination have vanished forever. Now that book is the only companion in her hour of sorrow. When everyone is asleep at night she washes and sits with the Koran. How can she read when her tears are wetting the pages? She has kept a blotting paper on each page. Nayeema, brought up in the lap of luxury, did not know that there is so much consolation in tears of penitence.

Her days are devoted to thoughts of her husband. Her husband has become everything to her. 'Oh God, throw me at the feet of my husband just once. Thou art Almighty, Thou canst do everything. Canst Thou do this little thing? The door for self-blame has not been closed even now. Accept the abasement of Nayeema, Oh Merciful!'

She has turned into Nurse Nellie in the hospital at Lucknow. She takes care of the patients during the day which makes it difficult to perform namaaz and read the Koran. She weeps all the time. At first the other nurses, even the lady doctors had tried to console her, but what consolation was there for one who has lost both this world and the next; one who has left her own kingdom and has turned into a despicable sweeper; one who has set fire to her own nest? Now no one tries to console her.

Seven long years have passed. Not one of these two thousand five hundred and fifty-five days of the seven years and eighty-four months, has passed without her tears. She just used to count the days, dragging her skeletal body. She would manage to spend her days somehow, waiting for the night. At night she will be able to pray and read the Koran; that is her only consolation. When she has night duty she is deprived of even this. Good God, she gets so much peace from doing namaaz at night and wetting her pillow with her tears!

I had not been able to recognize her at first since she had transformed into a skeleton. Then when she said, 'Bubujaan, don't you recognize me?', I had no doubts at all. Lightning coursed through my body. I sat down on the floor. Could I fail to recognize one who has been brought up by my own mother? Could I fail to recognize my own cousin? Does there exist a Bengali-Christian who can read the Koran, anywhere in the world? But alas, who could have wanted to see Nayeema, the bird of paradise, as a worm in hell? She had come to our home with five maid-servants, and is herself a servant now!

O Fate, so this is thy sportive unkindness
Casting to a pit of sorrow from peak of happiness.

8

I could not restrain my tears while listening to Nellie's saga of miseries. I was repeatedly telling myself that she was but suffering the results of her own sinning, that it was what she deserved, so why should it hurt me? But stones would have melted at the intense repentance and self-blame of Nayeema, let alone a human being.

After telling me everything and resting a little she asked me about her husband and her children. I told her everything in as controlled and brief a manner as possible. I said that Mummy took to her bed the day my Bhaijaan returned home defeated at the court. The only word she uttered to express her unbearable pain and despair was, 'Oh, Nayeema!' Bhaijaan, being a man, endured silently, without expressing any outward signs. He was like an angry lion, bearing all the shame, anger, and sorrow silently.

Mummy died after two months. Jamila fell ill with fever a few days later. She never dared to go to her father as he was always so forbiddingly grave. Her grandmother was her only refuge, and she broke down on losing her. She used to cry for her mother in fever, 'Mummy, why have you gone to the hospital again. Come back, please come back. Jafar cries so much for you and granny too is no here.' She did not suffer for long. Death released her from all suffering.

Bhaijaan became mad with grief on losing his mother and daughter within a fortnight. Endurance, too, has its limits. Jafar's weeping increased. Bhaijaan used to look after him very carefully. But how long can a year-old child remain healthy after losing its mother? He too passed away within a month.

Bhaijaan has not married till now. His family life is totally ruined. I am the only near relative he has. 'Oh Nayeema, look with your imagination at the burial ground you have yourself prepared and at your husband sitting amid destruction.' But before I could say it she fainted and fell down.

I was thinking of sprinkling a little water on her when Dulha Mian came and knocked at my door. His adolescent daughter Siddiqua was also with him. I did not dare touch Nellie in front of them. Siddiqua took me by the hand and took me to her mother.

9

By the grace of God, Khuki got well and we came home. Before we returned however we travelled to a few more cities, especially to Delhi, Agra, and Lahore. Anarkali's tomb at Lahore brought to my mind Emperor Akbar's might on one hand and Prince Salim's love on the other.[2]

Another thought came to my mind on seeing the Taj Mahal. However much women-hating men might rail against women's education, truth will triumph. Education is desirable for all, be it man or woman. Fire might burn down a house in a particular case, but can any housewife do without fire?

The Taj Mahal is renowned throughout the world, and is one of the Seven Wonders of the world. There are very few people in the world who do not know it by name. But how many sons know Mumtaz Mahal who is lying in eternal sleep inside it? Even such a beautiful edifice has not been able to make her memory eternal. And what about Begum Nur Jehan? Nothing has been done to perpetuate her memory. Her insignificant tomb is standing neglected and uncovered at a small unknown place in Lahore. Many do not know about its existence. But Begum Nur Jehan is eternally alive in our memories. What is the thing that had made her immortal? Why, it is education! The light of the world has become famous everywhere because of her education. God forbid, but the cannons of mighty energy might one day destroy the Taj but the memory of Begum Nur Jehan will never die.

All right, enough of digressions. Even after returning home I could not forget the earnest request of Nellie. She has clung to my feet and begged with tears to request Bhaijaan to bring her home. She wanted to spend the rest of her life as a maid-servant or a sweeper in the home of her husband. Too much of weeping has made her ill; she will not live for long. So during the Durga Puja holidays I went to my father's house, but father was no more, so I went to my brother's house.

One day I found my brother in a good mood. So I sat down near him and said, 'Bhaijaan, shall I massage your feet?' He smilingly said, 'All right, but with what motive?' I remembered my happy childhood days when if I wanted some kindness from him I would massage his feet and toes. That was why he asked if I had a motive. I expressed my motive with great difficulty, in as simple a manner as possible. I told him the heart-searing tale of Nayeema's sufferings and said, 'A faithful wife, Nayeema has been purified by the fire of repentance'.

After hearing everything he said, 'Then I have hopes of seeing Nayeema again? I am living just in the hope of seeing her once more. I remember everything—I haven't forgotten anything in these long seven and half years. I remember how my mother, saying, "Oh Nayeema!" and took to her bed never to leave it again. I remember how Jamila used to weep for her mother with her head on my chest. She did not dare to take her name in front of me and used to make this excuse and that for weeping. Finally she died in my lap, calling her mother in delirium. I remember my Jafar, my sole support, the last support of my life, sleeping on my chest for the last time and leaving it forever. He could not sleep except on my bosom and it was here he closed his eyes in eternal sleep. The fact that I'm leading this shameless life even after so much humiliation is just because I hope to see her once more. After leaving my job memories used to beset me on my days of idleness. I would have died before this because of broken health. I had filled this revolver with bullets the days Jafar died to commit suicide.'

Saying this he took out a six-barrelled revolver from his pocket in front of me. He went on, 'But I didn't. I'm still living, with these bitter memories forever torturing my heart, bearing all humiliation because I hope to see her once more in my life.'

I turned to him with hope in my heart, thinking that perhaps Nayeema's fate had taken a turn for the better, and that may be she will find refuge with her husband at last. But the expression on his face made me despair. His face was grave, his eyes giving out sparks of flame. Firmly holding the revolver he said, 'Can you manage to bring her somehow to me? I'll finish all my borrowings and lendings with her then. That is my last wish Zubeida; I don't want anything else. I shall kill Nayeema—or did you say Nellie—with this gun. I'll pour out all these six bullets on her and then hang for it. But no, that can't be. She has repented and become Muslim again. So she shouldn't be killed. I shouldn't kill a Muslim.' And he put the revolver down.

It was at this time that his servant boy brought him an urgent telegram. He read it. The Chief of the Lucknow Hospital had written: 'Keep the grave ready, we are sending the dead body of Sister Nellie.'

(*Saugāt*, Agrahāyan, 1326)

Notes

1. There is an unaccountable and disconcerting change of tense here, and later on too. For the sake of fidelity to the text I have kept it as it is in

the original. The reader will please make the necessary changes (added by the translators).

2. Anarkali, the beloved of Prince Salim, was buried alive at the orders of Emperor Akbar.

Childcare[1]

Dear Ladies,

It is necessary to say a few words about the epidemic, specially infant mortality, that can be seen every day. It is a matter for thought that last year in Bengal itself 16,41,111 people died, and among them 6,24,750 were children who were less than ten-year-old. Among those six lakh there were 2,78,370 children who were less than a year old. That is to say, one third of the deaths is that of children. Children are our future—if they die like this then what is left of our future? Even if we take the survey of Calcutta alone, then we see that last year six thousand, that is, sixteen newborn babies have died everyday. With proper care 14 of them could have survived. Twenty-five years ago fifty per cent of the babies born here used to die within a year. Forty per cent had died in 1895. Then the environment of the city improved and in 1900, forty-four per cent died. Last year the death rate was thirty to forty per cent among which fourteen babies died daily because of the carelessness of the mothers. Whatever the reason, child mortality is a very serious matter and something will have to be done about it.

We have the wrong idea that whatever our ancestors did was not good, that it was all bad, and therefore we have to do the opposite. Let me clarify. In my grandmother's days a woman of a Hindu family had to be enclosed within the birthroom for nine to twenty-one days and a Muslim woman for forty days. Now, in order to do the opposite a mother who has given birth only two days ago is taken out in a car for getting fresh air or told to do household chores. Our ancestors were by no means stupid. Their system was a perfect one and they used to live for ninety or ninety-five years. And these days, what happens? 'You are barely twenty and your hair is grey!' You have to wear glasses when you are only ten years old. We have gone to the other extreme. My dear, well-educated sisters, please compare the modern medical rules with the old ones, especially the old Muslim rules.[2]

See what our rules say:

1. Keep the new mother in as much privacy as possible.
2. Burn charcoal near the door.
3. Anyone entering the room will warm his hands and feet in that fire.
4. The new mother will spend forty days according to Muslim rules and twenty-one according to Hindu rules in a leisurely manner, sitting down or lying, not moving much.
5. Do not keep unnecessary things in the birthroom (whether for 'purity's sake' or anything else).

And now look at what the modern doctors say:

1. The patient's room should not be crowded and noisy. (Is not a new mother a patient too?)
2. Charcoal fire purifies the air. (Then what is the harm in keeping it near the new mother?)
3. People coming from outside may quite possibly carry germs, and the fire kills them.
4. The post-natal health of a mother remains weak and unstable for six weeks after giving birth, so physical movement should be limited. It is better if one is at bedrest. (Six weeks means forty-two days; then what sin has the Muslim rule committed by confining the mother for forty days?)
5. Extra things should not be kept in the patient's room—not even books and papers, for they may be infected or 'impure'.

Now if we fill the room with charcoal smoke, close all the doors and windows to keep the room warm or keep the mother in a goatshed, then is the fault ours or that of the rules?

A serious defect in our mothers is that they do not understand the importance of clean air and keep all the doors and windows closed. In villages there are huts made of bamboo, straw, and other such materials which are not so harmful for there are many holes and crevices for the air to pass through, but in the brick or mud houses of Calcutta air cannot pass if the doors and windows are closed. A lot of people should not sleep in one room for that will make the air go bad.

An important reason for the high rate of infant mortality in Calcutta is that the baby does not get mother's milk as the mother herself is not in good health. The baby is almost killed with cow's milk and other such rubbish. It is no good trying to save the baby alone; the mother should also be looked after. A family doctor has said that one should not become a mother without knowing the duties of a mother. A mother's first duty is taking proper care of her child. This does not have to be told for even animals are aware of it. But humans have to learn their duties properly, because there is a lot of difference between humans and animals. They do not make mistakes but we do—to err is human, after all.

Many infants die while still confined to the birthroom. They are not washed properly for fear of catching cold. The vessels for feeding those babies who do not get mother's milk are not cleaned properly. A lot of milk is prepared at one time and the same milk, even though grown cold, is fed three or four times. There are many such abuses one can go on and on about. When the whole body is diseased, where will you apply the medicine?

The baby should be bathed once every day. The water should be tepid, as warm as the armpit of the baby or as warm as would it feel pleasant if touched by the mother's elbow. Do not bathe the baby in an open place in winter or in a place where there is much wind. Massage mustard oil before bathing, but do not feed him. No need to use soaps, better use gram powder (*besan*). The baby should be dried as soon as the washing is over with a warm towel or a clean piece of old cloth. Places like the armpit, crotch, earback, etc., should not be wet or it will become sore.

Dress the baby quickly after washing him, in garments made of flannel or other such soft material. The clothes should be loose. Do not put woollen caps or socks on him. All the clothes should be clean and dry. Wet clothes, even those wet with sweat, should not be used.

Then comes the feeding—the most important task of all. Up until the age of one year, mother's milk is the best. If you do not get that, then dilute cow's milk with water, making it as thin as mother's milk. A feeding bottle is the best thing to be used. It is difficult for the infant to digest the milk poured with a spoon into his throat. When the baby sucks the breast or the bottle then some saliva also goes in. That saliva has some attribute which helps in digestion. In the same way diluted goat's milk or ass's milk too can be fed, but it would be good to remember that human milk is the best for a human baby. When feeding cow's or goat's milk, it should be sweetened with a little sugar, for it contains less sweetness than mother's milk. A three-month-old baby should be fed one and half *chatak* water and a little sugar. A few drops of lime water can be given so his stomach will not get bloated. If this does not suit the baby, that is, he does not grow properly, then lessen the amount of cream and increase that of milk and sugar. If you are feeding him tinned milk then make it every time you feed. You should not prepare a lot of milk at one time and feed the same milk many times. The formula for the feed is—about 75 ml of milk plus the same amount of cream, plus about 250 ml of water. Older babies can be fed Meline's food. This too should be mixed with milk and cream. In the same way Allenbury, Benger's food, and Horlicks malted milk can be given.[3] As the child grows the amount should be increased and attention should be paid as to his intake of milk. It should be remembered that the baby should never be fed cold milk or food.

Putting the baby to sleep comes next. Feed the baby directly after bath and then put him to sleep. A baby confined to the birthroom should sleep for sixteen hours every day. A two-year-old child should have fourteen hours and a four-year-old, twelve hours of sleep. It is not good to put suckers in a baby's mouth. Some give opium to keep them quiet, this too is not good. Do not let him get used to the cradle. The mother wastes her time rocking it and it is not good for the baby's health. Let there be good ventilation in the room. Fresh air should be there but strong wind must not touch him. There is great danger that a baby may catch cold. You can often see the baby lying on a wet bed. It is dangerous if the bed is wet when he is sleeping or if there is a cool wind and the baby is unclothed. Cover him with a piece of flannel. Do not keep a kerosene lamp in the bedroom. Better to keep a mustard oil lamp in a corner.

It is better to put the baby on a separate bed if possible. Then he can move freely. If he lies with the mother he does not get clean air, for the mother's breath pollutes the air. Mosquito curtains are very necessary to protect him from mosquitoes and other insects. If there is water on the floor or in an open vessel then mosquitoes will breed there. Rubbish heaped in the room encourages flies. One should be careful that mosquitoes and flies must not breed. Cleanliness is the only way. Put out your clothes in the sun every day. If there is no sun then air them by spreading them out. Warm the bed clothes in charcoal fire.

Attention should be paid to every ailment, even minor ones. One should see that his digestion is all right. Do not feed him the minute he starts crying, first see if anything else is wrong. Use as little medicine as possible—it is not good to become an addict to medicine. Do not call a doctor unless very necessary, and when you do call him, obey him to the letter. I know that housewives often deceive the doctor, i.e., do not follow his directions properly and later tell him, yes I have given him the medicine at the proper time, he has not taken anything except the right diet, etc. Whom does this harm—the doctor or the housewife? Think about it. If the bathing, eating, and sleeping are regular then the child would not fall ill. Clean air is most important. Man can live for thirteen days without food and for three days without air. We start to take in air, i.e., breathing, the minute we are born and breathe our last when we die. So clean air is the most important thing for us.

It is not that more people are dying in our country than elsewhere. This terrible downgradation of humanity was first felt in England in 1899 and 1902 at the time of the Boer Wars. When the doctors went on rejecting one man after another as being unfit for the army, the eyes of the authorities were opened. They became conscious of the need for protecting children; otherwise, they realized the people of the country will perish.

The last war[4] made France realize that her manpower has decreased. So, I have heard, they have passed a law that a grant of a certain amount of money would be paid to every mother for each child so that it may be properly cared for. A family having four children would be given a separate grant for the father. In other words, Europe has become aware of the need for protecting her men and now the turn has come for us.

I think another reason for this great rate of infant mortality in our country is child marriage. Dr Bharat Chandra has said, 'Let no one become a mother without knowing the duties of motherhood'. When a girl is herself a child of twelve to thirteen years, when could she learn about her duties? This respectable doctor says that girls should not be married before twenty years.

One should be careful that women have good health. There are provisions for physical exercise in girls' schools but they cannot be implemented because the parents of the students do not want them to drill. Girls should sit like dolls for twelve years and then get married, and when her baby dies it is because she is unlucky.

You will be surprised to know that this is not the first time I am saying all this. I had said, almost fourteen years ago: 'Those who think physical exercise unnecessary for their daughters still want to see their grandsons as strong and stout children, veritable wrestlers, do they not? Do they not want their grandsons to return a slap with another at fisticuffs? If they want this then they want a tender rose-creeper to produce a mighty jack-fruit!'[5] Anyway, I can see that two things are necessary for the continuation of our race—first, the spread of women's education, and second the stopping of child marriage. Girls should be taught to care for their own bodies, the marriage of young boys and girls should be stopped. Have you ever thought, why do married women die more than others? It is because their health gets ruined. Protecting the mother is of prime necessity in order to protect the child. One has to use good fertilizer to get a good harvest. Do you understand? Please take a little care of what your girls eat. Do not starve them to death because their marriage will be an expensive affair. They are the housewives of future homes, the mothers of the future generation.

(Dr Md. Shahidullah and Md. Muzammal Haque, ed., *Baṅgīya Mussalmān Sāhitya Patrikā*, Kārtik 1327)

Notes

1. This had been read aloud on 6 April 1920 at the Calcutta Town Hall at the Child Health Care Exhibition. I've written in very simple language so that everyone can understand it.

2. A few days ago Dr B.M. Bose, MD said in a speech about general health, 'Ladies, you must eat only one curry while eating. One suffers from stomach upset when many kinds of curries are eaten. Remember, take only one curry at one.' The *Al Aslam* periodical in its Shravan issue of 1325 on p. 198, in the essay *Muhammad on Health Issues* says, 'Hazrat Muhammad was so far-sighted that in order to stop overeating and abuse in eating he has advocated eat with just one curry. If men today complete their meals with just one curry then diseases like dyspepsia, diarrhoea, and such will vanish and this earth will become half a paradise.

Now see a living proof of this. Poor people used to eat with just one curry and so they were far less subjected to diseases than the wealthy. Rich people eat a great variety of food and turn their bodies into dwelling places for diseases.

3. I am reminded of an Urdu couplet in connection with feeding artificial milk like Benger's and Horlicks which means:

How can the poor baby smell of his parents?
He drinks tinned milk and is taught by the government.

How very true—how can the child be influenced by the mother's character if he does not suckle at her breast?

When you suckle your baby, Oh Mother
Sing of the heroes of the past.
Let him be thrilled to hear, Oh Mother
And his veins echo to the trumpet-blast.

These eternally true verses too sound false in such a case.

4. The First World War (added by the translators).

5. *Motichur I, The Better Half.*

The Fruit of Freedom

Kāṅgālinī[1] has been unwell for a long time. The flame of life is sinking lower and lower—maybe she is going to die. She can have no medical treatment because of poverty. Let alone medical treatment, she barely gets one meal a day and has but one worn out wrapper for the cold or even for covering herself. She who was the Rani of Bholapur one day has now been reduced to a beggar woman.

She is lying on the grass under a tree, flies and mosquitoes flying around her wounded body. She is so weakened by her illness that she cannot drive them away. Her little boy Nabin, beside her, is sometimes playing and sometimes fanning her. Where she tosses about in pain he embraces her, saying, 'Mummy, I'll bring lots of rice for you when I grow up. I'll put a Benarsi sari on you.' She forgets her pain and smiles.

A bird calls out—*caudda put, eta dukh* (fourteen sons and such misery)![2] Kāṅgālinī says, 'That bird is singing of my misery. I've so many sons and am still suffering so much. Oh, when will this dark night come to an end?'

Darpanand[3] came in wearing a new pair of shoes and told her, 'Mother, your poverty will be gone now. I've ordered a gold anklet for you.' She smiled even though in pain and said, 'First all I've to do is live. I'm so hungry—'

Irritably Darpanand says, 'I really don't know how to satisfy your hunger. What botheration it is to look after old people! You won't take beef tea and thin arrowroot biscuits. Then what will you eat?'

KĀṄGĀLINĪ: 'I'm a poor person. A handful of rice is enough.'

DARPANAND: 'All that's the food of poor people. If you don't take paneer, biscuits, marmalade, and pudding then you'd better starve. I can't do anything more for you. Let me see if your fever's gone. Take one dose of quinine.'

KĀṄGĀLINĪ: 'My illness will be cured by quinine? Never.'

Darpanand said, 'Then you'd better die' and then went away. Another of her sons Praveen came and sat down beside her. Holding her hand lovingly he said, 'Mummy, you are getting thinner and thinner day by day'.

Kāṅgālinī had been very hurt at Darpa's behaviour. Now, suffering from repressed anger and a sense of hurt she said, 'Why are you worrying about that? It's enough for you if you don't lack sherry and champagne.'

Praveen replied, 'Sherry and champagne will be drunk by your rich son Darpa, why blame me? I don't touch wine, I take only biscuits. And what are you saying, Mother, we will not worry for you? You'll starve to death when so many of your children are here?'

At this time once more the bird's call rang out. 'Chauddaput, eta dukh.' Praveen said in answer, 'No, bird, no. There won't be sorrow anymore; we'll drive away mother's sorrow'.

KĀṄGĀLINĪ: 'Yes, there will be no suffering after death. I'm ready to die.'

Nabin, unable to understand the conversation, was looking at his mother's face and that of his brother by turn. When he heard that his mother was going to die he cried out loudly. Kāṅgālinī caressed him and said, 'Don't cry. I'm not going to die. Go play with your brother.'

NABIN: 'I'm a grown-up now. I won't play anymore. Come dada, let's go and get some medicine for mother.'

PRAVEEN: 'The medicines we bring don't do her any good. What medicine do you take, mother?'

KĀṄGĀLINĪ: 'Let it be, son. Don't worry about me anymore. Death is what I want now. May you live long and may I die, taking all your troubles with me.'

NABIN (Weeping): 'I'll weep so much if you die. I won't let you die.'

KĀṄGĀLINĪ: 'Oh my son, it's because of you that I can't die. I wanted to die the day I lost my throne, the day I became Kāṅgālinī from a Rani. I didn't die because you all were helpless children. I can't even die leaving you like this. Otherwise I'm not afraid of death—death is a thousand times better than carrying on with a life as despicable as this.'

At this time Darpa came there with Ninduk[4] and said, 'How can a man live without food and medicine? Mother, you're so foolish, you don't understand anything. I want to make your feet shine with gold anklets but that doesn't please you. I'm telling you again, take some quinine.'

KĀṄGĀLINĪ: 'Now look, Darpa, don't bother me anymore. I'm a poor woman, begging for some rice. Your gold anklet is but a mockery for me. Besides, my illness is not to be cured with medicine. A worthless son like you can't do that which will cure this disease. You'd better think about your own comfort. What else is needed?'

NINDUK: 'Darpa never did anything to light up the face of his mother. Now he wants to light up her feet with golden chains and that too he could not do. He couldn't even make her mouth bitter with quinine.'

KĀṄGĀLINĪ: 'Get away from here, Ninduk. I can't stand your jabbering.'

PRAVEEN: 'Tell me what will make you better, mother, I'll do anything for it. My life itself is worthless unless I can bring you relief. Shame on my education!'

KĀṄGĀLINĪ: 'Now there's no need to worry. My Praveen is very eloquent. He will succeed through eloquence.'

NABIN: 'Oh Mummy, please tell us, what will make you better?'

KĀṄGĀLINĪ: 'What's the use telling you? Will you be able to bring the medicine?'

PRAVEEN: 'Yes, yes, I'll bring it. Don't worry while I'm here.'

KĀṄGĀLINĪ: 'Then listen. Long, long ago a hermit had come to my house. He saw that I don't treat my sons and daughters equally. When going away he told me, "Child, you take great care of your sons, but not of your daughters. That is very unjust. You will be made to suffer by this spoilt son of yours in the end." I had thought: What is the use of taking care of the daughters? Will they protect my kingdom Bholapur? I showed as if I had been very distressed and said, "My lord, you're cursing me!" He said, "What curse can I inflict on you? People have to suffer according to their actions. Can anyone sow thorns and reap flowers? You'll have to suffer for being the mother of worthless sons and showing partiality in your motherly love." I clung to his feet and asked, "How long will the curse last?" He said, "There's the tree of Freedom Fruit on the peak of the Kailash mountain. You'll be free of your curse on the day when someone brings you a fruit from that tree to eat."'

PRAVEEN: I'll go just now to fetch you this fruit.

PARVEEN: That mountain is now in the realm of the King of Mayapur. Mother, you've told us to do something beyond human capacity.

NINDUK: Nothing is beyond man's capacity.

PRAVEEN: I'll beg for that fruit from the King of Mayapur. I'll journey now to sit at his feet.

Kāṅgālinī's daughter Srimati wept and said, 'Alas, alas, our mother has been cursed because she neglected us. But that doesn't mean we won't work for her. Come, brother, I too will go with you to the king to beg.'

DARPANAND: 'Where are you going to go? You stay at home, don't proceed a step further.'

NINDUK (Clapping): 'Srimati won't stay in a prison now. No need for Mother to weep any longer. Now Srimati will bring the Fruit.'

SRIMATI (Aside): 'Darpa-*dada* won't let me go very far. Ninduk-dada's sarcasm is worse. I'll be able to serve mother only if God helps me. (To Ninduk) Ninduk-dada, I won't pay attention to your sarcasm. Rather, I'm pained at your evil intentions. I feel sorry for you.'

NINDUK: 'Very much obliged, I'm sure. If Srimati is kind to me, what else do I want?'

PRAVEEN: 'Srimati, give me a copy of two or three songs of yours. One needs songs when begging.'

SRIMATI: 'That's why I want to go with you. I too could sing.'

PRAVEEN: 'No, dear sister, I can't let you go to Kailash. You talk to me, read novels, sing religious songs with me—that's enough. I can't give you more equality.'

NINDUK: 'Be careful Srimati, don't cross the limits; don't be ridiculous.'

DARPANAND: 'See what a good girl Sumati is. She never comes outside the hut.'

SRIMATI: She's stupid, so she hides in a corner. She doesn't have the courage to come outside, has she?

Sumati had nothing to do so she was sitting inside doing some darning of old clothes and listening to all this. Hearing the last remark of Srimati she said to herself, 'I might be timid or stupid, but I'm not going to go outside without first getting enough strength, as she has done. And what great thing has she done by going out? Reading novels and singing with brother in tune—that's all.'

DARPANAND: It is because she is stupid that we have consideration for her.

SRIMATI: All right, I'll see for how much longer Sumati hides her brains. But Dada, you won't grow strong unless you allow us to raise our heads.

NINDUK: Be quiet, Srimati, we don't want to listen to your lecture. You do your own work. Go and wash the dishes.

2

The King of Mayapur has his luxurious gardens on the peak of the Kailash. Eighteen thousand giants, sword in hand, guarded the garden. Let alone man and animals, even birds and bees cannot enter the place.

The old king sent off his courtiers one by one after finishing the day's work. Now only the Prince, the Minister and a few important men were with him. At this time a giant came and said with joined palms, 'Your Majesty, can I present my information without any fear?'

KING: 'Speak without fear.'

THE GIANT: 'There's the tree of Freedom Fruit at the top of Kailash in the garden of Your Majesty which is the crowning glory of the djinns.'

MINISTER: 'All right, all right, so what?'

THE GIANT: 'That tree which is desired even by the gods, bears but one fruit after many years.'

AN OFFICIAL: 'We know. We also know that it is bearing a fruit now. Say what you have to say quickly, no need for a long introduction.'

THE GIANT (Trembling): 'We heard a rumour that a son of man is coming from Bholapur to pluck this fruit.'

THE PRINCE: 'Impossible! All false rumours!'

MINISTER: 'Even if the rumour is true, then what are you, eighteen thousand giants, for?'

AN OFFICIAL: 'What do we fear when such huge and alert guards are there, and more so when Bholapur is a very insignificant and misguided country on earth. Are the sons of men from that country stronger than you?'

THE GIANT: 'No, sir. I've just come to the capital to bring you the news. We are armed and ready. Rivers of blood will flow on Kailash if needed.'

MINISTER: 'Spoken like a brave warrior. You may go now.'

THE PRINCE (Rising): 'I've to say something.'

ALL: 'Yes; yes, please say it.'

THE PRINCE: 'I don't have the impertinence to say anything about the royal administration. But I can't but object to what the honourable Minister says. He has not been wise in encouraging the giants to let rivers of blood flow. It will not reflect any glory on a race as mighty as we are to destroy such insignificant weaklings as the men of Bholapur. On the other hand, the King of Mayapur is renowned in the world of djinns as a kind and just king. What will our neighbour Djinn Kir say if human blood is shed in the kingdom of Mayapur? The entire Fairyland will call us cowards instead of heroes, is that not so?'

MINISTER: 'What the Crown Prince says is very reasonable. Our reputations will be stained by human blood, and the whole of Fairyland will be polluted. But the daring of men is unbearable. They are coming to get the Freedom Fruit. How are we to stop them?'

AN OFFICIAL: 'Perhaps the Crown Prince has already thought about it?'

KING: 'My son, whatever you say is very wise. You have saved our Mayapur from possible ill-repute, which is the crown of the entire Fairyland. Now do whatever should be done. If you succeed, I'll hand the kingdom over to you and retire.'

ALL: 'One should adopt ways and means for killing two birds with one stone.'

THE PRINCE: 'It is said that humans are very ignorant whereas the djinns and giants are experts in magic. It is easy enough to enchant these ignorant and conscienceless men with magic. Muralidhar, who is an expert at enchantment, should play a pathetic tune on the flute of enchantment and men will start dancing to it. Then the other djinn singers will tell them, 'Come, we'll take you to Muralidhar. When the humans agree to it then it will be easy enough for the djinns and giants to lead them astray; it will be no hardship at all.'

The courtiers applauded the Prince's proposal.

Then the Prince, in consultation with the chief giants, guards, and Muralidhar prepared a secret plan within a few days. It was decided that the djinns will not harm the humans in anyway. They will just keep an eye on their movements and send the information to Mayapur.

Thorn bushes had been planted ages ago all around the Kailash mountain. As the djinns, peris, and the giants always travels in their own magical vehicles these bushes never present any obstacles to them.

3

Layak has become very tired after taking care of his mother for many days and nights. He has not been paying attention to his own meals or sleep, so his health is suffering. He is sitting silently and stroking his mother's feet. Kāṅgālinī opened her eyes at the loving touch of her son and said, 'Layak, you here? Who'll ache at the pain of the mother if not Layak! But, dear child, all your care is not going to do much good to me. I'll not be rid of the disease till I get the Freedom Fruit.'

Srimati brought some food on a plate and said, 'Mother, you've become very weak. Eat a little now and you'll get a bit of strength.'

KĀṄGĀLINĪ: 'I can't take anything before taking the Freedom Fruit.'

LAYAK: 'Who knows when Praveen will manage to bring the fruit! Meanwhile here you are, bed ridden and so weak that you can't even drive away the flies.'

SRIMATI: 'But perhaps mother will die before brother brings the fruit. What will the medicine do when the patient is dead?'

KĀṄGĀLINĪ: 'Don't worry about me, for who will bear the burden of suffering if I die? I'll have to live on even though starving, even though my body is the home of many diseases, even though I'm humiliated and insulted. This worn piece of cloth I'm wearing has one end of it in the hands of the djinn of Mayapur and I'm holding on to the other end, like half-naked Draupadi, with all my strength. I'll have to live even after such humiliation. Oh Allah, forgive me.'

Then Layak, not able to bear his sufferings any longer fell down on the ground. Srimati ran to him. Unable to understand that his last moment had come she looked helplessly as her mother and said, 'Mother, see, what has happened to him?'

Kāṅgālinī managed to sit up somehow and take her dying son on her lap and wept. She cried aloud, 'Oh Layak, my child, where are you going leaving me? You were like a tower of strength to me. You took death away from me for your own self!'

With half-opened eyes he said, 'Mother, don't lament so much. I thank God that I died looking after you. What can be better than this? He who dies for himself does suffer, but he who sacrifices himself at the feet of his mother …' Saying this he died.

KĀṄGĀLINĪ: 'This is the reason I'd told Layak not to nurse me. He got infected with my incurable disease, and died. Alas, who can remove the curse from the accursed? I used to love my sons so much and spoilt them so that one of them became *darpanand* (the Haughty One), one became *kritaghna* (the Ungrateful), one became *ninduk* (the Scandal-Monger), and one became *matridrohi* (Mother-Hater). The one who became fit to be called a man, my Layak (The Able One) has passed away. What hopes have I—'

SRIMATI: 'Don't despair, Mother. Even now brother, Dhiman, brother Praveen, and Nabin are still there and I, the least of your nurses, am still here. I can't give up hope; I'll go on hoping that your condition will improve.'

KĀṄGĀLINĪ: 'To whom can I lament, that I'm like a beggar while Darpa is so rich?'

Nabin stood beside Layak and called him. Not getting any response from him he went quickly to Srimati and asked, 'Didi, why is Layak-dada sleeping now?'

SRIMATI: 'Our Layak-dada isn't asleep—he has become immortal.'

NABIN: 'I too will become immortal, didi.'

KĀṄGĀLINĪ: 'All right. Now don't chatter, go and play.'

NABIN: 'I don't like to play by myself. When will Praveen-dada come back?'

KĀṄGĀLINĪ: 'He'll come bringing the Freedom Fruit.'

NABIN: 'He won't be able to bring it. I too will go.'

SRIMATI: 'You are a grown-up lad now. So all right, go. Come back quickly with the Freedom Fruit. We'll wait for you.'

4

Praveen sits at the foothills of Kailash and writes applications to the King of Mayapur every day. Seven litres ink have already been used in writing these and all the reeds of the forest have been nearly finished. There is no paper anymore. Now he is writing on the big leaves of vegetable marrow. Seeing that the vegetable marrow is also on the way to extinction the boars and the pigs have sent a letter of complaint to the God of Food.

Praveen sends his applications by a different giant every time but he is not getting any reply. The singer-magician consoles him by saying: 'The King will pluck the fruit with his own hands and send it. Rest easy.'

PRAVEEN (To the magician): 'Yes, I'm resting easy all right. But the minute I return home Darpa says sarcastically to Mother, "And has your wonderful son brought the Fruit?" Besides, these days Nabin has grown older, his importunities are getting unbearable. He doesn't let me be, asking questions, all the time, all the time.'

MAGICIAN: 'Can't you manage him somehow?'

PRAVEEN: 'If I get twenty-five to thirty giant guards to help me then managing will be no problem.'

MAGICIAN: 'It's difficult to catch him. He's very proud; he doesn't come to beg for the fruit from the giants. Moreover, he doesn't come near us. He is always avoiding us. Don't worry about the sarcasm of Darpa. He's almost always with us. He wants to become a monkey and needs a tail for that. He is worshipping the djinn to get a tail.[5] Now if we tie him by the tail he'll not be able to stir—he won't say a word. This year on the Crown Prince's birthday Darpa will be tied by the tail.'

PRAVEEN (Aside): 'I too could have got a tail, but I've to control my desire because Nabin will laugh at it. Darpa doesn't have a tail, so no objections to tail. (Aloud) See, Darpa is coming with all his friends.'

MAGICIAN: 'Let him, we have no objection. He's our friend.'

DARPANAND (Bowing down to the Magician): 'How are you, sir?'

MAGICIAN: 'Come and sit. How are you?'

DARPANAND: 'I'm fine. I hope His Majesty remembers about my tail?'

MAGICIAN: 'Yes of course. But there's one thing. Do you too want the Freedom Fruit?'

DARPANAND: 'No sir, am I mad? I'll never do anything that will displease His worshipful Majesty. You ask my twin Praveen.'

PRAVEEN (Alarmed): 'What have I done? Am I going to take away the fruit by force? I only written petitions to His Majesty with joined palms—he'll grant me alms if it so pleases him.'

MAGICIAN: 'Yes, that's right. Rest easy about the King's generosity. He will definitely answer your prayers. It'll take many years for the fruit to ripen. The moment it is ripe we'll ourselves bring it to you.'

DARPANAND: 'It's not we who need the fruit. Let my old mother die if she has to die. I and my one hundred and six friends adore the Djinn King, so we don't want the fruit. (To his friends) Now sing the hymn of praise you've written.

Darpa and the others, all one hundred and seven of them, played the sitar and sang together:

There are a hundred and seven of us
Djinn-worshippers, all of us

Deep in the heart
Does always rush
A river of djinn devotion in us.
The horizons ring with praise melodious
We do not care
For brother, sister
Let mother starve, we care not
Djinn-worshippers, all of us.

The magician was very pleased on hearing this song and said, 'Oh bravo, Darpa. You all are very clever. You have your own interests very well indeed. Why bother about the old?'

DARPANAND: 'No, I'm not worried about my old mother. It'll be quite enough if we are happy ourselves.'

PRAVEEN (Aside): 'That wretch Nabin will not let me be happy. Brother Dhiman too is continually telling me to hurry up. He says can't rest easy till we get the fruit. I had said I would bring the fruit only to pacify mother, but Nabin is quite sincere about getting it. (Aloud) Yes of course, we've to save ourselves fit.'

MAGICIAN: 'Look, don't worry about the fruit. We're guarding it only for your mother. Otherwise what do we have to gain from it?'

DARPANAND & PRAVEEN: 'Yes of course, how very kind you are!'

MAGICIAN: 'Praveen, we really love you. Please stay with us always.'

PRAVEEN (Sotto voce): 'As you wish. Keep a kindly eye on me.'

(Exit the Magician)

Ninduk had been listening to everything from behind a tree. He came out when the Magician left and asked Praveen, 'what, Praveen, have you got the fruit?'

A bit non plussed, Praveen answered, 'No, I have not, but I hope to get it. Be patient, don't lose hope. I will definitely bring the

Freedom Fruit for mother. Nabin has cleared part of the forest near Kailash, so I'll go along that road to see how far it is.'

DARPANAND: 'Be careful. You cannot travel along that road. The giants will create havoc if they see it.'

PRAVEEN: 'Nabin told me to cut steps over there. He is working so hard uprooting the thorn bushes. Can't I just go to see it?'

DARPANAND: 'Go and have a look if you like, but Nabin is so over enthusiastic he might be in danger because of this.'

Ninduk started smiling and said, 'Nabin and Praveen will very easily climb and get the fruit because all the giants are fast asleep, aren't they?'

PRAVEEN: 'I know how to hide, I'm not so imprudent as Nabin. I keep both sides satisfied. I tell him, "Yes, I'll build the stairs", and tell the giants I'll go a little further so that I may catch the fruit when you throw it to me.'

Both Ninduk and Darpa laughed aloud. Praveen was a little shamefaced.

5

The courtiers were present in the Assembly Hall at Mayapur palace. The king was absent because of illness. He was resting in the peris' inner court. The Crown Prince was looking after the administration.

One of the officials asked Muralidhar, 'So your fluting hasn't been able to fool the humans, has it?'

MAGICIAN: 'My honoured friend is perhaps ignorant of the news from the earth. The humans have certainly been fooled.'

OFFICIAL: 'Praveen says one thing and does another. He says, "Yes, yes, we are just begging from the king", but in actual fact he is building a staircase to climb the mountain. Does my friend Muralidhar know this?'

MURALIDHAR (Smiling): 'Really, you all are … Praveen is building the stairs just as a ploy to deceive children. He is making it with stones and only one step a year.'

CROWN PRINCE: 'Why waste words? Let's call the chief singer and ask him.'

The chief singer arrived at once in his magic car.

MURALIDHAR: 'Tell us, Oh Poet, how goes the earth? Has Praveen obtained the Freedom Fruit?'

SINGER: 'If he was to have taken it, what are so many guards for? But in future humans may succeed in climbing the Kailash mountain.'

MINISTER: 'Impossible. Quiet impossible.'

CROWN PRINCE: 'How does the singer known that Praveen will be successful in climbing the mountain?'

SINGER: 'He will not be able to climb it. All these days he has been content to write applications and deliver speeches. But now urged by Nabin he wants to build a staircase. Nabin does not allow him any rest. He is at the root of all disturbances.'

MINISTER: 'Even then we need not worry. Nabin or Praveen or Dhim or Ninduk or Darpa will not be able to do it, yet there will never be unity among them. So we don't have to worry. Also unless Kāṅgālinī sacrifices one of her sons she will not get the fruit and we know that she will not be able to give one of her sons in sacrifice, she loves them too much.'

SINGER: 'That's true, but Layak has sacrificed himself willingly.'

MINISTER (Surprised): 'What, Kāṅgālinī's worthless cowardly son has been able to renounce life itself?'

SINGER: 'Yes, his self-sacrifice is a true event. We have seen it.'

A COURTIER: 'Then we shouldn't deprive Kāṅgālinī of the fruit. That will be unjust.'

MINISTER (Sarcastically): 'Yes? Then let's remove the eighteen thousand giant guards from Kailash. Let the humans pluck the green unripe Freedom Fruit easily and taste it?

MANY COURTIERS TOGETHER: 'No, no, never. The humans don't know what's good for them, they can't even defend themselves. That they should put themselves in danger by eating the unripe fruit is something our kind hearts won't be able to bear.'

Thinking of this possible danger to mankind everyone present wept buckets of tears. The Crown Prince, the first to control himself, said to the Singer: 'Does the Singer think that the imprudent Nabin will be able to climb the mountain and pluck the fruit?'

SINGER: 'I don't think so. But I can't control my amusement at the vaunting braggings of the boy.

MINISTER: 'The Astrologer tells us that as long as Kāṅgālinī's daughters don't help their brothers no one will be able to get the fruit, and all of you know worthless and inefficient her daughters are.'

ALL: 'Then we can rest easy for a good many years to come.'

MINISTER: 'Of course. Now just look at the way. Praveen and Nabin are building the staircase. When Nabin says, "Let's make it a step higher", Praveen says, "No, let's go down and cut a step over there." Nabin says, "Let's go higher up", Praveen says, "No, let's go lower down." The two brothers are bickering like this all the time.'

A COURTIER (Laughing): 'And our friends tell us to be careful, when they hear the bragging of the worthless sons of Kāṅgālinī! If anyone is afraid of the roaring speeches of emptiness then he might throw a fit even on hearing the call of a cuckoo.'

(All laugh loudly)

MINISTER: 'We don't really have to worry. It's just that a few giants are spreading false rumours and annoying us.'[6]

CROWN PRINCE: 'So we don't have to worry, but it will not be wise to give up all caution. Let Muralidhar continue playing on the magic flute.'

Then Muralidhar, much encouraged, started playing the magic flute. The melody of the tune he played made the ocean forget the roar and become quiet. The ever-moving wind became quiet too and the trees, the moving and the still, all heard eagerly. The birds forgot to sing. Why then should Praveen not be enchanted by it? After all he is only human.

Nabin, Praveen, Dhiman, and Ninduk are presently in the Kailash valley. Dhiman is telling them how to build the staircase. Nabin, paying him no attention, is busily making a ladder with young bamboo shoots. Praveen is getting the material for making the steps very slowly together. Ninduk has not come there to do any work. He is only finding faults in the work of the other. This is how the four brothers are working for their mother.

NABIN (To Praveen): 'Brother, I feel very irritated at your slowness. Why, you've not been able to get the material together even now. When will you build the staircase and climb it? The prize of the Freedom Fruit is not meant for you.'

PRAVEEN: 'What! I've been looking after our mother for twenty-two to twenty-three years. I've been trying to climb the mountain, and you, a lad but a few days ago, are telling me the Freedom Fruit is not for me! You think you'll be able to climb up that broken ladder. That ladder will break as soon as you step on it and besides there's no way to protect yourself from rain and hail and thunderstorms.'

NABEEN: 'And won't you get wet in the rain when climbing the stairs?'

PRAVEEN: 'Am I as stupid as you are, going ahead without weighing the pros and cons? I'll make a closet under each step and shelter in it as soon as I see any lightning.'

DHIMAN: 'If we go on thinking of our own comfort so much we'll die before getting any work done.'

PRAVEEN: 'Do you know there are many thornbushes on the way?'

DHIMAN: 'One shouldn't hang back for fear of thorns, and why only thorns, there are snakes and scorpions in this forest. Higher up there's hail and thunder. We'll have to proceed despite them.'

NABIN: 'No, we won't pay attention to all that. Why should we be afraid with sharp weapons in our hands?' (Taking Praveen's hand) 'Come, brother'.

PRAVEEN (Aside): 'I'm not brave enough.' (Aloud) 'Your ladder isn't strong enough. Our legs tremble when we climb.'

NABIN: 'We can lean on these weapons and leap up.'

PRAVEEN: 'We'll have to hide these weapons, for the guards will be furious if they see them. We also have to take my petitions.'

NABIN: 'The amount of leaves you've used for your petitions will fill a dozen carts. It's impossible to carry them. No, brother we'll have to leave them behind.'

PRAVEEN: 'Can you hear the thunder? We'll get wet.'

NABIN: 'So what? What harm will a mere wetting do?'

[Enter three magician singers]

1ST SINGER: 'Where are you going, Sirs?'

PRAVEEN: 'Nabin here wants to climb the mountain.'

NINDUK (Aside): 'How clever Praveen is! He quickly tells them that Nabin wants to go, keeping the fact that he too is going a secret.'

2ND SINGER: 'Are you going to climb with the help of that ladder Sirs, have you run mad? And what is that weapon for? You'll have to leave it behind.'

3RD SINGER: 'Come with us, we'll show you a very fine road.'

PRAVEEN: 'Let's go, Nabin, they'll show us the way.'

NABIN: 'No, we won't take the help of others.'

PRAVEEN: 'We've heard that Muralidhar dwells in Mayapur and that he grants everyone his wishes, just like the Wishing Tree?'

SINGER: 'Yes, we'll take you to him if you want. He'll give you them Freedom Fruit himself.'

PRAVEEN: 'What about it, Nabin, shall we go?'

NABIN: 'We've heard of many such givers, but no alms will be enough for us now.'

PRAVEEN: 'Be sure that there are no such generous givers as Muralidhar. Why, he is like the divine Wishing Tree!'

NABIN: 'I don't believe that.'

(Flute from afar)

What do you want, men and women all?
The flute-player kind can give you all.
Come, come Praveen and go away, Nabin
We can't bear you at all.
Come friend inside my hall
What's there in the Freedom Fruit So many flowers and fruit
Do I hold in the palm of my hand
If you want even the sun I'll give it to you, my son.
And garland you with stars.
But no, oh do not ask for the moon smiling at dusk
It's the one thing I cannot give.
Come Praveen, Oh Praveen, come quick.

PRAVEEN: 'What more are you waiting for Nabin? Let's go with them.'

NABIN: 'No, I won't go. Muralidhar hasn't called me, and I would not have gone even if he had.'

Praveen said, 'All right. You stand there, but I'm going', and left him. The djinns took him deeper into the forest by a different path that went about and about.[7]

They told him that he will get freedom, even Liberation (Mokṣa) if he followed them. Ṭhe djinns will even make him king of the whole world.

PRAVEEN (Elated): 'You will make me the king of the whole world—as infinite kindness to me, unworthy as I am!'

MAGICIAN: 'Why just the world, we'll give the other kingdoms of the solar system also, gradually, to you. The realm of Saturn is very big. It'll give us a little trouble.'

PRAVEEN: 'Oh can I ever thank you enough? Even if you do not make me a king I'll be only too happy if made a minister.'

(Voice offstage): 'Dada, dada, where are you? How much further must I travel to find my brother?'

PRAVEEN: 'What's this, Nabin here! I won't answer.'

Looking this way and that, Praveen entered a cave. Nabin too entered it and saw him.

NABIN: 'Dada, you here! Why are you inside this tunnel? Here I'm tired looking for you. I've been walking day and night for three days and at last I've found you.'

PRAVEEN: 'You want to climb Kailash with a ladder. I can't do it.'

NABIN: 'All right dada, I'll do whatever you say. Let's go the way I want. I'll only take my native weapon with me.'

PRAVEEN (Aside): 'You might say anything you like; I'm not going allow you to be with me.' (Aloud) 'It's because of you that stairs couldn't be built. Otherwise I would have been half up by this time.'

NABIN: 'It doesn't matter, we can still build it. Let's get the stone and bricks together.'

Most unwillingly, largely out of shamefacedness, Praveen started to build a few stops along the hillside with Nabin. At the same time the magician singers a bit far off, all started to sing most melodiously:

Listen to the tune of the flute, Oh listen!
Why waste your time labouring in vain?
Take thy petition
And come to us, run
We'll take you to the flutist so high
Come, come the tune draws nigh.

Listening eagerly to the song, Praveen forgot himself. He thought, 'It'll be impossible to backtrack with Nabin standing there; it'll be impossible to go to Muralidhar. But Nabin won't leave me. What to do? Let me push him so that he will fall.' And so, leaving the stairs, he went and pushed Nabin violently. Unable to balance himself, he too fell and both of them rolled down into the valley.

Then both got up and dusted themselves. Ninduk started clapping and laughing. Dhiman did not laugh, he felt very sad. Praveen blamed Nabin, 'We fell because of you'. Nabin said, 'I like that! You're the one who pushed me'.

PRAVEEN: 'I know nothing. You fell and took me with you.'

NABIN: 'Well, really, here's pot calling the kettle black! Would we have fallen if you didn't push?'

PRAVEEN: 'If what you say is true then why did I fall after pushing you?'

NABIN: 'Because you lost control of yourself.'

PRAVEEN: 'The world's my witness. Will anyone say that the man who pushes falls?'

NABIN: 'The world understands your cunning. You are the cause of our fall.'

PRAVEEN: 'Quiet, you liar. I've been building the staircase for twenty-two to twenty-three years now, and I've become the cause of fall today.'

NABIN: 'No use abusing me. Using bad language won't make you great. Everyone knows who's telling lies.'

PRAVEEN: 'You've spoilt my labour of twenty-three years. Alas, I've served our mother for a lifetime and everything's been spoiled in just one minute. Come with me to mother.'

NABIN: 'Yes, let's go. Mother knows quite well what each son of hers is like.'

7

Kāṅgālinī is extremely ill. There is no hope for her life. Srimati and Sumati are looking after her. They look at the skeletal body and the ashen face and weep in despair. Again and again they think, maybe Dada has come with the Freedom Fruit. If a leaf stirs, if the least sound can be heard, Srimati feels elated with hope—'perhaps Dada has come!'

Sumati has spent the long January night without sleeping, hoping for the impossible.

Morning has come. Today Praveen, Nabin and the others will return with the Freedom Fruit. Oh, what a happy day this is! Sumati has washed her mother's face and changed her clothes. Now she is sitting at the door looking out upon the road.

Ninduk, arriving before the others, told the sisters that Praveen has got the Freedom Fruit.

SUMATI: 'I can't believe it. By my life, tell me the truth.'

NINDUK: 'I swear by your hair, Dhiman-dada has brought food for our mother on a gold plate and Nabin a Benaras-silk sari.'

SRIMATI: 'Oh, let them come quickly. Mother's almost dying of disease and sorrow. Oh, when will they come?'

NINDUK: 'Don't be impatient, Srimati. See, there's Praveen.'

Seeing Praveen at a distance Sumati ran to him, 'Where's the fruit, Dada?'

PRAVEEN: 'Better ask your pet, little Nabin. I could have brought it if he had not gone.'

NABIN: 'Then why didn't you bring it all these days?'

SUMATI: 'So what have finally done? Here's mother dying by inches, how could you come without the fruit?'

PRAVEEN: 'It's useless blaming me. It's Nabin's fault.'

NABIN: 'God knows, it's Dada's fault. He made me fall down.'

PRAVEEN: 'Nabin had been ready for the fall from beforehand.'

NABIN: 'Dada had been ready to push me from beforehand.'

PRAVEEN: 'Why make your sins heavier by telling lies?'

NABIN: 'You telling such a lot of lies in your old age ...'

DHIMAN: 'Our mother's dying; is this a time for quarrelling? You have come back as failures. Isn't that shameful enough?'

KĀṄGĀLINĪ: 'Mother Earth, split open and let me hide my shame within you!' (Aloud)

'Srimati my child, your brothers are tired, tell them to take some rest.'

SUMATI: 'Nindukdada, tell us the truth: Who pushed whom?'

NINDUK: 'What can I say, sister? The one who cannot stay at home when the enchanted flute calls, the one whom Muralidhar is forever calling to stand beside him under the Kadamba tree, he's the one who pushed and both fell.'

NABIN: 'This time Ninduk has told the truth.'

PRAVEEN: 'Then did I just cry in the wilderness all these days?'

SRIMATI: 'Dada, whether you've been crying in the wilderness for twenty-three years or whatever else, we don't know. We want to see the results. Who has climbed the forest stretching from here to the Kailash?'

DHIMAN: 'It's Nabin who has laboured for twenty-three years to clear that dark forest.'

NINDUK: 'Praveen had been sitting in that forest, writing petitions.'

SUMATI: 'All right, you had better stop now. See, mother's hut has caught fire, let's run and put it out.'

Kāṅgālinī is lying on the floor, silently wetting it with her tears. Her heart is breaking with shame and anger when Sumati tried to get her out of the burning hut she said, 'Is that Sumati? Why push and pull me about? Let me die in peace.'

SRIMATI: 'No no, you can't burn to death while we are here. That is unbearable.'

KĀṄGĀLINĪ: 'Oh you unlucky daughter of an unlucky mother, you know can't be freed of the curse unless I get the Freedom Fruit. Why torture me by keeping me alive?'

NABIN: 'Oh Mother, don't be angry. I'll try again to bring it. This time I haven't been able to climb the mountain, but I'll try again.'

SRIMATI AND SUMATI: 'We'll go with you this time. Is it a difficult road?'

NABIN: 'Not very. One can climb by ladder, for some distance.'

SRIMATI: 'All right, I get it. We won't need a ladder. Come Nabin, let us start right now.'

NINDUK: 'You surprise me, Srimati. Nabin has at least got a ladder. You don't depend even on that.'

SRIMATI: 'Why, dada, we'll depend on our own two feet. We'll climb catching hold of mountain creepers. If that is not enough, we'll crawl. We'll climb whichever way it is possible.'

PRAVEEN: 'How will you climb the steep slopes?'

NINDUK: 'There the two sisters will try to fly.'

SUMATI: 'Why be so sarcastic? Some way or other there will have to be. Nothing lasts in this world. Either it is cured, or one dies—but a disease doesn't last forever.'

DHIMAN: 'No use talking. Let's make a start, all of us.'

SRIMATI: 'Here, I'm undoing my braid of hair. I won't put my hair up till we've brought the Freedom Fruit for our mother. Oh Almighty God, help us.'

KĀṄGĀLINĪ: 'What is this I see? My delicate dolls, my daughters, giving up all thoughts of worldly pleasures are binding themselves to do my work. Now that Srimati and Sumati have joined their brothers in this work, I've hopes that my dark night of despair is drawing to an end. Perhaps my children will be able to bring me the Freedom Fruit now. Oh Hope, enchantress Hope!'

(Baṅgīya Mussalmān Sāhitya Patrikā, Jyeṣṭha-Śrāvan 1328)

Notes

1. The name, meaning 'destitute' is an allegorical one, as are the other names in the story. Thus Nabin, coming later, means New-Man or Neander (*pace* Dryden) (added by the translators).

2. Just as some birds' calls sound like '*cokhgelo*', '*baukathakao*', etc., so does this bird's call sound like 'caudda put, eta dukh'. Here allegory and realism shake hands (added by the translators).

3. The name means pride, i.e., Mr Haughty. It has been thought advisable not to translate the names (added by the translators).

4. This allegorical name means 'scandal-monger'. Cf. Sir Benjamin Backbite in *School for Scandal* (added by the translators).

5. There are many who take the help of djinns in order to get some earthly wealth and bliss. Djinns can be won by persistent worship. The story of Aladdin and the djinn is a well-known one.

6. Usually Muslims do not believe in ghosts, etc., but they do believe in djinns and peris. It is said that djinns often harm humans and at times

intermarry as well. Giants too are the enemies of djinns. Poets say that though giants are huge and very strong yet they are the subjects of djinns. It is usually heard that a djinn is the king and giants are the subjects, that the inner courts of such and such peri is guarded by a giant, etc. Whatever it may be, the giants try to annoy and disturb the djinns quite uselessly on account of this enmity.

7. It is said that the djinns do not want to be easily tamed by men and so when men are trying to get them by spiritual ways they present many obstacles. At times they frighten the devotee by assuming hideous shapes and also by taking them into the forest by hook or by crook. The Rishi Vyasadeva, suffering from hindrances in his devotions, had said to his goddess:

> I turned myself into a skeleton for you
> How has fooling me been good for you?
> With what surpassing craftiness did Goddess Durga give him the 'Donkey Varanasi'!

It is popularly known as Vyasa-Kashi (added by the translators).

Creation

The other day we talked till late in the night. The subject of discussion was: djinns, peris, and ghosts. Some have seen white-bearded djinns performing namaaz while some have seen white-robed peris and some others ghosts eating fried fish. Miss Nanibala Datta went to sleep and I was sitting on a sofa. Zahida Begum asked me to go to bed and went to her own room after putting out the light. I can't say whether I dozed off or not, but I think I was awake. There was a loud noise after some time. Nani woke up and, startled, asked, 'What was that?'

I can't say. A few days ago I saw a picture in a newspaper—an aeroplane had broken down and fallen on the roof of a building and the man in the aeroplane had fallen down on the bed in one of the rooms through a hole in the roof, with not a scratch on him. Who knows whether an aeroplane has fallen on the roof of this house too? Why don't you open the window and see?'

Mrs Binapani Ghose was in bed, sound asleep. I told her, 'Get up, get up quickly'. Before I had even finished saying this she scrambled up and asked, 'What's the matter?' I told her what I had told Nani.

Nani said, 'It's raining so heavily, how can I open the window? Besides, I'm feeling scared too, the way you all talked about ghosts!'

'All right. I'll open and see,' said Bina and opened it.

At once a strong wind and a lot of rain rushed in and made us wet all over. Along with the gust of wind came a meteor. We gaped at it. Hearing the noise Shireen had woken up and from another room Afsar Dulhin had come running. They too were dumbstruck. We didn't know what to do—where to run, or shout and waken the household. We all stood staring at that mass of fire.

Gradually the ball of fire took on a human shape. I seemed to have seen this bright god-like being somewhere but I could not recognize him. I cannot recognize people's faces and because of this I have been put to shame many times. The fiery being said, 'Daughters, you all are very frightened. Let me tell you, there's no need to be afraid.'

SHIREEN: 'The other day a detective, disguised as a hermit had come here. Are you one of them?'

NANI: 'You've taken up residence near the Maulana's house. That's why the detectives are there.'

The fiery being, most emphatically, replied, 'No my child. I'm nothing like that. I'm the Creator of the universe, Tvasti.'

The minute they heard the august name, Bina and Nani fell on the floor in homage. I too remembered that I had seen this shining entity when writing *The Creation of Woman*. We all humbly requested the God to sit down. Bina said, 'Lord, may we ask why thou hast visited this mortal earth at a time like this?'

TVASTI: 'The cause? (Pointing at me) This girl is the cause.' Frightened and surprised, I humbly said, 'Lord, me?'

TVASTI: 'Yes, you. You've created a lot of trouble by writing in Bengali about the history of the creation of woman. But you are not the only one to be blamed. Some of the blame must go to the office of *Saugāt.*'

NANI: 'How's that, Lord?'

TVASTI: 'It's like this: she had given that article to the monthly periodical Saugāt. At that time the editor was not present in Calcutta. The idiots in the office published the article without two of the footnotes given by her. The essay, not having these footnotes, has become difficult to understand in places. So the gentle readers have not been able to understand it. Then they said, 'Now call Tvasti, let him explain whatever is written in this essay'. See now what has happened. The minute they get hold of a planchette they call me from heaven at all times. Listen to what happened today. A few young men have enthusiastically adopted the 'satyagraha'. The authorities tell them, 'Instead of taking on Satyagraha (the way of truth), you had better take up *mithyāgrahan* (adopting falsehood)'. But these are foolish children, they wouldn't obey. As they didn't take mithyāgrahan the police started chasing them and two advocates have come here to Ranchi. Their house is very near to yours. But you know, they won't rest even now not even in this foul rainy weather. The whole day, with unalted energy, ploughing through mud and sand and water, they are continually lecturing against mithyāgrahan and in favour of devoting oneself to truth, thus disturbing the peace of the country. At night the two of them sit at a planchette and disturb the peace of heaven. I can't rest till midnight or 1 o'clock, because of the importunities of the two advocates. Here on earth you've got the police to punish those who disturb the peace, but there's no such provision in heaven. Tonight my chariot got stuck against your chimney when returning from their house and I managed to escape somehow. Getting wet in the rain is bad for my old bones, so the minute the brave daughter Bina opened the window I came in.'

NANI: 'But, Lord, there are iron bars in the window.'

TVASTI: 'Oh to dickens with those worm-eaten bars. Who can stop me?'

NANI: 'Lord, we're very curious to know the ingredients you used create man.'

TVASTI: 'No, child. I'm in a great hurry. I must go now. You go to bed.'

But all of us started importuning him. We would not let him go without knowing the mystery of the creation of man.

SHIREEN: 'But, Lord, you have got drenched in the rain, please stay for a cup of tea. Please tell us the story and I'll tell them to make the tea.' Then she called out loudly, 'Maro—'

Tvasti, startled, said,'What! Whom is she going to beat?'

Shireen, hard put to hide her laughter, left the place.[1]

TVASTI: 'Has she gone to call people who fight with staves?'

Bina, controlling herself, replied, 'No, she has gone to call the maid. Her maid is named "Maro".[2] Please tell us the story now. See, Begum Shireen has also come back.'

TVASTI: All right, since you just won't let me go. You girls too are not any better than the advocates. At least they pay attention to laws, but you all don't obey anything. But you won't remember what you hear. Nani, get some pen and paper. I'll talk and you'll write. But you must write fast.

While Nani was looking for ink and all paper, Bina got a pencil and paper and came forward and said, 'Lord, please don't worry about the lack of time. Please speak on and I'll take it all down in shorthand. I can write three hundred words in shorthand every minute.'[3] Divine Tvasti was pleased to no end on hearing this. He went on talking and Bina went on writing and the rest of us heard and looked at them quietly.

I saw God Tvasti was getting very sleepy. At times he yawned and spoke barely above a murmur with half-closed eyes. At times he rubbed his eyes and spoke loudly and examined whether Bina had noted down his words correctly or not. He corrected mistakes if any, and made her write again. It was as if he wanted to show, by all this pomp and ceremony, that he was not sleepy. He almost roared: 'Do you know, my daughters, I had hardly any ingredients when creating Woman. So I took the smell of one thing, the taste of another, and the vapour of something else. But I didn't have to worry the least when creating Man. I had everything in plenty. I took whatever came to my hand, as I stretched it out, for example—when making his teeth I took serpent's teeth down to its roots; when making his nails on hands and feet I took the claws of tigers; when I had to fill the brain cells I took the whole of a donkey's brains. When creating Woman I took just the heat from fire and for Man I took burning coals. My child, put that down.'

Bina wrote: 'burning coals'.

Tvasti continued,'Child, listen to me with attention. When creating Woman I took just the coldness from ice and for Man I took pieces of ice, the entire Kanchenjunga itself. Have you written that, Bina?'

Bina showed him the paper: 'Ice—Kanchenjunga'.

Shireen said, 'The volcano Vesuvius and the mountain Kanchenjunga have been used side by side—there is no doubt about it. We can see the description of man in his own words thus:[4]

The fire on his forehead flared out
Space and land all burned with the blaze.

The Rudra became the dreaded Destroyer
He held in his hand the terrible lance.

The very next minute we see ('He became gentle at Parvati's words'): He smiled and said to Indra then

O Indra, I should not slay this Britra.

The dictation came to an end. Tvasti the Divine said, 'My child, be careful when transcribing this into ordinary language. Don't change a word, even the punctuation.'

Bina replied, 'As you command, Lord. Please don't worry. I'll write very carefully for otherwise my Lord will be much troubled. At present only men call you, but then women will also annoy you.'

When the God went away we all went to bed. But, I do not know how, I fell down while climbing into my bed. The fall startled me. I opened my eyes and found myself still sitting on the sofa. The candle was burning in a corner and Bina and Shireen were sleeping like the dead. I heard the cock crow from afar and understood that the night had passed. 'Was it a vision, or a waking dream?'

(*Baṅgīya Mussalmān Sāhitya Patrikā*, Śrāvan 1327
Published under the title 'Introduction to the Creation of Man')

Notes

1. The nickname 'Maro' is from Mariam (Virgin Mary) as explained below. The word '*maro*' in Bengali means 'beat him up' which is how God Tvasti takes it. So the girls can hardly control their giggling (added by the translators).

2. The beautiful name of the poor girl has been turned into Maro from Mariam. I had had the doubtful felicity of hearing the names of some women from very aristocratic families in Bihar, for example Hasho, Lato,

Dallu, Ullu, Jubba, etc. If I do not give the original names it would not be fair to them, and the gentle reader might be startled or alarmed like the God Tvasti. So listen: Hasmat Ara, Latifunnisa, Daulatunnisa, Aliunnisa, and Zubeida!

3 One admires Begum Rokeya. Not only did she know that shorthand and typing had come as a means for emancipation for women, but she has made full use of it (added by the translators).

4 The lines quoted are from Hemchandra's Vṛtra Sanhāra, which I have ventured to translate. The poem is in blank verse and has been translated as such. The alliteration is deliberate (added by the translators).

About the Author and the Translators

Rokeya Sakhawat Hossain (1880–1932) was born in the village of Pairabondh, Rampur, now part of Bangladesh. Self-educated, she was a champion of human rights, women's rights in particular, and a pioneer in the field of social reforms and women education in modern India. One of the greatest feminists of her time, Rokeya also made significant contribution to Bengali as well as English literature, having written the first science fiction novelette and other fine literary works.

Ratri Ray was born in 1944. She had a brilliant academic career, winning three gold medals in BA English Honors and two in MA English from Patna University. In 1965, she was joined the department of English in Patna University and retired as the head of the department in 2004. She has published many books of literary criticism of English literature and on the literary works of Sri Aurobindo.

Prantosh Bandyopadhyay was born in 1944 in Bangladesh. He is the general secretary of the Rokeya Institute of Value Education and Research (RIVER), Kolkata, and one of the founders of Rabindranath–Rokeya Primary School, Paraspur, Murshidabad. Prantosh's quest for Rokeya began since the communal riot of 1964, when he joined a small group that propagated Rokeya's messages to the people. He took initiative towards 9 December, Rokeya's birth and death anniversaries, being celebrated as 'Rokeya Divas' in India.